UNMASKING THE MAYHEM

Battling Two Minds

By Christine Vennari

PREFACE

GREAT JOB NEWSWEEK! *The neurological science of improving memory is finally underway. I had mesial temporal sclerosis and lived more than 27 years of my life with seizures. Five years ago, I underwent almost seven hours of brain surgery and had some of my left temporal lobe and entire left hippocampus removed. I haven't had a seizure since. I live my life without some of the most pertinent components in the brain controlling short-term memory, yet I do not regret anything. The human brain has considerable plasticity and is capable of remarkable adjustments after trauma. With five years of pushing my brain to its maximum potential, my memory is about 80 percent normal. Please continue these kinds of reports for they will one day improve the quality of life for millions.*

The letter placed at the top of Letters from Readers in a 2004 issue of Newsweek was my response to three articles revealing breakthroughs shaping science and medicine, including potential future drugs to boost human memory. The letter befits a perfect arch, I thought, a concise narrative grounded by a happily ever after. Yet in 2010, eleven years after my brain surgery and six years after my letter got published, I encountered my neurologist and neurosurgeon at an epilepsy fundraiser. That evening made waves. The following morning, I found my body swiveling up and down on my office chair, and reverting to 1999, when that neurosurgeon, Dr.

Gordon, removed two vital pieces of my brain. Seven or eight hours of brain surgery, I told myself, as my 180-degree swiveling transformed into a 360-degree roller coaster loop backwards in time.

The short-term exhilaration from my Newsweek letter eleven years ago turned out disingenuous; I finally conceded, still grieving the inexplicable loss of self. In fact, my identity withered away the moment I gained consciousness in the I.C.U., I knew right away, while entering the first stages of unmasking; unconsciously living out my childhood, my long lost, forgotten past, all while mourning my lost identity. A brain fully unequipped to back up such a letter, I conceded that morning, leaning back on my home office chair, elbows behind my head, rehashing my years of denial, chaos, depression, and rage. In fact, I recalled tossing the magazine into the office closet just after reading it, knowing, if only subconsciously, that the reality I'd described in the letter was a false façade.

I walked into the extra-large walk-in closet, finally attaining the muscle to rummage through my old piles of medical research. I delved into dusty books, journals, articles, and letters, before inadvertently coughing up my original eighteen-page draft from many moons ago, the pages I'd shared with my neurologist, Dr. Adam Levy, at New York Presbyterian Hospital. Then titled Living Through Epilepsy, the draft represented a tunnel channeling through my twenty-eight-year epileptic adversities, before finally reaching the present outcome, the death of my disease. I was struggling to convince myself that eradicating my epilepsy correlated with happiness, health, and a better well-being, all while crying every hour of every day, suffering through deep emotional demise. I read my draft three, four times a day, and wept in grief, sorrow and despair as my teardrops wet my pages. My brain was tricking itself, tenaciously insisting that my narrative was authentic and well-suited for publication. Thoroughly researched, it persuaded itself, professionally written, and formatted with an ideal arc; a chronological construction of my life, holding exposition, rising action, climax, falling action, not to mention a happy ending. I saw it as a bona fide finished product, while silently clutching onto clouds and cotton candy. A brain stuffed with reveries, illusions, hopes and dreams. "It's magnificently written and quite useful," Adam professed after reading my story. So impressed that he began advising future patients of the unforeseen risk of personality changes and mood swings.

Who in the heck was I trying to impress to begin with, I asked myself eleven years after surgery, and what happened to improving my quality-of-life like the doctors all insinuated beforehand? My letter felt as intangible as my brain, a decomposed, non-existing entity inside of a seashell. I knew that life after epilepsy and brain surgery can become far from manageable. Sure, plenty of advances in surgical and pharmaceutical treatments exist to make epilepsy a more controllable disease, but unfortunately the seizures destroyed millions of my brain cells over time, as well as triggered The Severity of the Unknown, unidentifiable future consequences. Those destructive convulsions slyly damaged my memory, speech, decision-making, and judgement, while simultaneously managed creating a neurological guinea pig at the same time as well, trying to find her way out of a convoluted maze.

My brain was handed two distinct identities in the O.R.: The Old Christine and The New One, each battling for a place to call home. My brain seizure and medication free for the very first time suddenly perceived the dissolution of my marriage, and my husband Steven's lies, neglect, and passive-aggressive behaviors. The familiarity and perceptions of my loved ones tarnished as well, crisscrossed from love to unfamiliarity, as I failed to understand how or why. Half of my brain, my right mind, transcended in time and turned back the clock without my conscious awareness. My brain was gifted with clairvoyance, extraordinary intuition, and a new sixth sense. I transformed into a savant, brilliant in various areas while ignorant in others. But back then, as I endured the stages of shock, anger, and denial, helping Adam felt better than remaining idle. Bizarrely, I awoke from brain surgery perceiving Dr. Adam Levy as my newfound partner, as my face recognition and feelings unknowingly crisscrossed in the O.R. My perceptions of familiar and unfamiliar swapped!

Before going under the knife, Dr. Gordon informed me that two pieces of my brain would get removed, a portion of the left hemisphere specifically the temporal lobe and the entire hippocampus. Well, it turned out that brain surgery afflicted my entire cerebral cortex, where our four lobes in our sensory system all reside. Our vast cerebral cortex is the conscious part of the human brain, where the most modern, developed areas lie. Besides touching upon my damaged lobes in the cerebral cortex, the surgery touched upon older more primitive networks as well, specifically areas in the limbic system, containing the hippocampus, amygdala, basil ganglia and hypothalamus. As my hippocampus was being removed, my brain got simultaneously flooded around aged, buried memories of exceptionally long ago as well, holding deep-seated, unconscious emotions. These areas in my right hemisphere began mourning inaudibly, silently without consciousness, right beside Wilbur the pig who just lost his best friend Charlotte, in the iconic story Charlotte's Web by E. B. White.

The seahorse-shaped hippocampus keeps the brain in real time, and without one, my brain became a prisoner of the past sucked into a world of time travel. In 1999, The Old Christine from a specific point in time was reborn and placed right beside The New Christine without my knowledge. Over the next two decades, my right and left hemispheres coexisted separately, living out two distinct points in time: past and present. An indirect consequence of time travel was the dramatic change in identity and personality as well, going from conservative and accountable to free-spirited and bohemian. More conflicts instantly piled up: brilliant vs childlike, conscious vs unconscious, real time vs time travel, ancient versus contemporary.... Why wasn't I warned that such dramatic alterations could occur, I asked myself repeatedly, or of the multiple paradoxes taking place inside of my delicate two and a half pounds of matter?

The remains in my brain failed to braid together like before, I knew right away, when they were conjoining in unity and distributing their residual assets and liabilities evenly. "May I share your story with my colleagues at Columbia?" Adam asked me proudly. "Treating patients like you is what makes being a physician so rewarding, and your contribution is as great as that of any physician."

Yet this time around, in 2010, the educated Christine perceived his comments differently. In fact, I chuckled at them, before finding my old reply at the bottom of my stack of papers:

Dear Dr. Levy,

Thank you for all your time. I know this was tedious for you, but your input and criticisms put things into perspective for me. I agree with most of your comments since you are the doctor. It's just that the right and left hemisphere abilities for most people do not coincide with mine. Maybe it's the mixed dominance thing that made the surgery give so many people like me some shortcomings. Either way, I am now satisfied about putting this story aside for a while. Maybe at some point I will figure out what to do with it and how much I should really tell. Your comments were certainly not all black and white. I do understand your concerns about how my experiences and writing may deter people from having this surgery, when in fact the surgery would be beneficial. I believe you know that this was not my intention at all, and the surgery in the long run was beneficial to me too.

I think we both found a happy middle ground from all of this, where I better understand things medically and can move on, and how maybe as a doctor you can better understand some of the potential outcomes of this surgery. Goodbye for now to a very special person.

Christine

For now, because in the end, my heightened gifts of intuition, insight, and brilliance preceded all else. These right hemispheric gems were silently and unconsciously discerning that God's power bequeaths a human what it can afford, and that mine afforded Hell before I could find my Zion. Finally, equipped to embrace the storms of the past and future, that morning I was ready to challenge them. I picked up exactly where I left off and began writing again, only this time the truth, the facts, all gasping for air for too long. I sat down Indian style in my closet and truly began breaking my silence, and *Unmasking the Mayhem*.

In *Mind Games*, author Michael Powell expresses that, "Apart from food, water and love, human beings need a sense of empowerment in their lives." Over time and grueling challenges, I kept this in the back of my mind. Determination and strength will artfully triumph over my diseases, I continued reiterating, as well as over those of my husband, Steven. In the decades following the operation, my older brain cells were gradually dying off, shifting, rewiring, and providing more space for newer, healthier ones to develop. Trust me, however, with missing pieces of the pie, the brain fails distributing its remains evenly and harmoniously like normal. Yet from this lopsidedness emerged a savant, brilliantly gifted in so many areas yet childlike in others. Obviously, life does not always go as planned for reasons beyond our control, yet when things begin finally unfolding, they do so for a reason.

Since neurology and psychiatry intertwine like marriage and divide like divorce, focusing on seizures alone failed to improve my quality of life. While neurosurgery is vital, it is straightforward and mechanical as well, deflecting our emotions, as well as aspects of our well-being. The guinea pig felt inclined to help bridge these two sciences together, as well as stop my opposing hemispheres from disputing with one another and refusing to live in unity.

I genuinely believed that healing from epilepsy would automatically lead to a harmonious home environment filled with health, comfort, love, prosperity, and encouragement. However, it took brain surgery for me to begin to touch upon the reality of my eight-year marriage, which I later discovered got plagued by codependency, enabling, gaslighting and narcissism. Christine the epileptic had been incognizant of the marital abyss surrounding her, yet The New Christine instantly questioned why The Old One had married Steven to begin with. Not nearly ready to consider that he was struggling internally behind his own masked demons, nor that curing one disease does not cure another. Hell, I could barely take care of myself. I had not asked for a new brain, one promoting awareness and wisdom, and allowing me to evaluate my circumstances through clearer lenses. The seizures and antiepileptic drugs had been silently blocking my brain's pathways, I discovered rapidly, as the lifelong blurs dissolved instantly. My new brain was gifted with an alertness, vigilance, attentiveness, and more importantly, deeper right-hemispheric intuition.

Between living in a troubled environment and grieving an internal loss, my brain hungered for peace, rest, consistency, and love. Perhaps it craved a support system that would provide it with a sense of value or worth as well, including that of genuine friendships, rather than those challenging my gullibility, poor memory, judgement, and speech patterns. Failure to understand brain deficiencies promoted equal expectations of me from others and inner frustrations within. My failures allowed the marital, emotional neglect and financial abuse to pursue, and to make matters worse, Steven's parents continued to enable him, accepting his mannerisms, and spoon feeding his ongoing material desires.

Remarkably, the human brain holds miraculous plasticity for change, improvement, growth, and adaptability. But mine struggled exceptionally hard for this since I turned into a drifter as well, drifting back and forth between reality and delusion, real time and time travel, consciousness and unconsciousness, hope and despair. I labored with time, space, and boundaries.

Dr. Oliver Sacks, famous English neuroscientist, and renowned author of over twelve books, wrote books about patients like me that endured multiple head traumas over their lifetime. In one such book, he stated that:

The patients' lives would still have been shattered and irreparably broken...There is an ultimate courage, approaching the heroic, in these patients, for they have been tried beyond belief, and yet they have survived.... not succumbing to despair but maintaining an inexplicable affirmation of life...I used to think that hell is a place from which no one returned. My patients have taught me otherwise.... The effect of their experience is to make them not only deep, but finally childlike, innocent, and gay.

Childlike, innocent, and gay describes The Old Christine impeccably; The New One had a hunch the moment she awoke. Ironically, these three characteristics represented the childhood concealed behind my disease, the one that I never had the pleasure of living out as a child in the first place.

Without a doubt, a neuropsychological memoir began originating before me, holding the right to integrate two sciences together from a patient's perspective. But what would it look like? I asked myself, combining the fields of neurology and psychiatry together, as well as firsthand experiences and medicine? Dr. Alexander Luria, a Soviet neuropsychiatrist generalized the format of a good read by expressing that, "Two sorts of books need to be written, wholly different, and yet wholly complimentary of one another as well." One story should focus on medical analyses and testing, he suggested, and the other on personal and romance. I begged to differ.

While Luria believed in a need for two books, Dr. Oliver Sacks felt differently as well, which brought new challenges to the forefront of neuroscience. A New York Magazine article in November 2012 criticized Sack's medical contributions to science. These doctors disapproved of his style of writing by expressing that his full devotion was not only to medicine, but to storytelling. One critic wondered whether he truly improved his patients' lives, while another described his writing as a "diverting memoir and trivial contribution to brain science."

Sacks admitted he could not reach the top of his field in neuropsychology if it were not for other physicians challenging his ideas. His obstacles instigated "a strange mutism surrounding his work," as well, he expressed, but the "strange mutism" surfaced into New York Times Best Sellers, the Hollywood movie Awakenings, as well as theatre, opera, music, and not to mention extending lives. This world-renowned scientist tackled science and the media by delving into patient's multifaceted minds, through creative, artistic technique and personal acquaintance. He succeeded so well that it felt to me he was living among us, those with an injured mind.

Neurologists specialize more in seizure control than in the psychological ramifications of the procedures that can rid us of them, but I remained faithful to my own experiences. Sigmund

Freud noted that the ongoing nature of neurological illnesses and treatments cannot get fully understood without biography. And over the years, Dr. Luria's two-book opinions changed as well. He wrote Sacks a letter expressing his certainty that a good clinical description of a patient's case plays a leading role in medicine, specifically in neurology and psychiatry. Mechanical and electrical devices cannot replace the study of personality. It knew where it needed to go, but my brain took its own alternative routes and winding roads to get there. Famous poet Ralph Waldo once wrote, *"Do not go where the path may lead, go instead where there is no path and leave a trail."*

Famous English poet John Donne wrote the following just before being placed on bed rest: *"I observe the Physician with the same diligence, as he the disease; I see he fears, and I feared with him; I overtake him, I overrun him in his feared; and I go faster, because he makes his pace slow; I fear the more, because he disguises his feared; and I see it with more sharpness, because he would not have my see it...he knows that my feared may disorder the effect, the working of his practice."*

Doctors Luria, Sacks, Schiffer, and Doidge all integrate the medical with the personal, the psychological with the neurological, through the eyes of scientists and physicians, but now it's time to story-tell from a patient's perspective, from the inside looking out, from both the conscious brain and the unconscious mind.

I go with the flow and tolerate uncertainty and unfinished business, knowing full well that my gut instinct will usually prevail, and something valuable will emerge. My brain is fine being different now, as it utilizes the dissimilarities as a gateway to independence and success. A memoir is a historical biography of one's life, but this alone did not fulfill me. With my extraordinary circumstances and tools, I felt compelled to re-draft my story, and unfold my realities while enlightening readers with knowledge learned along the way. The facts thoroughly researched, and my book written to the best of my knowledge. Oliver Sacks once wrote, "Tell your story or it will never be known," and I dedicate mine to him.

<u>Acknowledgements</u>

I would like to express my deepest gratitude to these doctors and authors who helped me along my journey of *Unmasking the Mayhem*, because thanks to all of them, I am still alive.

Dr. Oliver Sacks   The Man Who Mistook his
                                         Wife for a Hat

                                         Awakenings

                                         Musicophilia

                                         Hallucinations

                                         The Mind's Eye

Dr. Norman Doidge   The Brain that Changes Itself

Dr. Fredrick Schiffer   Of Two Minds

Dr. John E. Sarno   The Divided Mind

Dr. Lisa Genova   Still Alice

Dr. Susan Nolan-Hoeksema   Women Who Think Too Much

Jonah Lehrer   How We Decide

Zadra, Antonio, Stickgold, Robert   When Brains Dream

Malcom Gladwell   Talking to Strangers

Zayn, Cynthia, Dibble, Kevin, M.S.   NARCISSISTIC LOVERS

Book Design   QuasimVirtual@gmail.com

Editor   Anne Koosed

Table of Contents

July 10, 1999 / 1971

*A*fter twenty-eight years of wretched seizures, and minutes before going under the knife, I endured a very last attack. My heart palpitating, fingers clenching, and lips pursing, all before my brain passed out into oblivion. While gradually gaining consciousness a few minutes later, I saw Mom wiping tears with her sleeve, praying for me in Italian. Yet, unlike every other episode over the past three decades, this seizure produced tranquility rather than despair. The deep chill resonating through my body felt as if I was listening to a soulful rendition of the Star-Spangled Banner. I felt a prodigious tie between my brain surgeon and God, both assuring me that my horrific disease would eradicate by the early evening. I clasped on to Mom's wet hands before placing them along my skull. "Don't worry Mommy, that was the very last seizure of my life," I promised. Then, in the blink of an eye a nurse wheeled me into the operating room for nearly seven hours of brain surgery. Mom, Dad, and my husband Steven stood behind, waiting. "I love you Chris," I heard Mom call from behind.

The operating room appeared small, crowded, and claustrophobic. "How does this tiny square room accommodate so many people?" I asked myself, "for brain surgery nonetheless!"

The icy box encased medical professionals, moving around like a colony of ants, individually engrossed in their own distinct

1

specialty. I saw caps, gowns, and scrubs. I saw x-rays, stethoscopes, and video screens. Thousands of ants led by the Queen, on a unified mission to invade and conquer my epilepsy once-and-for-all. The mix of science and compassion felt surreal.

Suddenly, the Queen ant appeared above my head without warning, Dr. Robert Gordon, dressed in protective gear and fully prepared to remove the spoiled pieces of my brain pie: about one third of my left temporal lobe and my entire left hippocampus, nothing else. As I gazed through his binocular eyepieces, I envisioned the technical competence lying behind them. He will cut open my cerebrum soon, I thought, the outermost layer of the brain, exposing it for a craniotomy, an anteromesial temporal resection. "The flashlight drill with the pointy metal edge will uncover my blood and guts," I imagined, "fluids and brain cells."

His presence not only commanded respect from every medical professional in O. R. but it filled my brain with delusions of his grandeur as well.

Then the anesthesiologist appeared behind me and jerked my head to the right and held it in place with some peculiar fixation device. It was a rapid and painful act. Oddly struck by two fears, distinct in nature, but equivalent in emotion. My heart palpitated. I panicked. "If I die, then my two small children will get left behind without a Mommy," I told myself, "and I will never see the hundreds of Holland bulbs I planted in my gardens bloom into glorious tulips the following spring."

A clumsy mask placed above my head from behind, like an old-fashioned bonnet dryer from the 1960s. I saw pretty angels and silver stars. By the early evening, The Old Christine from childhood was already reborn, rejoicing around a bright, vintage carrying case from the late 1960s; a plastic bonnet case adorned with fluorescent yellow and orange flowers. Multiple lifelong paradoxes slyly arranged themselves in the O.R., I thought, with nobody's knowledge. My oldest networks lying dormant in my limbic system for three decades fortuitously activated. The Partridge Family's brightly colored Chevy bus just made a very bold statement in my unconscious mind, representing a tiny preview of what lay ahead in my new life.

I woke up to hear a heart wrenching song from ABBA, and the band trickled through my brain and heart, so close and yet so far. It was a mournful plea for happy days, so hard to find, and of reaching deep into an aged, closed mind. The song, "S.O.S.," echoed from an unknown place deep inside of me, an insistent piano melody that continued to reverberate over the next decade, like a perpetual leaking faucet, drip by drip by... The 1975 song emanating from a distance felt emotionally jarring, ancient yet novel.

My brain felt like a raw slab of meat carved out meticulously by a butcher before tossed in the bin to rot. Tears of pain and grief streamed off my cheekbones. My seizures were just permanently sent out to pathology, The New Christine discerned, after an insidious twenty-eight-year run. Those sardonic ghosts ascending upward from my chest and straight through my corpus coliseum had

3

just died a golden death, but unfortunately, right alongside my sense of self, I knew without a doubt. Feeling alone, thirsty, and scared, I slipped my fingers between my left cranium and cast in-effort to massage my brazen, tender scar, before a nurse barged in and stopped me in my tracks. The Weighty Lady in the printed fabric jerked my arms downward before offering me a small cup of ice. "Measly crushed ice for a dry, burning throat!?" I alleged, "Put it on the over-bed table!" I shouted.

"Suck on the morsels," she adamantly expressed, "and get your saliva flowing again." But my bloody throat scorched from the endotracheal tube. I felt millions of neurons firing through my brain as well, like a rapid heartbeat of a runner after a long race. I pleaded for a painkiller, but The Weighty Lady in the printed fabric refused to budge. "Your scars need to heal progressively," she expressed, "so I can't administer any pain meds just yet. Plus, they could mask a seizure." Those jarring, ferocious seizures defeating my brain cells for three decades had just eradicated in the O.R., I knew irrefutably, right alongside my sense of time, space, and purpose in the world. "There are no more seizures!" I screeched, "so, hand me a darn codeine or Percocet for the pain!"

But she flared a spare-me-the-drama look before whisking away in a flash. The Weighty Lady in the printed fabric had the audacity to assume the worst, I thought, just to prevent a lawsuit against the hospital. My brain felt physically beaten. Impoverished yet overcompensated, as if it were skiing along steep mountain slopes. Too many angles competed against each other for me to sustain one thought at a time.

Besides the imbalance, two minds emerged in one brain, each holding distinct needs, tastes, and desires. I rocked my head back and forth and up and down, seeking balance and unity. I tried to force myself out of bed, feeling an imperious need to look in the mirror at the odd person inside of me. But I could not do it, since the signals between my body and brain resisted one another, clashed, and wrestled. When my left hemisphere reached for the crushed ice on the over-bed table, my right hemisphere flat-out resisted. I felt my right and left hemispheres competing, my need and execution jetting in opposite directions, and craving that vital hub to connect the pairs together again. Dr. Joseph Bogen labels such competition as *cerebral duality,* where each hemisphere maintains its own distinct mind, rather than interacting in normal unison and harmony.

Not surprised at all to learn that our vital gifts of cognition, perception, reasoning, and judgement stem from the left frontal lobe, allowing the brain to go from reaction and emotion and from action and decision-making. In addition, the corpus callosum, our thick brand of nerve fibers in the center of the brain dividing our hemispheres, got severed as well, I sensed without a doubt, affecting their ability to communicate back and forth in unison and make rational decisions.

It turns out that our magnificent corpus callosum responsible for transferring our motor, sensory, and cognitive skills from one side of the brain to the other, help to balance our emotions, decisions, feelings, and judgements. When I pressed the call button for aid, I found my body rocking back and forth like a pendulum on a clock, as my need and execution failed me once again. It turns out that simple decisions such as reaching for a glass involve complex body movements, and billions of healthy neurons and connections in the prefrontal cortex. Without them the brain jets back and forth in opposing directions, unable to make up its own mind.

Our marvelous prefrontal cortex holds our four lobes (frontal, temporal, occipital, and parietal), all located our vast cerebral cortex. Our cerebral cortex surrounds the layer along outermost part of the brain, our cerebrum. These areas hold an abundance of gray and white matter, both pertinent to our judgement, reasoning, decision making, planning, executing, and other tasks taken for granted every single day. When even a part goes awry, a domino effect ensues, and the entire chain slyly breaks down, causing multiple paradoxes and double whammies. Upon awakening, my brain craved incessant activity and stimulation, and when deprived of this at any point in time, it managed creating its very own, whether temporal, auditory, occipital, or visual. I'd just closed my eyes in my hospital bed to disengage from outside chaos when talented Tanya Tucker from 1972 promptly impeded, representing just another scratch on a phonograph record causing the needle to stay in the same groove. As I massaged my ears and rubbed my eyes, the disheartening lyrics continued chanting behind the scenes. My unconscious right mind riveted around a gypsy and her name was "Delta Dawn."

I heard Tanya Tucker asking me, what's the flower that she had on her flip flops? The gypsy's brown hair parted straight down the middle, just like Laurie Partridge from the 1970s television show. Long, straight, and jagged around the edges. Next, I found my brother Joey and I paddling together through the muddled water of Crescent Beach, back in Niantic, Connecticut. We were trying to reach the white raft where all the cool teenagers hung out, basking in the sun, or diving in the ocean. I noticed their tan bodies coated with Coppertone's "Let the Sunshine In," as I began living through the golden age of advertising. "Don't be a pale face," I heard on the commercial from afar, as the sunlight mirrored off their reflecting blankets.

With heroic effort, we paddled briskly back toward the shoreline. Our bodies began battling the sandbars, high tide, and dangerous obstruction of the New England Sea. The shoreline appeared miles away to little kids like us, and yet we made it back.

As Joey walked toward our blanket, I stood motionless, with water dripping down my fluorescent-pink bathing suit. My mind suddenly mesmerized by the stunning teenage couple walking along the stony New England shoreline. I gazed at the girl's unkempt style and saw a reflection of myself. She wore a fluorescent orange suit and matching paisley bandana wrapped over her head in the shape of a V. Her hair appeared greasy, as if the Coppertone Oil had penetrated through to the scalp.

The new millennium was admixing with hippie nostalgia, confusing my sense of time and space. I could not cope with the anguish of losing the person closest to me, the one who was so far away and yet standing near. Like all other implicit memories, this selective memory, frozen in my limbic system, began melting. It began melting at a snail's pace, leaving drips of riveting emotion behind for me to contend with. The hippie displayed the same plastic flip flops from my childhood as well, adorned with purple and white flowers. But for the life of me, I could not identify the flower, the magnificent bloom clutching on to my deep-seated emotions. It was on the tip of my tongue, but my lack of explicit memory prevailed. I felt a hole in my heart over the next fifteen years, unconscious inner anguish.

The Willowy Hippie was an emblem of The Old Christine. Her boyfriend's shaggy hair, dark sideburns and sprawling dark mustache went unchanged. Sill holding his Winston cigarette as well. Two advocates of nonviolence and peace for sure. She embodied the gypsy that I heard Stevie keep expressing from afar.

While mourning a grave loss, I also found myself amid anti-war rallies and peaceful demonstrations. I heard a call for love echoing through the land, calls for equality, soulfulness, and generosity. I saw nurses passing me, baring fringes, and chiffons, and I saw bloody patients in lacey shawls and billowy dresses. Spellbound by this new and profound evolution emanating from the late sixties and early seventies, I embraced esthetics and vintage through an ancient set of eyes. The era tasting as rich as an aged, red merlot.

The Weighty Lady in the printed fabric returned. "Let me check your heart rate and pulse." she said.

"What about my brain?" I asked. "It feels hollow."

"Please stop trying to rip off your cast," she replied.

"Like two pieces of the jigsaw puzzle just dissolved in mid-air. Can you please help me?" I begged.

"Your skin is bleeding again from your fingernails. Stop jabbing it!"

Mourning a grave loss of my pre-existing self while unaware that our left frontal lobe assigns each brain a distinct identity, personality, and sense of individuality, and that our hippocampus holds our long-term memories, which allow us to place our events in real time. As mentioned before, the operation left me with two distinct minds, and the transformations were far from minor neurological glitches that would resolve through time. My insight, as well as my ability to perceive these shortcomings, insinuated that my brain kept its higher right hemispheric powers. In addition, the keen astuteness remained well preserved throughout my epileptic life as well, I learned, buried deep in the right hemisphere. My brilliance, positioned on the other side of my jubilation, demonstrates savant syndrome. **

As I lingered in shock, denial, and depression, the ABBA song continued dribbling without recourse. My brain prodded by the

---

* A favorite part

song's insistence that something irreparably altered, far away yet still physically present. Dr. Gordon represented my unconscious villain or my conscious hero depending upon the day. In one moment, he made me feel alive for the very first time, but in another, I feared that something had died, as my brain was unknowingly, contextually, and emotionally grieving through lyrics from a specific point in time. The reminiscent backdrops held unknown common threads, too enigmatic and mysterious to define. The sedentary, persistent music felt soothing and peaceful one moment and gut-wrenching and traumatizing in another. Dr. Norman Doidge notes that music alone can exemplify its very own realm of perception, and Dr. Wilder Penfield notes that over time, we can draw upon various forms of memory through music, specifically those reflecting the earliest times in our lives. *

I probed my fingers beneath my cast again and again, feeling the blaze of fire on my bloody scalp. My brain felt addled. And what I lost…. I heard Fleetwood Mac express, and what I had, and what I….and what I…. My identity felt just about as solid as cotton candy.

A young man in a robe and stethoscope appeared before me, swiftly transporting me forward to real time. A college yuppie, I thought. "But I'm at New York Presbyterian Hospital," I told myself. "Ivy League Columbia, one of the most renowned hospitals in the world!"

"Who is our president, and what is today's date?" The doctor asked.

"Go to hell!" I whispered to myself.

"Bill Clinton, and July 9, 1999," I scoffed back.

Played for a fool. I knew that Bill Clinton was real time, and that Eminem just released his first debut album. I knew that some sported tearaway track pants with open snaps along the sides, offering the legs ample air for a long run, while others wore nylon vintage track suits in bright fluorescent yellows and greens. Some sported grungy acid-washed denim jeans; while others wore off-the-shoulder crop tops exposing the waist, navel, and other points of the midriff. And never mind the boy bands in 1999, dressed head to toe in pure white, and best left in the past. The presurgical Christine wore nothing but collared shirts and pleated pants like an understated conservative.

But real time was no longer mine to grasp on to. It felt vague, blurred, and out of sorts. Rather than Bill Clinton, I perceived Richard Nixon as the current president, but I did not dare share this with my doctor. I cracked up in front of him instead, as my immature right hemisphere became enamored by Archie Bunker, President Nixon, and Watergate. I began savoring the contemporary itch of an ancient joke as well, a simple pun, unembellished and free of abstract thinking. As the doctor glanced down at my chart, the beloved comedian from four decades ago popped out of my memory bank, returning me back to my childhood home in Niantic. Fluffy, my long-haired Maine Coon cat, was sitting on beside me as we

11

watched a comedian on television in a crisp white shirt and black bowtie, preparing to perform a standup routine.

Fluffy was cleaning her dense fur and the white threads got caught on her sandy tongue. "Where did those strings come from?" I asked her, modeling them so well.

The short, nerdy doctor had me touch my nose with right pointer finger and balance it back and forth with his, assessing my balance and coordination. But simultaneously, the comedian elicited my funny bones, as I cracked up during the assessment like a madwoman. While attempting to summon up his name, Doc jerked my knee with a rubber hammer to evaluate my reflexes and forward me to real time again.

Moments later he walked out, and my body began sweating. The perspiration caused my legs to stick to the sofa cover in the living room, the sticky plastic preserving Mom's velvet cushions. My brain was incognizant of touching upon another defining mark of the brand-new generation, pure and utilitarian. Apparently, the aged generators in my right hemisphere ignited again eliciting new passés, and off-the-wall logos. Struck by new emblems such as *Flower Power* and *We Shall Not Wilt.* Rather than sticky and cheap, the sofa felt pragmatic and sensible. Rather than gluey discomfort, the cushions sticking to my bare skin represented utility and preservation. They were about preserving "what you have" and "using it to the best of its ability."

I didn't know that these new convictions alluded to my brain's gift of neuroplasticity as well, and to Dr. Doidge's more modern concept of 'use it or you'll lose it.'

I finally recalled the comedian's name. "It's Bob Hope!" I shouted out to Fluffy, my cat.

"Nixon's leaving office in a Ford pickup truck!" Hope joked on the stage, as I laughed so hard that saliva dripped off my chin.

The novelty loitered in my unconscious mind for years to come. Hope's periodic stopovers failed to age, because the primitive areas in the limbic system hold our earliest implicit memories of our childhood stuffed with unconscious emotions. Feelings of joy, bliss, grief, and despair all targeted in the operating room began undergoing major psychological reorganizations in a grueling attempt to move forward to real time. The pace was slow, like a snail in molasses. "Nixon is leaving office in a Ford pickup truck!" continued reiterating like the very first time! "It's because he got impeached!" I discovered about eight years later, at the end of the unmasking process. "And replaced by President Ford!"

I covered my eyes from the bright fluorescent lights above my bed, and covered my ears from the buzzes, beeps, and voices. The medical terminology and jargon not only produced stimulation overload, but it disrupted Stevie's coveted velvet underground holding lace and paper flowers. Suddenly, I heard lightning striking maybe once…then maybe…. while I feared for the lives of my goldfish up in the tree. My befuddled brain lost calendar time and organization since it had no more hippocampus to sense time or filter out mindless junk. "The lightning will strike the trunk!" I shouted aloud to a passerby. "Maybe once, maybe twice," Stevie warned, as I quickly climbed the trunk to save Dr. Seuss's fish in the tree.

For years and years after the surgery, my brain continued to transpose childhood scenes and songs, integrating them a bit differently each time. "I will never let you die up there on the branches!" I promised my fish from below.

And then I met The Little Man for the very first time. "Remember Christine," he expressed to me from far off, "Fish breathe by taking water into their mouth and forcing it out through their gills."

I failed to identify The Little Man, rambling timely jargon from inside my right mind. "When the water passes through them," he unconsciously conveyed, "the dissolved oxygen moves into their body, before traveling through their cells."

Then The Little Man evaporated, just as another Dr. Seuss figure appeared in my slot machine of figures. The figure reminded me that, "*I indeed have a brain in my head and two feet in my shoes, and that the path will be mine for whatever I choose!*"

I smiled joyously, before suddenly weeping again, as I witnessed my precious, colorful fish suffocating up in the tree in the sweltering heat without water and nourishment. Daddy resurfaced next, willing to provide them all with beer rather than fresh water. I saw robes and masks, and I saw Daddy's empty tin cans suspended on strings from the ceiling above. His old, rusty Schaefer Lights were bashing into my fish in the tree, further wilting their dried-up scales. My alcoholic father began suppressing my wheezy-breezy childhood all over again just like long ago, replacing it with mental and verbal abuse. "Bitch, bitch…" I heard, as my childhood anxiety re-surfaced in my right hemisphere, where my backflows of pain all resided. My operation, my third brain trauma as well, caused my father to pick up exactly where he had left off in my early childhood years.

I witnessed the helplessness from below, as they witnessed mine from above in the branches. I looked up at them and they looked down at me. I yearned to rescue them and they yearned to rescue me, but we all suffocated collectively in my unconscious limbic system, with no means of escape.

My conscious brain began admixing with my unconscious mind, communicating to me through dreams, memories, flashbacks, and hallucinations, all holding elaborations and fabrications. Sigmund Freud stated that, "We may assume, perhaps, that in each case the dream was the expansion and complete development of a vague fugitive wish of the waking mind…the dream becomes a revelation. It strips the ego of its artificial wrappings and exposes it in its native nudity. It brings up from the dim depths of our subconscious life the primal, instinctive impulses…"

In addition, he noted that further head trauma occurring later in life (such as my operation) causes the brain to regress and re-experience memories in childlike ways. I was not conscious of my chaos, disarray, and misperception of time, nor that they all represent the initial steps of the brain's unmasking and recovery processes.

Unlike the heart, the brain must undergo chaos before redeveloping and healing. It is all about regression before progression. * The clock on the hospital wall read 11:06, as I lay alone on my first night as The New Christine, in raw pain and emotional grief. But rather than yearning for my husband Steven, I desired Adam instead, just Adam. I longed for the man I'd met just three months ago to make things normal again like before. Within seven hours, he converted into my lifelong partner, best friend, and better half, as my perceptions and feelings attached to the wrong people. I must have fallen asleep again, because shortly after midnight, I heard another nurse, a kinder one than The Weighty Lady in the printed fabric. I was fully cognizant of my surroundings, and keen and mindful of real time.

"Where is he?"

"Who Dear?" she asked.

"Adam Levy!" I expressed.

My feelings broke, before reattaching to the wrong person. Rather than my real husband, I coveted his doppelganger instead. "So, where is he?" I asked again.

"Oh, Dr. Levy checked on you twice today," she expressed softly. "But you were out cold. The doctor will be back in the morning sweetie, so get some rest now."

"But I need Adam right now!" I cried out.

I begged for The New Steven to take my hand, kiss my cheek, and assure me that everything would be fine. As I learned five years later, my brain had unknowingly undergone an extremely rare psychological condition, Capgras Syndrome. But when the nurse left, I forced my logic to prevail over my emotions and perceptions, and I decided to call my husband. Unfortunately, I couldn't recall his cell number, so I hung up the phone. Then, as I tried pressing 411 for information, I accidentally pressed 911 instead. An emergency dispatcher answered, so I hung up the phone a second time. When I finally recalled the digits 411, I failed to recall my address and hung up a third time. Last, I failed to recall the digits 411, so I hung up a fourth and final time. Neither man was present to console me. Beneath my bewilderment lay a mother, wife, daughter, and friend that dissolved into the vast universe.

Goodbye to me it's hard to die. I heard as another tic from afar, this time Terry Jacks from 1972. The elevator music resonated through my unconscious mind for years to come. When all the birds chanting up in the....

<u>July 11, 1999 / 1971</u>

Oh crap, my recognition is broken   M.P. Bryden

The following morning, I tried getting out of bed, but my brain and body tussled. The Passive Frame Theory states that it's not about perception, but response; and it's not about desire, but execution. Every thought and decision we make, The Passive Frame theory suggests that it's performed by many parts of the unconsciousness. My desire to get out of bed challenged my hinge in execution, since desire requires a central neurological hub in the unconsciousness first-and-foremost. It hears before it acts. The unconsciousness provides a venue of different opinions and suggestions, before integrating them with consciousness, and making a final decision. And once the unconsciousness makes the decision, the consciousness simply implements it, before congratulating itself on a well job done! * It's phenomenal that our unconsciousness must run smoothly when it decides, even when making a nitty gritty one such which color shirt to throw on in the morning. The consciousness doesn't solve conflicts or debate outcomes, but simply relays them! It turns out that damages to the prefrontal cortex and cracks in the corpus callosum like mine, trigger ambiguity and incongruity, causing the driver and horse to muddle in controversy.

When the horse finally forced the charioteer out of bed, my body darted up fleetingly, without thought or reflection. It darted directly toward the mirror to observe the unfamiliar being reflected there in front of it. She gazed at the attractive woman with hazel eyes and long brown hair, shaven along the right temple, but we failed to connect. "Do I know you?" I asked the strange woman, lacking the mind body connection I had the day before. My image appeared vaguely familiar, and I knew I wasn't suffering from insanity, but bewilderment and misperception. It wasn't a minor, neurological glitch by any means, but a permanent pseudo effect, an imposter looking at her false Self. Possibly intelligent or important, I considered, but possibly misleading as well. My brain felt mutilated, but paradoxically held a hunch. It sensed a very bizarre syndrome correlating to my grave perceptions between my family and friends, and acquaintances and strangers. As I lost my mind body connection as well, I sensed that this peculiar dilemma was crossing the bridge from *neurology* to *psychiatry*, from *mind* to *personality* and from *personality* and *self.* Dr. Fredrick Schiffer notes that the oddity can feel like "Two people inhabiting one body." *

When I glared at my Mohawk, I heard a techno-pop tune from twenty years earlier mumbling in the deepest part of my limbic system. I saw my eyes… they made me... My dreadful Mohawk resembled famous New Wave singer from the 1980s, Mike Score from A Flock of Seagulls. And for a little while, I thought I was falling….

Dr. Levy strolled into my room to pay me a first post-operative visit. "You have the nerve to leave me destitute on my very first night as The New Christine!" I exclaimed, "and now you meander in ever-so leisurely, Adam style!"

The gall, I thought. "Chris, I checked on you twice last night, but you were out cold," he said kindly, smirking his adorable smirk.

Adam represented the good egg and Steven the bad one, the joker failing to show up at the hospital on my very first night as The New Christine. Just Mom and Dad were present to console me. Adam's handsome reflection in the mirror reminded me of actor Edward Norton from *The People vs. Larry Flynt*. The familiarity and ease felt very comforting for me to say whatever I wanted. "You should have provided me a heads-up about my shaven head!" I expressed.

I turned my body around and finally faced him. He is my neurologist, I *knew*, but he is also the man that just replaced my husband, I *felt*. The imposter felt lucid and clear, while Steven felt ambiguous and hazy. The swap, triggered by an unintentional surgical technicality, bizarrely had me expecting equivalent support from them both, equivalent patience, validation, and security. Even after snapping at Steven's counterfeit, Adam remained composed as usual. "Chris, we discussed your hair shaved along the left temple, remember?" He softly asked, the way a loving husband should.

"It's only a small portion on your left side, and it should grow back within three months," he assured me.

"Yah and silver, like the tinsel on a Christmas tree!" I snapped, "silver since I turned twenty-one Adam. You already know that."

He rolled his eyes and smirked his adorable smirk, before performing the tedious three-word test on me once again. He stated *book, door,* and *finger*, before asking me to repeat the words ten seconds later after the conversation diverted elsewhere. My short-term memory got assessed again. "But my are seizures gone!" I snapped, "so the test is useless now!"

Relationships are about compromise, I told myself, give and take, so stop shouting at him.

"The surgery wasn't about recovering any of your short-term, explicit memory Chris," Dr. Levy kindly reiterated a second time. "Although it may improve slightly through time."

"I love you, Dr. Levy, either way," I blurted out.

*A*s he vanished, I watched Nana slipping into her layers of dress all over again, placing the crinoline beneath her garb. The stiff fabric flared out like a bride. Just like twenty-eight years before, Nana resembled a woman of high standing, living in and around the mid-19th century. I found my arms draped around her hula hoop waist, so broad that failed to braid my fingers behind her. The wide waistline was desirable back then. After dressing, I watched her twist her thick, silver hair into a high bun, and clip it with bobby pins and

21

brown barrettes. Nana's face was round, eyes aqua-blue, and skin a radiant, ivory silk.

Just like Nana, The New Christine swiftly banned makeup and nails. From groomed and wholesome, my personality shifted to a free-spirited bohemian, lapsing backward to a period of freedom, altruism, and liberation. Our long, natural waves, our biggest assets, were offset by a liability as well, and mine was heftier than hers. Nana and I both greyed at twenty-one, but unlike her, I failed to rock my silver roots gracefully. Every three weeks they sprout into white, dense weeds, costing a lot of money for professional coloring. But I thank God for Brielle in Woodcliff Lake NJ, and her stylists Christina, Emily, Suzie and Mary *at House of Beauty*, who all color my hair professionally every three weeks and blow it out any darn way they choose. They know how much I love them but despise sitting at a hair salon for thirty-five years as well, so they know not to ever ask me how I want my hair blown, or what shade of brown to choose. Each makes a choice based on their own mood.

The cast draped around my head like a mummy, and as a little girl again I marched up the three little steps onto Nana's handicap toilet. The colossal chair mounted to the mahogany wood floor welcomed me back with a happy squeak. "Hello Christina, it's so nice to see you again after so many years!" he expressed. "Did you hurt your head?" he asked.

Belle, Nana's mini-chihuahua, appeared swiftly, barking to go outside again to play with Stuffed Pink Piglet. We circled down the spiral staircase, singing *London Bridge is....my fair lady.* Nana was already in the kitchen rinsing the home-grown garden vegetables, while Mom snipped off the ends of the string beans. Mom's finely sliced eggplant with glossy purple skin was topped with olive oil, fresh garlic, mozzarella cheese, and a sprinkle of breadcrumbs. Richly decorated for baking. "Eggplant is a fruit like a tomato," The Little Man informed me in real time. "It's not a vegetable, rather an egg-shaped, berry fruit with coarse, flat stems."

I wasn't cognizant of this unconscious pest feeding me scraps of information seconds before real time and correlating to my present circumstances like a sixth sense. Nana, the family matriarch, and head of household sported an apron around her broad waist, as Belle peeped up the crinoline from beneath, raising her head for morning droppings. I loved watching her sniff for crumbs, knowing full well that treats were seconds away. She knew the day Nana would drop her three mini meatballs, sprinkled with seasoned breadcrumbs. Her drooling mouth and sad puppy eyes free of verbal exchange felt free of judgement as well. She warmed my heart like the child I relapsed back to. She triggered my ancient limbic system and together, we despised verbal tongue, language.

Nana and Belle were not only rewarding my pleasure system, but repressing my painful childhood emotions as well, entombed in my unconscious mind for decades. Just like chaos and disarray, my brain began undergoing regression and disassociation as well, vital steps in the unmasking process, of reliving past events and grieving them for the first time.

Nana was born and bred to marry and have lots of children. The bleeding effort to please her cheating husband and maintain some family peace overshadowed her inner sense of freedom, independence, and idealism, The New Christine discovered over time, like the way my disease overshadowed mine. *

As a five-year-old again, I failed to understand the family alcoholism, as well as the modern characteristics associated with it, including gaslighting and narcissism, codependency and enabling. However, this failure to discern things early on did not imply that my childhood turmoil wasn't getting stored for later recall. Dad's father, Grandpa John, passed away before I was born. We never met, however, twenty-eight years later when he struck my unconscious mind, I began to loath him the same way that I loathed my father, his brother, and step siblings. It took years for me to understand the underlying reasons behind the hate, but just hours to feel them.

The sacred and precious memories of childhood; how impoverished life would be without these.   Esther Salama

Our memories represent an information system flowing through our corpus callosum, before branching out like a tree to other areas of the brain. However, blocks, damages or removals in these nerve fibers cause the channeling system to crack, preventing the brain from processing explicit/declarative memories. Further, damage to the hippocampus, or lack thereof prevent these memories from getting saved. Dr. Steven Glazier compares a severed brain to a cheering wave at a baseball stadium breaking in the middle of the bleachers, before hitting a dead end.

A normal channeling system works like this: _____

While mine works like this: -- ----- - --- -------

Author. Jonah Lehrer spins this into an effective tool: "The broken mind helps us understand how the normal mind works."

Our brains hold distinct types and subtypes of memory, emanating from separate parts of the brain. Our short-term memories form in our left frontal lobe, before they transfer to the hippocampus for long-term, permanent storage. These memories encompass life's events, including times, places, names, and emotions. Our *declarative/explicit* memories, located mostly in the left frontal lobe near the surface of the skull, are most susceptible to outside danger. Unlike our implicit memories, our explicit remain more neutral, within the confounds of conscious awareness. Our first form of *declarative/explicit* memory called *episodic* memory, stores events that are all linked to our feelings, emotions, decision- making and judgement. They contain autobiographical events, including times, places, occurrences, and feelings. This pertinent form memory allows us to remember life's experiences in full and sequential order so they can reconstruct at a future point in time. For example, my seizures erased my memories of my older brother Joey, leaving little emotion for me to fall back on later in life. This began taking place at around eleven years old, around the time our family moved from Southeastern Connecticut to Long Island. Unfortunately, the emotions generated from this form of memory are just as significant as the memories themselves. Think of the emotional charge we feel when recalling our senior prom or birth of our first child, or the pain and despair everyone encountered in 2001 when The World Trade Center collapsed before us.

Unfortunately for me, this form of memory remains sparse or erased. My memories of high school and college disappeared, beside those of my wedding, honeymoon, and births of my two children. Nobody was aware that each seizure damaged my episodic memories over time, those used to create and maintain an autobiographical self. When a child is born, the parent not only recalls the event, but the love, pleasure, pain, and pride beside it as well. Over time these feelings heighten and broaden, through a complex process including encoding, storing, and retrieving. Our memories build our relationships with family members, friends, peers, classmates, and coworkers. Our moods, personality, attachments, and identity all stream from life's events, and without full explicit memories the brain slowly detaches from the world around it. We trip through life in an off-balanced state, driven by neediness, codependency and enabling.

Our second form of *declarative/explicit* memory is *semantic* memory, holding structure, facts, and concepts unrelated to firsthand experiences, such as records, data, and formulas that we learn at an early age. Ironically, this form of textbook learning remains well preserved after brain injuries and often even pop out of the woodwork later as well, after several blows to the brain! * These memories are independent of my spatial environment and daily activities. I woke up one day telling myself that the medical tax deduction is the excess of 7.5 percent of adjusted gross income. I learned this years ago as an accounting major. Such remaining memories turned sporicidal.

I was unaware that my oldest networks got underhandedly targeted in the O.R. after a long stretch of inactivity. But as years passed, I noticed that this form of memory began interacting with other forms of memory as well, and the coincidental timing felt like temporal lobe flukes.! "When the water passes through their gills the dissolved oxygen moves into their body, before traveling through their cells," I heard from afar, crying out for my fish in the tree again, crying out for my Self.

This semantic memory, this tidbit of knowledge spitting out of my unconscious mind silently connected to my present implicit memories fostering in my unconscious mind. I was mourning my fish in the tree, their dried-up scales and thirst for water, as my emotions began to slyly leaking out without my knowledge. These aged Dr. Seuss characters even coupled together with other characters later on, and the timing was as spot on as a car collision. This is how The Little Man was born. *

It was another early evening in the hospital. My raw flesh was burning, swelling. My head tightly wrapped in gauze like a mummy, and the pressure sizzled like frying bacon. The New Christine felt empty and void, and there was still no sign of my real husband Steven. I fell in and out of consciousness as I watched the classic movie *Crocodile Dundee*. I hallucinated once again, this time with an ominous need to locate the furthest point on the globe from my hospital bed at New York Presbyterian. At some point I heard myself shouting, "It's Madagascar," during my non-REM stage of sleep, "the large island nation off southwestern Africa!"

But The Little Man elbowed my unconsciousness again to correct me, "No! Go back to fifth grade silly, Mr. Peterson's geography class."

I still failed to notice the pattern of semantic discharge, especially after such a long epileptic retirement from them. Still ignorant of my eldest implicit memories resurfacing, and later reattaching to other forms of memory. Parts of my brain felt short circuited while other parts began to take longer detours to reach their destination. My brain felt like the lights of a Christmas tree, mentally and physically blinking.

"The furthest place in the world from New York lies just a few hundred miles southwest of Perth, Australia," The Little Man expressed with a blink, "deep in The Indian Ocean!"

My eagerness to reconnect with Perth Australia held underlying meanings that I failed to touch upon just yet. All I knew was that my brain suddenly hankered for maps, specifically landmarks, borders, and tangible boundaries. It yearned for the partitions separating continents, countries, states, cities, and towns along the vast planet Earth. "Welcome to New York, The Empire State" and "Welcome to Connecticut, The Constitution State." They feel perplexing and invigorating to a brain that views the planet as one humongous entity, lacking definitive edges and lines.

When Belle finished devouring Nana's droppings, she waited at the table for me to finish my Apple Jacks and banana. After excusing ourselves from breakfast we walked out the back door to meet Stuffed Pink Piglet for our morning excursion. We all locked eyes. She came to back to life right before us! Stuffed Pink Piglet was no longer made of synthetic fiber and plastic pellets. She was moving, breathing, smiling, and picking up exactly where we left off before my horrific accident at five years old. We squeezed one another tight. She heard Belle's leash dangling, before circling round and round in childhood elation. Belle howling and Stuffed Pink Piglet licking his ears. "How did you get out here before us?" Belle asked after catching her breath.

"I snuck out the east side of the house with the bread when Nana went outside to the vegetable garden," Stuffed Pink Piglet replied. "Do you have water?" she asked, "I'm thirsty?"

"Me too," Belle said.

I filled the terra cotta pot with water for them before we all headed down to the ocean. We stepped vigilantly down each rock one by one, avoiding the erosions descending from centuries along the ocean. When we reached the bottom, we each carefully stepped over the yellow, rocky New England sand, made of sharp grain and quartz. Just before reaching the dock, I released their leashes, as they sat beside me, waiting for me to put on their bright orange life preservers. But I jerked my head around to scratch my back. I saw the back of Nana's house atop the cliff through richer occipital lobes, holding greater depth and dimension than before. Nana's Victorian lay atop a steep overhang, atop the vast Atlantic Ocean. My imagination began re-transcribing my memories again, altering and embellishing them to befit my present needs. The calm New England shore turned into a swelling ocean, with waves ascending parallel to the coastline. I began seeing and hearing with my brain, rather than just my eyes and ears. I heard the waves gushing fiercely, swiftly. I turned back around for a safety check and found Stuffed Pink Piglet and Belle at the end of dock. "Why did you wander without your life preservers!" I shouted anxiety stricken. "You know better than that!" I lashed out.

"Because you didn't put them on for us like usual," Stuffed Pink Piglet innocently replied. "I nudged you twice," Belle said.

I ran up to them and hugged them tight, before buckling them on their bodies. My brain was drowning in fear again. "Awakening from sleep full of anxiety," Dr. Schiffer notes, while signaling changes in hemispheric dominance.

From this point forward I existed in this endless cycle of fear and anxiety. Fear of losing my marriage and children, fear of losing my innocent creatures of the Earth, as well as the person attached to my heart, brain, and mind. I was falling in and out of consciousness, dreaming, hallucinating, and awakening in fear of the unknown. "Please don't wander off without your life preservers again, do you understand?" I shouted.

"I'm sorry, I love you," Belle replied, before licking me again.

This passive activity dredging up every day without my permission never replaced my present activity. It was background, elevator action. Weightless and yet hefty. Stuffed Pink Piglet and Belle never distracted me from the plot of Crocodile Dundee on the television screen in my hospital room, since dreams, hallucinations, and backdrops of memory don't carry perception, order, judgement, awareness, attention, logic, or coherency. It turns out that in rare cases like brain surgery, the unconscious mind draws upon a very specific point in time. It remains deadlocked, unable to shift gears. *

On the brighter note my brain maintained the ability to provide safety measures for me and my loved ones, I later learned, during real times of crises, threat and upset. The higher the stakes, I discovered, the better my decisions become. I put on our life preservers. Their licks and oinks, kind gestures and tones all soothed my anxiety. "I'm sorry," I said, "for turning my head on you both."

We walked carefully along the splintery dock, before plopping ourselves on the edge. I sat happily between them and rocked my legs up and down. "The high tide is crashing in again, I expressed, as waves of threat and upset evoked in my limbic system again out of nowhere. Peace and solace turned into fear and anguish.

"It's The Sound," Stuffed Pink Piglet whispered, "not the ocean."

"New London water is just an inlet," Belle expressed, "a channel just like Niantic water."

"Look again Mommy," Stuffed Pink Piglet said, "no waves like the open Atlantic Ocean."

But my illusions did not pair with the facts like before. My brain regressed backwards with childhood angst. Perhaps it knew that the range of water is far from fierce, and the winds aren't strong enough to transfer their energy to the water and create the choppy waves I'd imagined, nor the dangerous ocean swelling. Yet my right unconscious hemisphere snowballed me again, burdened me with worry and concern. I wanted nothing more than Nana's Sea to remain the simple channel lying between two bodies of land, Connecticut, and Long Island. I wanted nothing more than the truth, so I diverted from anguish to pleasure again. I feasted on the ecosystem lying before me and imagined the millions of habitats living in the water: the plants, dolphins, whales, octopus, otters, seaweeds, algae, and kelp.

In the immediate moment, The Old Christine was blocking her father's drunken rages again with God's marvelous creatures of the Earth. The intensity and power behind my repressed childhood feelings provoked again without my knowledge. Like Freud and other psychological masterminds, Dr. John Sarno noted the problem lies in that one cannot experience something that it's not consciously aware of. "We live in a world of the conscious, and most of us think it is our only world," he stated. "We acknowledge only what we are aware of, what we feel consciously."

By dinnertime on my second night as The New Christine I got a surprise visit from you know who, as he strolled in with our two children, watery eyed and without a care in the world. "Thank God you're OK," Steven said, pecking my cheek like a child of eight years. His thinning blond hair and round face appeared only quasi-familiar to me, as my perceptions unknowingly transformed during surgery. Steven doesn't smoke, I told myself, smelling something peculiar. But my husband's stoned, The New Christine discerned. "Kiss me on the lips." I commanded, glaring through his lying eyes.

He bent down disparagingly. "Your breath reeks of pot!" I exclaimed.

I would have never guessed that the odor signified the beginning of the end, or that my sudden discovery paled compared to what lay ahead in my new life. Dad stood right by me, watching his son-in- law march in like a prize, pounding the floor and high as a kite. Dad was seething, with eyes bulging out like two sacks of a black goldfish. He held his breath, before suddenly shrieking. "Her brain surgery was yesterday. You left right after your wife went into the operating room. You never came back! We stayed with her until ten o'clock on her first night. Where were you these past two days, Steven?" he raged.

Steven presented himself as grandiose and beyond reproach. An overt narcissist, I soon learned, and victim of childhood emotional

33

neglect, fueled with monetary privilege, delusions, and entitlement. An attention-seeking, exploitive boy that never left the schoolyard.

"Where were you over the past two days?" Dad asked again.

"And where were you?" Steven replied, squinting his eyes from the false allegation, before turning away and devaluing him.

"Not now Al," Mom expressed.

Steven swiftly turned away and began ripping open the bags of Chinese food. The odor sickened me as much as his breath. I never cared for Lo-Mein. Narcissists always turn the other way when challenged, I soon discovered, glancing around for outside distraction rather than focusing on the conversation or task at hand.

"Ralph down the road never went to work again," he said next, giggling, "what a life!"

His brain dodging rhetoric and jargon, I told myself. Dad was an overt narcissist, loud, aggressive, verbally abusive, and easy to read, while Steven is a combination of overt and covert, of clear and dubious. Both are passive aggressive, and outright charming, craving admiration and lacking empathy. Half blatant abuse and half silent abuse. Robustly animated when seeking pity, and quiet as a mouse when financially mischievous.

Dad was a victim of childhood neglect, raised by an alcoholic, physically abusive father and enabling mother. This upbringing made him prone to belittlement and delusions of persecution. Steven on the flip side, raised with a silver spoon, turned unscrupulous and coy over the years. Both bullies, I later discerned, struggling for control and identity, while failing to understand that contempt denotes insecurity and inner self- loathing. Narcissists like them are measly chips off the old block, children that never left the playground. "I was fourteen years old and smoking pot in my bedroom with the door wide open," Steven expressed to me various times, "waiting to get caught in the act."

So, I snuggled and protected him the same the same way Mom did with Dad. I kissed his cheeks and eyelids each time we crossed paths in the house. I patted his back each time I convinced myself to believe another little, white lie. Dad and Steven, bred from the same litter, were polar opposites as well, on each end of the sphere. Blue collar versus white, an understated life versus one fueled by hyperbole. Dad held himself financially accountable for his family, while Steven never gave a rat's ass about anyone but himself. Never lost a wink of sleep over money or the lack thereof. At various points he earned a shit load of money, but he always managed pissing it away, knowing that his wealthy parents would fund him.

That evening Mom and I watched the two proverbial kittens turning into lions, raging back and forth in vindication. Jason appeared pensive, engrossed in thought. I found him staring at his Mommy with wet eyes. "Go give her a hug," Mom said.

He bent his body over my bed, and I kissed him while Stephanie whined for her dumplings. My emotional confusion affected everyone and caused a long-term cascade. Rather than Jason, Stephanie and Steven, my brain ached for Adam, to walk in and clear the dark clouds for me. And wouldn't you know it, he wandered his way in shortly afterward? I smiled from ear to ear, because rather than linking my positive emotions to my husband, parents, and children, I linked them to a virtual stranger in a white, ballooning shirt instead. My brain underwent a sudden change in face recognition, together with my feelings attached to it.

"Would you like an egg roll, Dr. Levy?" Steven politely offered.

"Are you crazy!?" I barked. "He can't eat an egg roll, he's Kosher!"

"I would love one," Adam sighed. "It's been a long day. I'm Jewish, but far from Orthodox and Kosher Chris."

He smirked another adorable smirk, and I smirked right back. Insulted by an article suggesting that a neurologist holds a reputation of "not doing so much for their patients."

When everybody vacated, I felt my brain mentally and physically shifting, thrusting, and reconfiguring, like a pair of wet sneakers thumping in the dryer. In order for my fragile remainders to maintain their cortical real estate, they had to desensitize themselves from reality. They were undergoing shock, anger, and denial, and refusing to accept the identity crises. My brain thirsted for empathy, simplicity, compassion, and peace, and aside from Mom, my primitive right hemisphere was the only source providing me all of this. The animals, trees, flowers, water, and lands from my childhood all flourished again after decades of latency. They amplified and augmented. I saw my crawly caterpillars from Niantic sticking along the leaves of my three magnificent weeping willow trees again, this time developing new spinnerets and thinner antennas.

My enigmatic brain was using its childhood as defense mechanisms to reduce the grief during my threat and upset. Incognizant of my ego and superego, the decision makers of the mind, each trying to contain these unconscious feelings in my id. My id was replacing reality with happy childhood dreams and memories, often embellished to befit my present needs as well, in order to avoid greater distress and hopelessness.

Uncle Louie appeared in our shadows as well, feeding us a few tidbits about the ocean. Stuffed Pig Piglet, Belle and I were still sitting along the dock in our life preservers and listening intently to him. "The tides change every six hours based on the pressure from the moon," he said, "and its gravitational pull generates a tidal force."

"Joey and I don't fear the force of the water," I replied.

"Chris it's because this a calm, muddy ocean in New London, mixed with salt and fresh water. It's The Sound, not the ocean."

By the early afternoon, our flock of seagulls appeared right above us on the dock. We watched them lift and lower in ideal accord, before gesturing us from few feet above. Stuffed Pink Piglet raised two fingers to his forehead and saluted them like an American soldier. Every Sunday afternoon Nana placed a loaf of fresh Italian bread on the corner of the dining room table, but by the time the family sat down for our four pm dinner the crumb of loaf had already vanished. The crust hollowed. The three Robin Hoods stole from the humans to feed the fowl. "Our flocks deserve fresh crumb as well," Belle whispered up to me.

Next, Belle and I scurried outside to the wraparound porch with our crumb in tow. I mashed the doughy crumb into mini meatballs, before burying them between the plastic sofa cushions for our weekday morning expeditions. Stuffed Pink Piglet already outside to grab the Sunday morning dough.

We watched our seagulls eating fish, insects, and other rodents with their gulls, and after obtaining their primary nutrients, they flocked directly toward us for a last fix. Stuffed Pink Piglet threw the crumb far and high above the water, as we saw them snip the remnants in mid-air. "Perfect timing," Belle said.

We never dared to pilfer the crust, because God forbid our precious herrings would chip their teeth or gag on the loaf. Our seabirds thanked us with chirps and squawks rather than verbal language, which I despise as a right brainer. Our seagulls are far from scavengers or beasts like narcissists, I knew, squandering our basic needs including food, water, gasoline, and clothing. Seagulls hold different hunger than the narcissist, no repugnant language or verbal tongue.

Nana appeared outside, hanging the wet clothing on the clothesline. She used old fashioned wooden clothespins with galvanized wire springs. The flock flew toward her and circled above the clothesline in accord. She looked up at them, before glancing at us with the corner of her eye. Belle had one last dough in tow. Nobody budged.

Famous French Philosopher René Descartes noted distinct differences between the brain and mind. The brain is made-up of laws, judgement, reasoning, substance, and consciousness, he noted, while the mind is the soul made of unconscious and intuitive reasoning, vital right hemispheric assets lacking space and weight. Human beings hold this duality, Dr. Norman Doidge explains, the marriage between the material brain and immaterial mind.

Yet the Descartes theory that dominated science for centuries never truly clarified how the immaterial mind directly influences the material brain. Doidge noted that our immaterial thoughts have a physical signature, which must someday get explained in physical terms to understand how they can change the brain structure. As a neuropsychological guinea pig unmasking my old life right beside my new one, I can attest to the distinctness, as well their effect on one another. After all my unconscious mind remained enveloped around childhood joy or sadness, and this time it was watching Dorothy and Toto balling in the 1939 film The Wizard of Oz. I just escaped a lifelong epileptic cyclone, I told myself, and now Dorothy and Toto are attempting to escape their very own. "It's a twister! It's a twister!" I kept hearing from my bedside, clandestinely suffering more fear and distress.

"Zeke!" I heard.

"Oh Henry, Henry, I can't find Dorothy," shrieked Auntie Em. "She must be out somewhere in the storm! Dorothy!" she shouted.

"Auntie Em!" Dorothy shouted back.

Dreams and hallucinations are indeed subjective, impossible to measure in space and time, however brain injuries can hold remarkable exceptions. Dorothy and Toto felt very close to me again, concrete, and vivid. They evolved from that very specific point in time as well, I later learned. This unconscious arousal represented a fifth dimension, a standstill of memory and emotion, quantifiable and measurable. Hearing the tornado ripping through Kansas again only renewed my childhood panic. I saw the flying houses above my bed, feeling frozen back in time. The uptight socialite neighbor Ms. Amira Gulch was still trying to kidnap poor, little Toto right before us, as time in my right mind stood still.

This rarely occurs in a normal scope of life since the id is timeless. Freud noted that, "There is nothing in the id that corresponds to the idea of time."

Our hippocampus has everything to do with the brain's stream of consciousness and awareness, I learned, and without one, the brain becomes cunning and coy. It plays tricks with time measurement and space. In a case like mine, the id takes over the ego and superego, as the unconsciousness rules the brain. The visual cortex, in the back of the brain, helps to measure time as well, and this area to me feels like its very own stopwatch. As much as it tries to understand the Earth's axis slightly tilted in-relation to the orbit around the sun creating the seasons, it still fails. It fails to understand seasons, boundaries, space, rules, and edges. They all froze, which proves again that the brain is so localized that just a little jolt can change an entire perception of the world.

I heard visitors on the other side of the curtain wall in the hospital and I saw Dorothy battling the pelting rain. I heard laughing and I saw the picnic basket on the back of Gulch's bike, and I saw little Toto peeking out from under the lid in distress. Another weeping spell erupted, leaving me defenseless again, with nobody to console me for the pain.

Much of this stems from what's called infantile amnesia, the inability to retrieve full episodic memory, due from seizures or other forms of brain injury. After decades of deadlock my brain started recalling random fragments of here and there, but over time these memories of events, times and places began weaving together with other forms of memory not drawn from subjective experiences. The Little Man storing these semantic memories began silently succumbing to my present circumstances.

A Sacks patient, Ms. O.C. had frontal lobe damage as well, and he conducted an E.E.G. in attempt to provoke her long, lost memories. Sacks wanted to prove that when the temporal and frontal lobes strike again later, long lost memories will trail behind. The moment he stroked her lobes with the instrument she displayed an overwhelming sense of pain from her lost past living back in Ireland. Her memories were profoundly nostalgic. Wrapped in my mother's arms again, she later expressed, listening to her sing to me like a small child.

This represented an aura, Sacks explained, a rapid relapse in time: passionate, immature, and empowering. After gaining consciousness she expressed that the figment was present and real, and she felt blessed with the pleasure of being a child for the very first time in her life. She developed a distortion in time, but unlike me, she awoke and resumed her life exactly like before. She didn't get sucked into time travel, nesting in a covert world instigating real time.

In the late 1800s neurosurgeon Wilder Penfield, dubbed "The Greatest Living Canadian" began using tools to instigate brain tissues of wounded soldiers. Like Oliver Sacks he induced their seizures, and even labeled them "experimental seizures." He probed into two lobes in the cerebral cortex: temporal and frontal, and in the immediate moment he asked them what they felt, sensed, thought, and experienced. He wondered what factors attributed to their memory selections; what specific period they took place in; and what emotional significance they held. This form of cortical conditioning in the cerebral cortex traces the brain's memory and emotions, as well as the present reactions to them. At first, he found the patterns quite random and abstract, lacking an emotional counterpart. As a guinea pig, I agree with Penfield's first conclusion: "quite random and abstract," but I wholeheartedly disagree with "lacking the emotional counterpart."

English writer, H.G. Wells wrote a segment about Ms. O.C., expressing her door was indeed very real, just like her wall. Her stimulated lobes held an emotional counterpart, opening an old can of worms from back in Ireland. Over time and further testing Penfield's conclusions and opinions changed as well, as his own patients experienced similar recollections to ours: joyful, dismal, elated, and distressed. These implicit memories remained preconditioned, he finally discovered, holding deep meaning, feelings and ties. They are not fantasy at all, but concealed memories later accompanying emotions, which are both accompanied by our original experiences.

Although Grandpa John passed away before Joey and I were born, I woke up at thirty- three years old detesting him anyway. The effects that his unorthodox values and wraths had on Nana affected me deeply. It turns out that my Uncle Nick, Aunt Ray, and Aunt Rose are our half aunts and uncles, while only Uncle Louie is our blood uncle. Before dispersing to New York, Tennessee, Georgia, and Mississippi they all lived under the same roof in New London, as a large dysfunctional family. Grandpa John raised the first three of Nana's children from her deceased husband, but she collected a hefty price in return. Nana, benevolent and selfless, tolerated her husband's adultery. Apparently, John had another child, born out of wedlock. Before my very eyes Nana's altruism overshadowed her self-worth and liberation the exact way as long ago.

Nana's name was Guinevere, Italian for Jennifer. They were born and raised on a farm in Calabria, Italy, the southern region of the boot, and raised pigs, lambs, and goats. Grandpa John grew olive and fig trees on their land as well, growing over the fence of the neighbor's yard. The neighbors were Gilda and Angelo, with four kids of their own. Nana and Gilda were best friends, and over time each family immigrated to America, seeking a better quality of life. Gilda shipped her crew off to America in three small herds while Nana immigrated her family all in one shot, her first three children: Nick, Ray, and Rose. Both family members boarded the boat docked in Naples at various points in time, proudly immigrating to The United States and never turning back.

Their Italian culture followed right behind: the vegetable gardens, dangling sausages on strings, fig trees and vines harvesting grapes for seasonal wines. The element of drama that cropping and harvesting provided my family failed to match any produce department at a supermarket. Nana and Grandpa John settled in New London, Connecticut while Gilda and Angelo settled two-and a-half hours southwest, in Far Rockaway, Queens.

Decades later, on a drive up to New London, Gilda and Angelo lugged along their fourth child, Maria, nineteen years old. Maria was miserable, wasting a summer weekend with her parents at a stranger's house in Connecticut, while her younger sister Sina faked a fever to avoid going. Upon arrival Maria's father Angelo instructed her to carry two bags to the front door and ring the doorbell. Mom cursed Sina under her tongue, I later learned. Sina was the youngest of five, only sibling born in The States, and raised with a silver spoon. Nana's youngest son, Aldo, born in The States as well, was instructed by Nana to open the door. It was love at first sight between my parents, and the rest is history. Gilda became my Nono and Angelo my Papa.

Both families sustained dysfunctional love. Angelo was an alcoholic like John, but a closet drinker as well, concealing his whiskey bottles in the old, torn up shed in their back yard. Two enabling grandmothers created generations of the same. Two big happy families on the outside, but they were pros at sweeping their glitches under the rug on the inside. One day The New Christine recalled Dad dawdling around the house, whistling a tune from his all-time favorite musical, West Side Story. Maria, *I just met a girl named...*

*W*hen our gulls flew off and circled the sea with stuffed bellies, the three of us marched to the west side of the house for our next excursion. We reached the muddy pond where even more living organisms of the Earth settled: our frogs, toads, ducks, insects, and fish, as well as our autumn cat tails and spring pussy willows budding right beside one another. Hallucinations hold no sense of time. Instantly, I saw our yellow butterfly, Lemon again as well, flying right before me as if no time had passed. "It's Joey's pal Lemon again!" Belle shouted. "Joey loves when Lemon reaches deep into the flowers to drink the nectar. He told me that butterflies use their feet to taste!"

The muddy pond represented an ecosystem of living particles, an abode of shallow water surrounding the wet grasslands and organic compounds. Once again, we saw our tall golden grasses and pink and green lily pads. Soon enough we found our turtles salamanders, and spiders just as I heard Itsy Bitsy Spider climbed up the waterspout ringing through my newly heightened temporal lobes, responsible for hearing. The unconscious precision is another gift, a sixth sense.

"It's Jeremiah!?" Stuffed Pink Piglet shouted in glee, "Our childhood playmate and bestie!"

We walked closer, and there he was, our sandy-skinned toad floating peacefully atop a pink water lily. Jeremiah was positioned the same way as we left him moments ago, decades ago. Still sunbathing belly up in his vintage round sunglasses and still holding his fancy, peach-flavored drink. "And the same red, white, and blue straw from 1971!" I shouted.

Jeremiah was a.... more white noise emerged, this time from Three Dog Night. Just like Lemon, Jeremiah occupied space in my limbic system as well. Ironically "Joy to the World" never ceases to play in my unconscious mind, and for some reason, still feels brand new in 2021.

I bent over the pond to peck his bulgy eyes, carefully not disturbing Lily and Louis, my two dachshunds taking their afternoon nap on the swing. The New Christine rocked her hot dogs back and forth in real time, while soaking up the outdoor pleasantries of yesterday. "He got fat!" Stuffed Pink Piglet whispered in my ear, before oinking in glee.

At once Jeremiah recognized her high-pitched squeal and lunged upward from the lily pad, croaking in elation. He landed on the swing right beside Lily, Louis, and I, as my re-transcribing hit me once again. I was unconsciously re-transcribing old memories to befit my present needs. My depression, losses, anger, and shock, mixed together with my present time. Stuffed Pink Piglet pecked Jeremiah's bulgy eyes. We teared, we oinked, we barked, we croaked, we swung, and we smiled.

"I'm so happy to see you!" Jeremiah exclaimed. "Where have you two been?"

"Is he a bullfrog or a toad?" I silently asked myself confused.

"Toads are fatter and live on both water and land," The Little Man replied in background, "and frogs are smaller and spend most of their lives in the water."

"Where's Belle?" Jeremiah asked.

"She's on her way," Stuffed Pink Piglet replied.

Then I heard the baby croakers croaking from the pond. I heard Louis, my dachshund, snoring beside Jeremiah on the swing in real time. I heard joy to the fishes in the deep and joy to you and...by Three Dog Night.

Suddenly, Belle appeared, nervous. "Dad got drunk again and slurred out vulgar words at Nana!" he exclaimed, out of breath.

"Again!" Stuffed Pink Piglet shouted.

"And Mom was calming Dad, trying to keep the peace again." Belle replied.

"She's still enabling?" Jerimiah sadly asked. "Of course, she is, dumb question."

Jeremiah hopped toward Belle for licks. Time stood still.

"I want to lunge at that rotten man again." Jeremiah croaked, "and use my sticky tongue to snag him once and for all!"

"But we have a long way to go," I replied.

"Yea, I know Christine," Jeremiah said, "but we will break the generations of curse. I am ready, willing, and able trap the bugs flying around in all those men, in John, Louie, Al and Steven! Our women don't deserve to be bullied," he said, "but they must learn to stop enabling as well, taking the easy way out."

I won't allow men or brain surgery to deplete my freedom, nor ability to stay in-touch with my Self, I thought. Nana and Mommy deserve better too, so I have a soaring role ahead of me.

*D*reams and hallucinations like these are complex areas of neuroscientific study, and brains with abnormalities make them more complicated to grasp. The brain cycles in and out of Rapid Eye Movement (REM) sleep about every hour and a half throughout the night, and the length of each cycle slowly increases as minutes pass. There are distinct areas in the lower brain centers that remain active during REM sleep as well, specifically the hippocampus and amygdala, which allow us to recall our dreams and their emotional content after waking up. During these stages of sleep the brain incorporates details, events, and emotions of waking life of the day or of the previous day, which Freud labels as day residue. The brain can incorporate these details through the dream-lag effect as well, using events from the previous five to seven days. These processes are accomplished by the hippocampus and amygdala, which help store our short-term memories.

Yet even with damage or removal of these two parts of the limbic system, I woke up from surgery dreaming very vivid dreams, expressive, mystic, prejudice, prompt. During REM sleep rather than unmaking my past few days or weeks, I began lucidly unmasking an ancient period of my life without even knowing after a three-decade-lag. Other unknown areas of my brain began to slyly process these emotions and memories for later dream content, I discerned years later.

Further, there appeared to be distinctly clear connections between my present waking life and my dreams: impeccable timing, attachment, and continuity. Sometimes I laughed aloud at myself, and other times I snarled, shouted, or lashed out. The dream glee got directed at events from long ago, I noticed, while the nightmares got directed at events from long ago, as well as my present waking life, just before I had fallen asleep. Impeccable timing. An impeccable combination of aged glee and present sadness, and over time I learned that these odd patterns have everything to do with hampered temporal lobes and lack of hippocampi and/or amygdala.

As an epileptic it took an extremely long time for me to realize that my seizures and anti-epileptic medications were slowly destroying my memories. It turns out that when past events like mine get erased, our perceptions and the emotions attached to them get erased as well, silently affecting long-term relationships. This destruction in memory and feelings made my unmasking process even more arduous. Neuroscientist Dr. Paul-Y-Rita, known as The Father of Sensory Substitution, made powerful discoveries in neuroplasticity, one labeled, *Unmasking.* Unmasking the past, reliving and re-transcribing it is the principal way that the brain reorganizes itself, promotes peace, and heals, specifically those afflicted with multiple brain traumas. Later traumas, he notes, often trigger original memories of earlier life, and in my case brain surgery represented my third trauma. *

My biggest unmasking tools included unconscious dreams, hallucinations, memories, and music, all concealed by very profound emotions holding future lessons and drawing me closer to real time. The process took nearly two decades, as my brain, lacking full episodic memory, got forced into the role of a private detective. Without the basic elements of episodic memory, my brain turned to dreams to fill in the missing pieces of my past. My dreams and hallucinations representing the life of The Old Christine slowly helped me understand how I landed in my present turmoil to begin with. Over time these selective dreams and hallucinations helped link my emotions of love and hate to the right people. They indirectly aided in my decision- making process and judgement as well, which waking life failed to do for me the majority of the time.

Unlike my implicit, emotional memories unmasking right away, my episodic memories took an exceptionally long time to retrieve, years in fact. They too popped out randomly, and out of sequence with my actual events. These selective traces remain ambiguous, sporadic, fuzzy, but paradoxically, powerful enough for me to learn valuable lessons from past mistakes. Yet in their book, *WHEN BRAIN'S DREAM* Zadra and Stickgold state that episodic memories are not available for later incorporation, which is another contradiction to my peculiar experiences.

Victims like me without a hippocampus hold traces of memory from other parts of the brain, they note, but remain unable to bring them conscious awareness. I agree with the first half, but certainly not the second, after all, I'm writing about my childhood events with Stuffed Pink Piglet, Belle, Jerimiah, and my flocks of seagulls decades later, after they were all brought to conscious awareness. I saw myself stealing the dough from Nana's loaf again like long ago and using her wooden toilet to pee. It turns out that my injured brain's dreams and hallucinations, later explained through my dream notes and dream recall, were the most powerful tools of my unmasking process, as well as to science.

In the beginning, The Old Christine relied on embellishments and coverups as well, both in my dreams and waking life. With the lack of explicit memory, formed in the frontal lobe and stored in the hippocampus, my brain was always on a quest for fill-ins. But as my fill-ins completed my sentences and helped express my opinions, they held some misinformation and contradiction as well. My speech turned both tarnished and polished, having nothing to do with lying, and everything to do with filling in gaps of memory.

That evening Mom and Dad kissed me goodbye at around 9:30, and walked out with the kid's, leaving Steven and I alone. "See you in a few days Mom!" Jason said, while Stephanie appeared distraught and sad. I watched my little four-year-old girl cry, possibly from witnessing her Mommy's pain, possibly from seeing the hard cast wrapped tightly around my head and the IV around my arm. Even so our relationship changed from this point forward, as she lost her Mommy to brain surgery.

I glared at Steven directly in the eyes again, this time wishing I was a tiny creature of the Earth, arrested in the fragments of my infancy. But I wasn't. I was not only fully conscious, but I speculated peculiarity as well. Did it take brain surgery for me to notice the flaws in my husband and our relationship, I asked myself, that were distinct from Capgras Syndrome alone? I saw red eyes and yellow teeth. I smelled pot. I witnessed him high and noshing on the crispy noodles, stuffing them in his mouth, and making crumbs like an infant. Maybe he was kind and caring, I tried convincing myself at various points in time, or maybe not. But he certainly appeared lethargic.

When I looked at him as The New Christine, I recalled patting his husky Santa Claus belly with nonsense T.L.C. just a few days before, and endlessly smooching his cheeks and eyelids. In fact, I loved kissing his sweaty eyelids. I called his stomach "cute," as well, the way a child calls a puppy "cute." The baby soaked up my gestures with open arms. He chuckled, I chuckled, we chuckled together as codependents and enablers. Every time he sneezed; I watched the gook splattering out from his nose like a sprinkler head. Rather than covering his face or excusing himself, he giggled, I giggled, we giggled together. I called him "cute" once again. Our excess hovering disturbed his parents, but our mutual adoration for one another discounted their opinions.

Not any more though. No more seizures blocking my cognizance like before. It took no time for me to notice that after eight years of marriage, the gook was rude. "Cover your darn face when you sneeze!" I shouted.

We never kissed on the lips like a genuine couple, I thought next. We pecked like children, but never romantically touched, nor treated one another with mutual respect. This didn't imply that we never loved one another at the beginning of our courtship, I learned many years later, but we loved the only way we knew how, the way got taught how to love during our earliest, childhood developmental years, when our brains began developing. Over time, I picked up on the lack of empathy as well, disguised behind our diseases, my epilepsy, and his narcissism. Certainly, the empathy and lack thereof emanate from parents and primary caretakers during the brain's early developmental period as well. What most don't know is that empathy is a defining characteristic of emotional intelligence.

July 12, 13 1999 / 1971

I woke up the following morning, July 12, and heard Tina Turlington, our childhood neighbor in Niantic calling Joey and I "Telepathic Irish Twins" once again. Tina, The Dandelion Lady was spying on another one of our outdoor excursions, awed at our ability to communicate intuitively through natural gesture and mime, rather just words, lying solely in the left hemisphere. That morning her son Chuckey joined us, as we ran down the hills in the backyard toward the stream, where our three Weeping Willow thrived. As they soaked up the wetlands, our caterpillars pilfered their leaves. Our tadpoles lost their tails and left the stream before my eyes, fully equipped to become toads, leave the water, and live on land.

The stream behind my house bore narrow, trickling water, but by the time it reached Chuckey's it broadened, making it impossible to hop over to the woods to the other side. But that morning from my hospital bed the boys dared me to jump over it for twenty-five cents. The seven-year-old me leaped over the expanded muddy water again and fell flat on her face, flat on her new sky-blue Donald Duck sweatshirt from Bradlees. I walked home wet, dirty, crying, and fooled.

After a warm bath and apology, we tried again later in the day, this time jumping over the narrow area in my backyard. We carried blankets, canteens, and firewood from a neighbor's stockpile, and found space in woods to build a tent. The boys communicated with their plastic walkie talkies while I wandered off to chat with the tiny white worms, crawling between the logs. The hospital phone rang, but I talked to the beetles instead. In the immediate moment, The Little Man explained how the larvae lay their little eggs in the cracks and crevices of the wood, until hatching into beetles years later. Then I saw squirrels just as a lady checked my blood pressure. "How do you catch a squirrel?" I inadvertently asked the lady in the blue nursing scrub with Winnie the Pooh prints.

"How?" she asked, after giving me a pill.

"Climb a tree and act like a nut!" I responded cracking up at myself.

I must have conked out again, because Gilbert O'Sullivan was circulating round and round from above, leaving me alone again naturally and with a heart so badly broken. Feeling empty as a shell for years and years, and unable to manipulate the guilt hiding behind O'Sullivan's profound words. I saw Joey, just eleven months my senior, bawling in front of me like long ago. He was five, I was four. He ran out the front door to catch the school bus, while I sported my Burger King Crown, white knee socks and fuzzy pink slippers. The Old Christine watched him depart for kindergarten, twirling her pigtail around her finger and acting like a big shot. I stuck my nose up in the air as if I won the fight.

Tears of guilt dripped off my cheekbones again, as I woke up grief stricken. I wiped them with my bloody gown while throwing Joey's Hot Wheel pickup truck against the dining room wall again. It smashed and splattered into a million little pieces. After the school bus departed, I skipped to Tina's yard to pick some yellow flowers from the crabgrass. This time around, the blades of grass visually magnified due from my heightened occipital lobes, responsible for seeing. They felt denser and sharper against my skin as well. I wiped my tears again, before gathering the glorious staples of springtime and creating a special bouquet for Joey. The Old Christine sensed some bullying taking place that morning. When Joey finally walked through the front door after school, I approached him with my Burger King hat and sad face. I handed him the beautiful bouquet of yellow dandelions from my hospital bed. "I'm sorry I broke your truck," I said.

But unfortunately, the rubber road wheels failed to stop flying above me, failed to come to a halt. "I'm sorry Joey," I said repeatedly over the following two decades, but he couldn't hear me. Something knocked me down, O'Sullivan confirmed, and reality came around. Songs of solitude and despair muddled through my brain again and overlapped. Next, Bette Midler crooned about the nights too lonely and roads too long. The lyrics profound.

Author and musical philosopher, Victor Zuckerkandl writes from an injured brain's perspective: "Every melody declares to us that the past can be there without being remembered, and the future without being foreknown."

*T*hat evening my cousin Angela and her husband Larry appeared with flowers. Struck by the blood, cast, screeching and weeping spells. The skin-tight cast was generating burning tension in my brain, like a balloon ready to explode. Mom tried redirecting my attention to the beautiful lilies they had brought me, but my emotional and physical outbursts prevailed. Mom dialed Steven again helpless, but still no answer. Over an hour passed and no answer still. Larry, a large three-hundred-pound, Italian man holds a mild temperament, unless you strike the wrong nerve. "Where the fu- is her husband?!" I overheard him, "his wife had brain surgery for God's sake. What a coward!"

Steven was a no show again, so Mom changed her plans and spent the night beside me on the recliner.

*B*ig shot reappeared the following day or two, I'm still uncertain. He was ready to pick me up from the hospital and take me home as if all was good. The only thing I recall about our drive home is my two opposing hemispheres, past and present, acting up like siblings, one giggling, the other sobbing, one happy, the other angry. My brain and mind felt like an emotional roller coaster, like one long, run-on sentence with no real beginning, middle or end. As we were crossing over the George Washington Bridge, my primitive hemisphere had already noticed the great, white shark swinging his tail fiercely from side to side, preparing himself to menace the community of ocean goers. This time my right hemisphere retreated to 1977, I later learned through the unmasking process. The Old Christine was screaming in angst from the great white shark, as Mommy handed me a cloth from the back seat. She woke me up from another hallucination and wiped my sweat and tears. Somehow, she indirectly assured me that *Jaws* is a mechanical shark, unable to chew up the remains of my head.

I delved back to humor in the same breath, embracing myself in another silly pun. I heard myself cracking up aloud, not only at the pun, but at my Self as well. The oddity remains, and this is a common pattern in brains holding temporal lobe deficiencies.

"There's a problem with the control tower!" I heard from far away, but not from my ears, rather another unknown place, somewhere in my temporal lobe.

"What is it?" I heard the man ask from the passenger seat of the car.

"It's the big tower where the air traffic controllers talk to the planes."

The classic spoof *Airplane* from 1980 prompted uncontrollable laughter in my immature right hemisphere, diverging me from anguish to absurdity in one breath. I turned into my biggest buffoon, animating and mocking myself around childhood muse. One day I came across a Dean Martin play-with-words, stating, "I would rather have a free bottle in front of me, than a prefrontal lobotomy!"

"And who wouldn't," I asked myself aloud in euphoria,

Speaking of humor, both my old brain and my new one failed to appreciate *Seinfeld*. My face remained straight throughout every rerun, and at some point, my nickname became Little Ms. Literal. I kept listening to Steven and the kids cracking up at George or Kramer with a straight face. I struggled to understand the abstract humor. My brain fixates on classic parodies like, *Airplane*, and marvels at the effortless stupidity and one-line gags. My brain is an enigma, perceiving in entirety while remaining rigid, sharp, and contextual all at the same time. Dr. Doidge labels such asymmetry as The Plastic Paradox.

I always waited for the punchline in utter bemusement while hearing Steven and Jason choking in laughter. Well, it turns out that a complex joke needs to be analyzed and perceived through a healthy frontal lobe. Generally, a joke gets perceived as funny the first time it's told, before quickly becoming stale, with the exceptions of spoofs such as *Airplane*. This slapstick humor brilliantly written with satire and distaste holds no deep plot to follow or punchline to anticipate, rather simplicity tickling our immature funny bones. The observational comedy in *Seinfeld* manages capturing the significance of the insignificant, about commonplace events and everyday life, which feels universally familiar to everyone. It revolves around minimization and blatant inexperience in acting as well, which compelled me to further analyze the content and search for what was missing.

It turns out that a severed frontal lobe has the brain overthinking in the wrong moments and probing for something that does not exist. And a brain without a hippocampus wastes so much time and energy on analyzing the unimportant, that it misses the main content presented right before it.

Yet, one *Seinfeld* episode continues to strike my funny bone in 2022. Jerry's episodic memory went blank just like mine, as he failed to recall his own girlfriend's name. All he knew was that it rhymed with a female body part. She walked out on him insulted, and soon enough he shouted out from his apartment window, "Dolores!"

A simple rhyme requiring zero cognitive ability. At another point in my research, I came across a complex joke by Niels Bohr, a Nobel-Prize-winning physicist. A visitor walked into his office and noticed a good-luck horseshoe hanging above the door. "Surely you don't believe in that superstitious nonsense, Doctor Bohr!" the visitor exclaimed.

Bohr replied, "Of course not, but I've heard it works, whether you believe it or not."

The authors of the book explained the joke like this: Bohr's had a rational disbelief in the good-luck-power of a horseshoe, as well as the apparent belief that it may hold such power, after- all, which are both mediated by a sober pragmatism allowing him to have it both ways.

It turns out that both sides of the brain get used to comprehend humor, and it requires cognitive shifting through a healthy corpus callosum. It requires left-hemispheric language, abstract reasoning, and visual searching. It requires the ability to keep a story intact, so the punch line *connects* to the stem of the joke. Left brain deficiencies lose the meaning of the story somewhere in between, so by the time the joke reaches the punch line, the brain is already spent. Its why puns are wonderful for children, autistics, and the elderly. They occupy a special place in the brain for positive thinking and social interaction. Winston Churchill described a joke as *a very serious thing*.

Dr. Doidge had a patient with problems in abstract thinking as well; she felt that her silly humor was the dearest price to pay for an overcrowded right hemisphere. One day I tried to explain to Steven the medical reasons behind my fixation with puns. "You just had brain surgery Chrissy," he replied, without listening. "Relax about the nonsense," he giggled back.

Ok, I thought, you say it's good, but I see our relationship as a treadmill to nowhere!

*T*he following morning my *Airplane* euphoria persisted, until the point when my brain and body clashed, and battled one another again to simply get out of bed. It began living in the immediate stimuli, losing the ability to plan for future events or execute decisions. Even a simple decision such as getting out of bed gets surrounded around knowledge, feelings, reason, consequence, opinion, consistency.... I felt rushed and yet lethargic at the same time. So, I popped up from bed in urgency before walking myself downstairs. I headed through the large foyer toward the kitchen, where Mom turned around still. "How did you get downstairs by yourself Chris?" she asked disturbed.

I stood silent, puzzled by my odd surroundings. My two unfamiliar children sat on the stools, waiting for their pancakes. "Didn't you hear her cracking-up upstairs Gramma?" Jason replied matter-of-factly.

I felt trapped in a life that seemed to be longer mine, lacking clarity, familiarity, perception, and feelings. My brain was overstimulated by gazillions of neurons firing unpredictably at once. The white noise scrutinized every single spectacle, word, glance, action, and reaction, all seducing me into overthinking in the wrong moments. The lack of filter to discern between prevalent and petty made me express anything that came to mind, which was often misunderstood.

I gazed over at Mom's quasi-familiar features and pale complexion. I felt empty. No feelings. "Mommy!" Stephanie shouted in excitement, "look at the chocolate chip pancakes Gramma made us!"

Although my knowledge remained intact, I failed to connect her voice to my feelings of love and familiarity. Next, Mom reached out her arms to hug me, kiss me, and massage me, but I glared through her face like a mannequin unable to reciprocate emotion back. My mother and children instantly turned into bystanders, as my bewilderment dusted the room. I recalled praying for them and for my tulips before going under the knife, all while three sets of eyes ogled me. "Who selected us all to be together? Who made these arrangements?" I asked myself ambushed, with a dire need for alone time.

Neurosurgeon Gary noted in *WHEN THE AIR HITS YOUR BRAIN* that: "If a patient isn't dead, you can always make him worse if you try hard enough."

And that's how I felt, dead. A mother pining for personal separation while her two small children sought her attention, hugs, kisses. One hemisphere opened the drawer and began fidgeting with the forks and spoons while the other decided to pick up the pair of scissors, with no goal in mind. Circuits fired in opposing directions at once, and my impulse prevailed over my common sense. I left the drawer wide open only to circle around the island with the scissors in tow.

Ironically, psychologist Herbert Simon compares the human mind to a pair of scissors, where one blade represents our cognitive limitations, and the other represents the structures of our environment. In-essence, the blades may very-well fail in connection. Mom tried to take them away from me, but I jerked myself around her instead, and strolled down the hallway to the laundry room with my scissors intact. I longed for Adam Levy, my newfound partner and best friend, to embrace me and assure me that my life will be ok.

The dryer was full, but I decided on removing only three items: Steven's briefs and two pairs of Jason's shorts. I left the dryer door open and headed back to the kitchen with the damp clothes and scissors. I placed the articles on the center island, before moving my body right, left, right, left with the blades pointing outward. Mom took them away from the immature child, who looked at the three actors playing their parts. Perhaps my vision is blurry, I tried convincing myself for years, rubbing my eyes over and over, in hopes to gain back some recognition, retrieval, warmth or familiarity.

Our brains hold billions of neurons, individual cells generating emotions, thoughts, and perceptions. They guide and regulate our behaviors, choices, and opinions. They direct and execute our actions. My perceptions got clipped in the O.R., I'd already sensed, before accidentally crisscrossing to the wrong people. So, I circled around the island one last time, before finally deciding to speak.

"What?" I asked Mom, who stood staring at me with wet eyes.

She reached out to embrace me once again. "I love you so much Chris," she wept.

"Get away from me and don't touch me again!" I snapped back.

Departed the kitchen as silently as I entered. I walked down the long hallway to the office and plopped on the couch. I looked out the window into the back yard through brand new lenses. I gazed at my canna lilies in full bloom while seeking some nonverbal peace. No oral communication involved, I gazed at my bright yellow and orange flowers surrounded by my tall green grasses and pink sedums. I imagined my grasses turning gold real soon, and my sedums turning burgundy. My occipital lobe flattered with deeper visions, illustrations, hues, and depths. By this point in July, my marvelous cannas peaked at nearly six feet high. Just one stem, measuring as thick as a water pipe. The flowers bloomed along the stem, surrounded by massive shiny leaves branching out in shimmering solids and camouflages. Cannas stem from a bulb, cultivated in the shape of a Y, I told myself. They're called tubes, and their variations in shape differentiate their leaf structure and pattern. There are nineteen classified species, my new information system notified me, and they grow best in warm tropical temperatures and islands....

This information system runs in my right unconscious mind like one long run- on sentence.... Next it informed me that over the decades, horticulturists developed the tube to live and adapt to more temperate climates in the northeast, and even among most countries in the world! Each season I had specific bulbs shipped to me directly from Holland, fully primed for immediate planting. Each spring my glorious peaks of tulips replaced my daffodils. Tulips have no rivals, because unlike the daffodil, the tulip never gets dominated by surrounding shrubbery and weeds. Their displays are too striking to get overshadowed. Every spring I watched hundreds and hundreds of tulips heaping up and descending. The sprinkler heads showered my beds haphazardly, to create colorful mini mountains. It's no wonder that the tulip signifies elegance and grace.

Mom showed up in the office. "Let's walk through your gardens and get some fresh air," she suggested, before placing my slippers gently on my feet. She took my hand and walked me outside. Although I didn't perceive her the same as before, I clung on to her anyhow, and together we strolled through the plush landscape. Then we saw her through my pines, my colorful neighbor staring at us from her driveway. The witchy short-haired brunette with bulging fisheyes inspected my hard cast and shaved head. Just a month before I had asked her adolescent boys to lower the belting music from their outdoor stereo system. I had asked them to stop partying after ten on a school night, since Jason and Stephanie were just four and five years old. I was angry and hurt, but looking back now, I realized the epileptic had asked a lot from them. After all, they had every right to celebrate their kid's birthday parties without me hovering over them.

But by this point she had already turned on me, vengeful and wicked. When Dr. Levy weaned me off my medications, I was enduring multiple seizures every hour, and the neighbor knew this. When I walked outside to roll in the garbage cans, I heard her mock me from across the street. "Did you take your fuc.. medication today?!" she shouted.

All heads bowed down, as she laughed aloud. Then she saw my cast days later, and Mom and I noticed her change in tune.

I found my body rocking Stephanie back and forth on her rocking chair beside Petunia, our Norwegian Forest cat. She was purring alongside us while Nana was rocking me back and forth on hers, with Belle snoring alongside us as well. Stephanie and I, both four years old, snuggled beside our priceless furry creatures and listened to their rhythms. Stephanie began dozing off right beneath Nana's crocheted quilt, in chocolate brown with bright yellow and orange flowers. It turns out that such temporal lobe dreams and hallucinations need to get unmasked hundreds of times before getting classified by time, order, and context. But this arduous process took place during my children's most pertinent developmental years. Even worse, my doctors never warned me I'd endure such grief in the first place, such emotional detachment and extreme change in personality. "The healing process is about two months," Gordon told me matter-of-factly, when in reality, it failed to end.

How does it feel for a small child to see their mother in such anguish, and unable to come to terms with losing her? The New Christine asked herself a decade later. What happened to my Mommy, Stephanie asked herself in silence growing up, I later learned, suffering from her own masked depression and withdrawal.

And then there was Jason, suddenly asking his new Mom why she keeps talking about *Willie Wonka and the Chocolate Factory*, and singing, *I want to lock it all up in my*…over-and -over again.

"Mom we love the movie too, but you're being annoying, childlike!" he continued.

I must have nodded off beside Stephanie and Petunia, when The Little Man intruded on real time again, this time reminding me that Timbuktu is in Mali, a country in northwestern Africa, which is also known to have one of the first universities in the world. In addition, "Constantinople is an ancient city in Turkey," he expressed, "that dropped its name in the 1930 and replaced it with Istanbul."

More old, scattered tidbits of information arose, unrelated to my present circumstances. It turns out that our recent memories and impressions disappear the soonest after head injuries, Sacks notes, whereas impressions of long ago get recalled properly, "So that a patient's ingenuity, his sharpness of wit, and his resourcefulness remain largely unaffected."

Soon after, I found myself plopped in the back of Mom's Buick Skylark again, beside Stuffed Pink Piglet. I strapped the lap belts across our bodies, and off we went on our morning ride to Nana's house. Re-experiencing the sheer delight of crossing over Mr. Bridge again, with Mr. Sun's rays gleaming from above. Mr. Sun beamed right through The Cumulus Clouds to warm the Earth with his bright yellow rays. He provided us with beautiful reflections of the trees and boats along the water. Mr. Bridge and Mr. Sun bore the same grin as Dr. Levy, the implicit concern for people's welfare. Stuffed Pink Piglet and I were living through our unconscious memories again, our long, forgotten pasts.

A depleted hippocampus doesn't insinuate that the remaining primitive parts in of limbic system can't take charge. In fact, Sacks notes that our selective aged memories get stored in other subcortical structures as well, such as the basal ganglia, in addition to the more modern parts of the brain like the cerebellum and cerebral cortex.

Our tires rubbing along the metal grids sounded sharper than long ago, sturdier, and holding timbre and resonance. I'm sure that Mr. Bridge's grids corroded over the decades, but not according to our embellishments. In fact, his shiny metal grates gripping our tires provided our car with a melody, as it danced from side by side. *This land is your land....* Mr. Bridge hummed, as our lives were stuffed with old melodies and compositions.

My brain took word "land" literally. In the immediate moment I found my arms raking the autumn leaves alongside Joey, jumping in the piles, and cherishing the sacred lands all over again. Mr. Bridge respected the lands as well, since he relied on them for structure, stability, and accessibility. I noticed Mom smiling behind the wheel, a manufactured smile, I considered, lingering in the outskirts of her pleasure system. "Her brain is not like ours," Stuffed Pink Piglet whispered to me, "aged and ripened."

Unlike Mom, Mr. Bridge, Mr. Sun, and The Cumulus Clouds all continued to enhance my journey through time travel, alongside Stuffed Pink Piglet, Belle, and my flock of seagulls.

Everyone knew Nana's residence well, the decaying Victorian lying sedentary along the water on the New London side of Mr. Bridge, home of the famous East Coast Naval Submarine Base as well. Like every other weekday morning, we crossed over Mr. Bridge to Nana's at precisely 8:45. We watched the drawbridge closing as we drew closer to him. Mr. Bridge was always prepared to block the water traffic sailing beneath him when we passed, and like every other morning, Stuffed Pink Piglet gave him a peace sign gesture with his fingers, like a V.

A lovely, silver drawbridge with lovely, galvanized silver grates communicating to us in volumes. Stuffed Pink Piglet rambled with the flocks swooping in unison above. I opened my window and extended my arm up and out to touch the seagulls and The Cumulus Clouds. Sure, my brain knew perfectly well that cumulus clouds do block the sun's rays entirely, but my mind was undergoing transference again for its own self-preservation. It insisted that The Cumulous Clouds would never dare block the rays of Mr. Sun.

During this dream, this drive, I perceived my fluffy friends floating three thousand feet above enhancing the clear-blue sky with delicious white foam. I had a dream of clouds in my.... and the steamed milk swirled with cinnamon tasted delightful. From this point forward, Carly Simon's famous 1971 hit "You're So Vain," became one of the two songs taking up the most space in my brain. As a prisoner of the past, it still fails to age.

By this point I got pissed at The Little Man, who was notifying me that cumulus clouds obstruct the sun's emissions and trap in the Earth's heat. This type of thunderstorm cloud holds tremendous amounts of energy as well, he expressed, and provoke thunder, lightning, and even violet tornados like Dorothy's.

But Stuffed Pink Piglet, and I insisted that The Cumulous Clouds provide shade to the animals, and vegetation through the dog days of summer. My brain confirmed Sack's theory of reminiscence once again, proving that each recollection got fed to me in the wrong order, and was prone to revision and re-categorization. Further, our rare selections of music and memories reflect the taste of the *times,* rather than the taste of the *individual.* *

*I*t was Gordon's dexterity and skill reconnecting me to the taste of the *times* rather than the taste of the *individual,* to an old time and place filled with plenty of lace and paper flowers. I found myself in my walk-in closet wearing clothes that Mom dressed me in that morning, a navy collared shirt and beige pleated shorts from Land's End. As a conservative prep that's pretty much all I owned. Navy's, beiges, browns. Collared, pleats and turtlenecks. And of-course brown and black penny loafers from Cole Haan. Steven and I dressed like golfers and accountants back then, two peas in a pod. But that morning home, my shoes, belts, and apparel mismatched my image. Stevie elbowed me, pleading for me to stand up for who I am.

The New Christine searched through my racks for clothes with bohemian flair, but saw tailored grey and black suits instead, and blue and white button downs from Eddie Bauer. How are these collared shirts on my shelves impeccably folded and ironed? I asked myself. I am a hippie, I knew, a nomadic wanderer, holding an impetuous need to abandon conservative clothes like these. I exist on one vast planet, my unconsciousness knew, absent of rules, borders, and censorship.

The doctors never advised me of something so glowingly apparent, the simple yet complex fact that the frontal lobe shapes our identity, personality, and sense of self, and that the hippocampus helps keep the brain grounded in real time! * While all four of our lobes are crucial for survival, the frontal lobe remains the most critical, specifically the left frontal lobe, assigning each person distinct individuality and character. It identifies Jack as Jack and Rachel as Rachel. I never knew that my frontal lobe had been spoiling throughout my lifetime from the effects of seizures, oxygen deprivation and heavy-duty antiepileptic medications. It was a cunningly sly process, which led me to more questions later on: Were my seizures and medications blocking my personality and individual characteristics over time? Were they aiding in the altercation of my original Self as well, arising from birth, as well as from my earliest childhood years with Nana, before my dangerous accident took place? Perhaps my id, the most primitive parts of the brain got targeted in the O.R. as well, I began considering, activating the unconscious mind.

I looked at myself in the full-length mirror on my closet door and felt an urge to swap the beige golf shirt for a blouse with fringe and ruffles. I hallucinated a floral bandana draped on my head, backwards in a V, just like Rhoda Morgenstern, from the present sitcom *Rhoda* in 1974.

This new liberation and autonomy brought on some impulse as well, which started prevailing over my common sense, triggering random, impetuous decisions. I chucked my clothes into large Hefty bags, feeling a sudden, urgent need to replace them with unconventional, carefree articles, such as fabrics and styles from Free People and Anthropologie. Mom stood from behind, silently watching me chuck out my oversized clothes without decoration. I had lost my old identity and gained a new one, and endured grief and liberty at the exact point in time. "I'm a skinny size-zero Mom," I expressed, "with an ideal, hour-glass figure!"

"So why do these clothes feel so off-balance with my body?" I asked myself, perplexed.

"What's going on with you, Chris?" Mom asked, shaking her head back and forth in dismay.

"Mind your own business," I snapped back.

73

"Put the clothes back!" she yelled.

"Go away!"

"I've lectured you your entire life on your oversized clothes, and how they cover up your beautiful shape. So, stop yelling at me now!" she shouted before walking away.

From this point forward I gravitated to tablecloth fabrics, tie dyes, bell bottoms, and geometric prints. More earthy tones resurfaced, including burnt oranges, chocolate browns, and mustard yellows, as well as earthy prints like paisleys and florals. My brain began having trouble distinguishing leisurewear from formalwear, and summer wear from winter wear. This is because it lost much of its left-hemispheric edges in the operating room, holding the ability to delineate boundaries, including those of sizes, seasons, and points of reference. My right hemispheric edges softened, relaxing my confines and restrictions. These problems in perception make it difficult for me to adhere to rules and protocol. It turns out that left frontal lobe injuries offer the right hemisphere freedoms and allowances that don't always adhere to standard etiquette.

Paradoxically, my form of brain injury despises rules and restrictions on one hand, while craving them at the same time on the other hand. It acts like a child. In addition, my left hemisphere views the planet as one massive, undivided entity all while my right depicts rigidity and inflexibility. Another fine example of The Plastic Paradox, of two minds continuously contradicting one another like oil and water and making me often contradict myself in one sentence.

But in a way it doesn't matter because I pay homage to my right hemisphere, to the flower child of very long ago refusing to permanently wilt. The surgery provoked my right hemispheric idealism, creativity, and zeal, all overpowering my left realism and pragmatism. My mind reverted to a counter-cultural revolution of sorts, to the late 1960s and early 1970s. It suddenly struck by off-the-wall logos and new emblems such as *Flower Power* and *We Shall Not Wilt*. Real time and time travel admixing together in one brain, fully unaware of holding two distinct entities, and a damaged correlation in between.

Unlike psychiatry, neurology doesn't focus on battles raging in the unconscious mind, the residual primitive pieces remaining in the id after brain surgery. Psychiatry focuses more on the ego and superego, reason, and mortality. The epileptic Christine just happened to name her pets Petunia, Pansy, Daisy and Lily, without foreseeing that the names presaged my future. They must have covertly represented My Flower Children all along, way before the logo depicted real time. When The New Christine mentioned her newfound discovery to Steven, he laughed, as if he knew something I did not. "*Flower Power* isn't your emblem to patent Chris," he said, chuckling.

So, I went online in late 1999. For the very first time I reached out to Larry Page and Sergey Brin, who founded Google the same year! I Googled Flower Children and Flower Power and the metaphors generated profound emotion, feelings of freedom and emancipation, attachment and belonging. After fighting with Mom, I walked around the house braless and barefoot. Suddenly, I felt socks and bras cramping me. I perceived high-end brands as mere objects of vanity, rather than tools to make me happy. I knew without a doubt that these feelings and perceptions were real and would never alter again. I was now a drifter, I knew, despising regulations, and drifting back and forth between resolution and uncertainty. Over time I began wondering if the oldest networks in my brain got triggered, those representing what God had created in the first place, back in 1966.

Three Months Before
Surgery and Forward

Time progressed and my seizures were worsening. I turned into a full-blown epileptic with complex partial seizures, passing out three to five times a week and losing consciousness with each attack. Although I knew these evil forces were too powerful for me to maintain a healthy quality of life, it was the only life I knew. Epilepsy stems from the Latin word *Epilepsia,* meaning to seize, take hold of, or attack. Every seizure represented an attack on my nervous system, altering my personality over time, and degrading my overall sense of well-being. Nobody grasped the severity of the danger, that just one seizure while I was driving on the road could land someone in the grave. It never dawned on me that I could drown while swimming in a pool from an unexpected seizure, or die from Sudden Unexplained Death in Epilepsy, (SUDEP) when a seizure ignites during sleep, causing one to choke to death from loss of oxygen. By thirty-three, I had endured hundreds of seizures in my sleep and always managed waking up alive, but my luck was wearing thin.

In 1999, my neurologist on the New Jersey side of the George Washington Bridge advised me to cross over to the New York side to meet with a specialist at New York-Presbyterian/Weill Cornell, one of the top four hospitals in the nation. "What if we just tweak my meds one more time," I suggested first, "lower the Dilantin or up the Tegretol?"

But he scribbled on his notepad without looking up. "I'll rest more," I promised. "I won't drive when I feel an aura … I'll stop downing shots at the bar with my friends … Just one more tweak," I pleaded.

Unlike my new, up-and-coming partner, Dr. Adam Levy, my New Jersey neurologist's bedside manner was heartless. When he finally glanced up, he leisurely said, "Most likely the next step will be brain surgery."

"What's the worst conceivable outcome?" I blurted out, shocked.

"Death," he replied matter-of-factly.

I rode down the elevator feeling dazed and traumatized. After a fourteen-year relationship with this neurologist, I thought that a softer approach would have gone a long way. He could have explained why brain surgery would be the most viable option to eradicate my seizures and provide me with a safer quality of life. As I let it sink in slowly, my feelings began contradicting one another, shuffling around, and overlapping. I wanted to blame my parents, and I went from appreciation to anger, and to denial once again. "How could they watch their child trip through life passing out in the public eye for so long?" I wanted to know, "in the classroom, supermarket, and at her very own sweet sixteen party?"

"As parents you took the path of least resistance," I shouted at them, "leaving me to reckon with the consequences by myself."

"Yet, if I didn't recognize or foresee the long-term consequences myself, then how can anybody else?" I asked myself, "and if I suspected danger, I discounted it just like them."

Another fear suddenly stirred the pot, fear of crossing over the George Washington Bridge to the upper west side of Manhattan. Intimidated by those vast structures resting prominently at arm's length from the bridge in Washington Heights. Apparently, The Old Christine perceived them as an immeasurable mass of buildings, stocked with muscle, sway, brilliance and sovereignty. She never imagined that one day she'd walk through the doors of the Neurological Institute at "Ivy League Columbia." These peculiar sentiments were evidence of an impaired hippocampus and parietal lobe, both used for daily navigation, in addition to understanding and recalling where objects appear in space.

Our brain holds both grey and white matter. The grey matter that lies in the cerebral cortex and limbic system process our information through sight and memory. The white matter represents our links used to communicate between these two regions of the brain. When these areas skew like mine, our perceptions of the world become skewed as well.

In addition, a brain envisioning reality in entirety rather than piecemeal gets baffled by over-convoluted streets and dense populations. Since our memory banks can't fully store details, we often wind up in sensory overload. Neuroscientist Dr. Eve Valera performed a study of the brain's white matter on twenty women experiencing brain trauma and psychological abuse, and her results show less white matter in their brains, resulting in severe abnormalities in learning and memory. While male victims like athletes often go public about their brain injuries, female victims of physical abuse conceal their pains for an exceptionally long time, leaving studies inadequate and limited.

Everyone's brain needs white matter for cognitive abilities, including negotiation, bargaining, decision making, judging, and conceding. The lack of white matter produces *both* rigid, left hemispheric restrictions and liberal, right hemispheric freedoms. My factual contexts kept me focused on my research while my infinite possibilities spread across the divine universe, holding empathy and idealism. Over time I began considering that perhaps these two distinct mindsets were already active before the brain surgery and camouflaged by my illness.

Those buildings hold infinite power and genius minds, my idealistic old self thought each time she crossed over the George Washington Bridge. Minds that could spread across the planet to heal everyone in pain.

*O*n one-hand, my confidence was building, because I couldn't wait to get my short-term memory back, and to improve my job skills and relationships. Yet, on-the-other-hand I was still mad. I continued to question my parents about my care, however, their defenses never shifted. "Chris, we went to different specialists and hospitals, and tried different medications...."

Well, they indeed schlepped me to Yale New Haven Hospital from Niantic twice a year to seek all available options, I told myself, and back then brain surgery wasn't one of them. In fact, no name assigned to my condition back then. Of course, everything changed when we met Dr. Levy a few months later in March 1999. On that cathartic afternoon, I donned my signature ponytail and chocolate brown penny loafers.

Dr. Adam Levy was preppy as well. He looked like a young, overworked physician moving up the socio-economic ladder. When I walked into his office, the bright sunlight was reflecting through the windows. Too young to be sitting behind two large mahogany desks, I thought. I smiled at him, just before he grinned back at me with his first adorable grin. He looked to be around his mid-twenties, and too young to be sitting in a corner office at Ivy League Columbia, I told myself. The two desks positioned in an L, and I watched his head moving back and forth between two large computer screens.

When he finally arose in his long white coat and stethoscope, he shook my hand professionally. Unlike my first handshake with

Steven in 1988, he looked at me directly in the eyes with confidence and warmth. Very humble as well, and I soon discovered he was a man of a few words. He bore an impeccably tailored suit beneath his robe, and crooked tie. Noticeably young and overextended, I thought.

"How old are you Dr. Levy?" I blurted.

Perhaps my verbal filter was already waning, The New Christine later considered. He grinned again, before replying, "Thirty-four."

"Oh my God! I'm thirty-three!" I answered. "When's your birthday?" I asked.

"March."

"Oh my God!" I said again, like a child. "Mine too!"

Wow, thirty-four years old, I went home thinking, with a medical degree, residency and fellowship from Harvard, Yale, and Columbia. Dr. Levy didn't mind my curiosity, in fact, he seemed to like the shock value and compliments, all growing into a true friendship over the years.

Like every other neurologist over the past twenty-eight years, he began evaluating my short-term memory with the same kindergarten test I'd failed since childhood. He stated three words aloud to evaluate my declarative memory, having me recall them back moments later, after the subject diverted elsewhere. He stated: *"Apple, rain* and *headband,"* and once again my memory failed me, as I retrieved only one. On my second or third visit, I made a comment to him in front of my parents, one that still sticks to me today like maple syrup: "I can't wait to get my short-term memory back!" I exclaimed.

*H*is response changed my life. After smirking another sweet smirk, he said, "Chris, (He called me Chris from the onset) that's never going to happen."

He began explaining to us that a concussion falls nothing short of a permanent brain injury. Brain surgery might very well eliminate the seizures once-and-for all, he expressed, but it will never restore your short-term memory, nor make it more effective than it already is. It would be like trying to make a dead plant come back to life. It turns out that the antiseizure medications had slowed down my brain's psychomotor development, memory, and scholastic achievement during my most critical learning years as well. The age that a child's brain can no longer transfer functions from one hemisphere to another is around five to seven years old. Younger, underdeveloped brains hold more plasticity to recover, but I did not pass the paper-thin threshold. After seven or eight years, each piece becomes individually specialized. The corpus callosum is already fully developed by this age as well, allowing each hemisphere to communicate effectively with one other and share their tasks efficiently.

He stunned me once again by saying that I may have already had a pre-existing abnormality before my fall at age five, making me more vulnerable to future seizures. It was then that I learned something brand-new. Mom told him about my 104-degree febrile convulsion at two months old, and this was a a-ha moment for everyone. This is what most likely increased the susceptibility to a permanent, lifelong injury in the future, Dr. Levy expressed, should another brain injury ever occur. In-other-words, my seizures may have been brewing long before anyone imagined.

Injuries like this will usually begin in the frontal and temporal lobes, the anterior parts of the brain, positioned on the top of and behind our forehead. This makes them most susceptible to outside danger. For some odd reason, the hippocampus shrinks over time as well, specifically in brains with dementia and Alzheimer's. Unlike our peripheral nerves, which can heal from injury over time, the brain wasn't naturally designed to take so many insults without permanent repercussions. My seizures not only struck these known areas, but they indirectly struck other unknown areas as well, The New Christine discovered slowly, and once again, creating a savant over time as well.

With the human brain, critical implies time, because time increases the awareness of the disease itself. * It is why it took until my teens for me notice the deterioration in my memory and speech. By high school I finally realized that I had trouble memorizing facts for exams and recalling the right words to my complete verbal sentences when speaking. The damage is silent for years, but over time, inevitable. Dr. Tracy McIntosh describes the phenomenon of epilepsy as a *chain-reaction,* where mysterious effects occur in the brain, but don't truly manifest until later in life. She calls this phenomenon *programmed cell death* or *cell suicide.* If one cell becomes damaged, the damage will spread progressively and underhandedly to other areas, including regions responsible for language, judgement, memory, and cognition. My earliest diagnoses simply read "functional abnormalities and seizures," even more reasons that epilepsy is as *The Silent Epidemic.*

Remember, every seizure presented itself with an imperative warning, an aura representing my threshold of escape. My elementary school in Niantic was a one level brick building shaped like a maze, holding fewer than one hundred students. A building of that size and design was a relatively safe environment for a student in my condition, but Lawrence Junior High School I attended years later in Long Island, is a massive two-story brick building. It holds striking white pillars belonging in Washington, D.C. The building was too massive for me to escape during a seizure without notice.

During one social studies exam, I felt the oxygen darting upward from my chest right through the center of my brain, and yet I remained perfectly conscious of my surroundings, as I quickly excused myself to go to the bathroom. I sprinted through the long hallway, raced down two flights of stairs, and escaped from the gym door. I knew I had less than thirty seconds to disappear from the public eye before a seizure erupted in full force. Every seizure represented a short, isolated event, I recall, a meaningless moment of physical and mental nausea. Over time, though, these pertinent thirty seconds shortened down to fifteen...before ten...before.... I am screwed, I knew!

Ironically, the ideal description of a seizure was written by a social critic and novelist that never suffered from one before. Thomas Mann, born in 1875 described a seizure so precisely that I felt he lived amid one of us. "It's a crude, random, psychological event, wholly unselective without feeling or meaning," he wrote beautifully.

The aura was a phase of lucidity, a semi-conscious state of mind making me feel removed from my body. Another famous 1800s scientist, Dr. Hughlings Jackson, described this semiconscious period as the *manifestation of disassociation*. It's that miniscule point before the epileptic enters their *'dreamy state,'* he noted, which for me included crude sensations of smell and taste, as well as fingers palpitating, ears ringing, and odd sensations swarming through my stomach. After the nausea drifted upward to my brain, I passed out, unconscious. This rapid switch from consciousness to unconsciousness felt bittersweet, because on one hand I knew I was going to pass out into oblivion, but on the other hand I knew I was going to pass out into oblivion as well. In other words, the auras epitomized sardonic holy spirits holding feelings of grave disgust *and* gratitude. The auras functioned as buffers, warning my brain that it was going to shut down within seconds. "Ha, ha," they seemed to warn me in a bittersweet pitch. Another imminent arrival, I knew.

The sardonic holy spirits told me when to pull my car over to the side of the road to avoid a collision or death. They allotted just enough time for me to find a haven before the seizure erupted in full force. These spirits made me such a pro at masking my seizures that my closest friends in school remained oblivious of my disease. But as the auras' *mental beginning to the end* shortened, the risks heightened.

I wasn't mindful of sustaining two types of seizures, holding notable distinctions like life or death: *semi-conscious* and *unconscious* seizures. As an irresponsible teenager, I flat-out disregarded my symptoms, and rather than listening to my sardonic holy spirits, I drove around, barhopped, and misbehaved with my friends to satisfy my immediate pleasures. One ailing afternoon I drove to Point Lookout Beach to meet them, but that morning the nausea, dizziness, blurred vision, and lack of appetite all overcame me. By this point, my critical strands already shortened, and my risks became deadly. Less time for me to pull over to safety, so my driving privileges should have revoked. Yet, I remained a selfish, irresponsible teenager with an obstinate mind.

I slammed the gas pedal to get on to the Meadowbrook Parkway, sensing bad vibrations of an oncoming seizure. This aura didn't allot enough time for me to pull over to the side of the road to safety, and yet nothing happened. It's because I'd endured a semi-conscious seizure rather than an unconscious one, The New

Christine learned, allowing me to maintain full control of the wheel. I was living in the immediate moment, so my brain maintained the ability to continue driving straight down the middle lane of a busy parkway without full mental cognition! *

In the immediate moment of attack, one half of my brain remained conscious, while the other half completely shut down and detached from the event. Living through the *dreamy state*, as my mental cognition turned off and on at the same time. This dreamy state allowed me to continue performing the complicated task of driving safely in one lane of a busy parkway with cars passing on both sides. Since I remained mentally responsive to my immediate stimuli, I reached my destination in one piece. Dr. Jackson labeled this as a mental state of double consciousness.

Mental state of double consciousness, I told myself. Our brains hold an anterior cingulate gyrus, (ACC) that wraps around the corpus callosum, connecting to both the cognitive prefrontal cortex and the emotional limbic system. It helps us control and sustain fear during times of threat and upset. My research, history and recollections all led me to believe that my ACC got affected from seizures throughout my lifetime and it got activated in the operating room somehow as well. Here's my take. The ACC helps to integrate our consciousness and unconsciousness, our knowing and feeling, and it alerts us when we are in danger.

A damaged ACC is bittersweet, but far more sweet than bitter. On one hand my ACC mutes the emotional sting of a hazardous situation, but contrastingly, it rapidly reacts to it as well, and accesses necessary alternatives if, and when needed. It acts as the intersection between left hemispheric knowing and right hemispheric feeling. The ACC regulates signals of potential danger and has the unconsciousness alerting the consciousness of potential danger, before persuading it to respond immediately.

But my immediate is shorter than average. Look at what happened during my semi-conscious seizure when I drove on the Meadowbrook Parkway. Nothing. It's because a tampered ACC gifted my brain with speedier anticipation and detection than normal during the highest levels of decision-making, the high-risk decisions of the right hemisphere, those holding the greatest consequences, and in this case, human life. The ACC is also known to counterbalance the overstimulation of a seizure. All of this prevented me from veering off course on the road. All of this allowed me to drive safely on a parkway while processing my immediate stimuli. My unconscious working memory kept my mind in tunnel vision as well and saved my life. *

Dr. Jackson spoke of his patient, Dr. Z., who shared one of his own cases with him. On one occasion, Dr. Z. explained that while he was diagnosing a patient for a respiratory complaint, he sensed a slight fit impending. "So as a doctor, I just turned away and left the patient's room," he told Dr. Z. (like me in the classroom). Even in a semi-conscious state, Dr. Z. kept the ability to diagnose his patient properly with pneumonia. "It was good that my patient didn't notice anything strange in my behavior," he told Dr. Z.

Yet he still felt the need to check his patient's original diagnosis again later in the day, just in case. It was then he noted that his conscious diagnosis was the same as his unconscious one. In the immediate moment, neither Dr. Z. nor I grasped real-time, because our left, sophisticated state of mind was turned off! Remarkably, though, our earlier working memory in our unconscious right side remained perfectly intact, which saved us! I continued to drive while semi-conscious and the doctor continued diagnosing his patient, and to top it all off, we both felt like nothing peculiar happened in the first place! *

Unfortunately, this vital period decreased while my number of seizures increased. Over time I began passing out more and losing complete cognizance with each attack. As I felt the uncontrollable grips of force inside my body and brain, I realized that the doctor on the Jersey side of the bridge had been right the entire time. I needed brain surgery. Over the following three months I met with an entire team of specialists at New York Presbyterian Hospital working to locate the areas causing my seizures. Dr. Levy slowly weaned me off my medications to trigger them so that an electroencephalogram, (EEG) could observe my brain's activity in the immediate moment. The EEG followed the electrical impulses along the surface of the skull to pinpoint the lesions in split second's time. Then things got tricky. Scheduled for a two-night hospital stay, in hopes to trigger the seizures, so the doctors could target them spot on. Yet, the reckless Christine delayed the entire process, as her impulse prevailed over her common sense. My poor frontal lobe and hippocampus felt the need to expedite the doctor's orders, and win over the entire Chocolate Factory, just like the irresponsible cast of characters trying to fool the genius himself: Willy Wonka!

Weaning myself off meds on my very own volition only proved my already existing poor, impulsive tendencies. The hasty decision provoked an early a flux of seizures before the scheduled testing. My brain was making its own rules already, I later discovered, while knowing full well that it shouldn't have. My willingness to cross barriers without the sense of normal fear and consequence was evidence of an injured amygdala as well. In fact, the entire cast of characters in *Willy Wonka and the Chocolate Factory* are all swarmed around risk and chance, The New Christine grasped later on, and in the end, everyone paid the hefty price for their lack of constraint. The timing of the attacks is the most pertinent factor of the EEG, Dr. Levy explained kindly, and I felt pleasantly surprised that he pardoned my mistake and gave me another chance.

The Wada Test stood out the most. The goal of this test was to locate areas responsible for expressive language and memory. Remaining awake throughout the test, I witnessed my own neurological shortfalls. After the neuropsychologist inserted a barbiturate into my left hemisphere, the right half of my body and brain experienced a sense of nothing, nil. Next, the neuropsychiatrist placed ten flashcards in front of me, before quickly removing them from my sight. She asked me to recall back each picture by pointing to it since the right hemisphere cannot speak. It turns out that my right hemisphere successfully recollected all ten pictures. Yet, when she paralyzed my right hemisphere, my left recalled less. This test determined which hemisphere dominated my speech and memory. It confirmed what the doctors already sensed, an impaired left hemisphere.

Neurosurgeon Frank Vertosick made the striking comment, "To a brain surgeon," he writes, "There are two cerebral hemispheres: the left one, and the one that isn't the left one."

The right is merely desirable, he notes, while the left is indispensable. Damage in the right spares our intellect and personality, but damage to the left, he says, thrusts us forever into a foreign land, where no one will ever speak our language.

After a comprehensive evaluation by the team, I met the expert himself, my brain surgeon, Dr. Robert Gordon. A name flowing in a synchronizing stream, I thought. Brilliant like Levy, but more refined and scientifically bred. Clearly not as warm or polite, but dry and poker faced. I waited in silence beside my parents. For over forty-five minutes we sat in front of his large desk and listened to him ramble jargon on the phone with a medical colleague. He barely glanced up to acknowledge us. Dad was getting fidgety, frustrated, and beady eyed. He's a neurosurgeon and scientist, I thought, larger than life.

When Gordon finally stood up, he slid his body ever so gracefully around the desk, too distinguished to pick up his feet. I recall his khaki pants, striped button down and navy-blue tie. I recall his thick mass of hair as well, prematurely white, like mine. I recall his round, oversized glasses reflecting accomplishment. I recall his monotone voice, seemingly unconcerned. Just like his walk, Gordon's diagnoses fell short of effort and exertion. He slurred out his words with knowledge and conviction. Although the final decision to cut open my skull for a resection rested with me, we all fell at his mercy. After twenty-eight years of bewilderment, we all finally heard my diagnosis. *Left Mesiotemporal Sclerosis* and I needed an *Anteromesial Temporal Resection.*

*"D*o you want to improve your *quality of life?"* Levy messaged me a few weeks later. "Just a routine question he asked his patients undergoing a resection to treat epilepsy," I told myself. "It's just standard protocol."

When Dr. Levy called, my brain was coincidentally engrossed in a college textbook called *Basic Neurology*. It was like an *Auditing 101* textbook that I read in college. After Gordon diagnosed me, I made Steven schlep me into Manhattan, I recall, to the one-and-only medical Barnes and Noble in the Tri-state area. Like a big shot, I wanted to learn about the frontal lobe and hippocampus, even before beginning my two-decade journey. What I read scared the daylights out of me, but I had no more brain room left for worry or concern. So, I just rolled my eyes at Levy from the receiving end of the landline, and answered his very important question, "Do you want to improve your quality of life?"

"No," I answered sarcastically.

We chuckled together before hanging up. I sat back to read. It was all good.

*B*ut it all backfired one more time. At 7:30 am on the morning of the surgery, the phone rang. "Because of a power outage, your operation is delayed for an indefinite amount of time," the woman expressed matter-of-factly.

By then, my brain and body felt like a ticking time bomb, craving my anti-seizure drugs like a junkie. It turned out that New York Presbyterian Hospital had a full-blown power outage for the first time in its history, and their back up system failed them as well. So, the lady had more calls to make, notifying parents that school will be cancelled due to hazardous snow conditions. My brain was battling life every waking moment, struggling to stay afloat. Menial chores like emptying the dishwasher and running the vacuum hose along my cat Petunia felt impossible. While feeling fidgety, Violet Beauregarde from the *Willie Wonka and the Chocolate Factory* wound up spiking another poor decision. Her amygdala torn like mine, I concluded years later, provided us problems with self-control. Violet did not think before she made the hasty decision to pop Wonka's experimental gum into her mouth without his permission, before turning into an inflated blueberry! Violet, the chatterbox, was fueled by competitive and impulsive tendencies.

Two days later, I found my body sitting on the side of the tennis court, holding an ice pack on my head. By this point I felt sickened by my impulse. I had driven to my weekly tennis clinic in very poor medical condition, as my knowing and executing failed me once again. My boredom and impulse prevailed over my common sense. During my second set, I had a seizure on the court. It disrupted a deuce. I awoke to sympathetic teammates and tennis pros loitering around me, one handing me ice and another holding my hand. But one team member was angry at me. I overheard her walking past me, murmuring, "She's wasting our valuable court time."

I guess I couldn't blame her since she spent a hefty sum of money to play, just like the rest of us. Feeling ashamed, I walked off the court and left the building. I promised myself that this would never happen again. I slammed my car door shut before banging my head on the steering wheel. "God, please keep me conscious for the next seven minutes," I wailed, "and get me home in one piece."

Plato noted that when impulse prevails over common sense, the horse begins taking the reins away from the driver. The two lose the important ability to function together in harmony. When internal accord cracks, external discord follows. As a driver, I had to find new and alternative routes to lead me in the proper direction, rather than allowing the horses to do it for me.

Dr. Orrin Devinksy once asked a patient, "Do you want to be the mother of two children wondering when your next seizure is coming?"

Coincidentally, Jason and Stephanie were five and four respectively, so this statement generated more fear. Over the next couple of days, my brain was afflicted with more seizures and symptoms of withdrawal. I was confined to bed rest. Faint and socially isolated. My body began detaching from my brain.

On July 10 I stepped outside in the sweltering heat to sweep the deck, before feeling another aura about to commence. Exasperated and angry, I pitched my water bottle a fast ball. My fingers twitched, lips smacked, and automatic reflexes declined. The burst of electrical activity ignited another seizure, and I passed out. A few minutes later, I heard Steven barking in my semi-consciousness, "We have to leave the house at once, and head directly to The Milstein Building at Columbia Presbyterian, so move!"

"But I just had another seizure. Can you give me a moment?" I replied.

"Move!" I heard again and again.

Rather than accompany me to the car, he ranted his normal rant. The rant not accompanied by rage just yet, not until his withdrawal symptoms kicked in at the height of his addiction. That morning his screaming characterized anticipation of the unknown, as well as thrust, exhilaration, and control. From the onset of our relationship my disease and meds were already muting my energy level and independence, and he thrived on this, The New Christine soon learned. My body and brain felt like a hollow clam resonating in the cavity of a shell, but although he and his family provided support, it wasn't the emotional support that my brain so desperately craved. It was just their presence.

Ron and Sam flew up from Florida to babysit the kids. Nobody expected a power outage or planned an extended stay. The kids being kids were fresh, rebellious, hungry, and bored. Steven was busy smoking pot on the deck, he admitted years later, so the parental supervision was limited. His parents tried, but it was apparent that they couldn't wait to go home.

"The power outage is over!" I heard again, as I ran upstairs to change my clothes. I threw my blown hair up into a high ponytail, and the timeless style never disappoints. I threw on Old Navy sweats, and another collared shirt. Before leaving the house, I made a quick stop into the formal living room to kiss Petunia goodbye. I gazed at my Norwegian Forest Cat resting peacefully by the bay window, beneath my six-foot-tall Dracaena tree. As I started kissing her beautiful ball of fur, I expressed, "I'll be back in a couple of days for another vacuum session."

My moody beauty loved when I vacuumed her dense coat with the central vacuum cleaner hose. Each time she heard the system turn on, she leaped from anywhere in the house, darting directly toward the hose. When we did not vacuum her body, she sat on the newspaper blocking our reads.

My flower child was a Main Coon, striking and distinctive among other pedigrees, with oblique, almond eyes, and an equilateral triangular head with white fur bursting out like a firework. This morning was like every other, as she rested peacefully beneath the tropical green leaves growing from their thick canes. She relished the rays of sun creeping in from the east end of the house and relished her privacy from our other two flower children as well, Pansy and Daisy. Just like my weeping willow trees growing near the river behind my childhood home, the Dracaena provided Petunia with security and comfort during all four seasons.

Steven continued honking, so I had to leave Petunia. "I just had a seizure on the deck," I whispered to her. "And your daddy didn't even walk me to the car."

"Hurry Chrissy!" Sam expressed from the top of the staircase.

"I love you Flower Child," I whispered with a peck.

Petunia relished the heat emanating from the Christmas lights in December, as she rolled her body beneath the tree and gazed above at the blinking illumination until her lids grew heavy and fatigued. Unlike my future Flower Children, Daisy, Pansy and Lily, Petunia was a one-man worshipper, and I was her God, creating light, energy, and love. Unlike all my other pets, Petunia *knew* The Old Christine. I kissed the tip of her wet nose one last time, as she tilted her head inquisitively. "There will be no more seizures," I promised her, "and when Mommy returns in a few days our bruises will have already disappeared."

My quality of life will improve significantly, my doctors convinced me, and relief for everyone is just around the corner.

I'm sure my pre-seizure autisms frightened Petunia during her first few years of kittenhood, when she watched me smacking my lips, clasping my fingers, and passing out into oblivion. Her purring came to a halt atop my body, as if she lost oxygen beside me. Her body felt heavy. She didn't flinch, forbidding me to get up. As I gained consciousness minutes later, I saw her almond, green eyes staring right through mine. Her body loosened up, her head tilted sideways, and she began purring. I felt her sandy tongue licking my face, and the gesture was her stamp of approval, which allowed me to get up and resume my daily activity.

The New Christine never realized that Petunia ached for the rest of her life for her Mommy back, ached for the vacuum cleaner hose to run along her dense fur like before, suctioning up her loose hair. She craved daily massage time, and even worse, I allowed the pain.

At some point years later, The New Christine touched the surface of The Old One, and turned back into the Mommy that

Petunia adored, but by this point it was too late. At the ripe-old age of eighteen her weight dropped significantly, from eight pounds to three within just two weeks. I nurtured her again, like the five-year-old cat she once was. But I found her beginning to fall asleep under my bed, rather than beside me. After a week, a frail body appeared. She purred loud and rapidly, before wrapping her frail limbs around my neck and dropping her head on to my left shoulder. I kissed and kissed and kissed her, and the purring didn't cease. Our inexplicable love rejuvenated again. Moments later my Flower Child stopped breathing. I shouted, sobbed, mourned, and shouted, again and again. I knew that deep down Petunia had been happier with her epileptic mom. But she was just as comfortable on her very last breath as well, I knew, when she sensed that her old Mommy finally placed her emotions to the same place as long ago.

I finally scurried outside, barefoot like usual. I put my sneakers on in the car like slippers, with heels crushing the backs. I never had the patience to put my foot inside the sneaker or retie the laces. "Get in the car already," he shouted, "Jesus!"

We backed out of the driveway. My hair professionally blown and twisted into a high pigtail, ready to get shaved off.

1999 / 1971

We were celebrating Christmas at Nana's, as Joey and I plopped ourselves beside her grand piano, and unwrapped our Barbie and Ken campers, snow white and chocolate brown. I heard the word "dynamite" trickling through my new temporal lobes, and I saw colorful rainbows, peace signs and happy-face logos with my new occipital lobes. I saw myself unfolding the mini plastic tables and chairs and preparing for a picnic with lemonade and watermelon. Our sibling bond was mutual, undeniable, charged with entertainment, love, annoyance, secrets, trust, and intuition. As Irish Twins we spoke truths without filters. Joey kissed me all the time back then, but the reciprocation slowly died off during my twenty-eight-year brain lock.

We bore our gold foil King Crowns from Burger King and began dancing around the Christmas tree. I heard Rod Stuart, asking a friend to lend him a guiding hand. The white noise turned out to be another musical seizure, another reflection of the taste of the times rather than the taste of the individual. Another preconditioned echo of an earlier life, I learned years later, holding unconscious meaning and association, and pleading for consideration.

A half hour later our cousins, Cindy and Lynn strolled in, and soon enough she began handling our new dolls harshly. This time around though, The New Christine noticed Mom's irritation out of the corner of my eye. We stopped dancing and ran back to our campers to protect our dolls. I suddenly recalled that Cindy always managed to convince me to swap my expensive Barbie clothes from Bradlees for her faded, torn up ones. The chain discount store was founded in New London in 1958, The Little Man informed me, which was precisely where we bought the dolls!

I saw Mom's eyes glaring, before ceasing the exchange. This time I didn't budge. When the rain stopped, we ran outside to break Nana's clothes pins in half, before rubbing the wood along the sidewalk to make sharp knives for cops and robbers. Nana's wrap-around porch circled three quarters of the house, and everyone avoided the metal nails popping up from the splintered wood, ready, willing, and able to shear through our skin at any point in time.

After dinner we headed back home to Niantic, where Joey and I played with our new Volkswagen Bugs, stuffed animals with long troll hair, black eyes, and red smiley faces. Joey's brown and mine white. Dad managed a Volkswagen dealership on the other side of the bridge in Groton and gifted us the stuffed animals as an "interracial couple" on Christmas morning. The Archie Bunker bigot managed reinforcing and reducing racial bigotry at the same time. Dad was a conservative, hardworking American patriot, filled with hyperbole. He hollered at the television every evening, blaming the current President or Congress for his "rotten" life." A hopeless soul, The New Christine eventually learned, mentally incapable of change.

In the interim the New Christine was struggling to retrieve her present, short-term memories, together with the emotions attached to them. What happened to the common force of nature between mother and child, I asked myself again, the unconditional bond between my kids and I from the month before? I woke them up in the morning with tickles and smooches, before baiting them out of bed with blueberry pancakes and bacon. Jason pressed the tube of toothpaste from the center just like me, rather than from the bottom up. He tossed the tube back in the drawer capless, just like me. But overnight the scene went from amusing to madness.

Back then I helped them tie their shoelaces and allotted playtime before dinner. I was patient, warm and maternal, but within the blink of an eye, motherhood became grueling. I failed to complete the simple task of heating their fries and chicken nuggets, due my declining ability to follow a process step-by-step. I failed to preheat the oven before placing the food on the rack. As a whole thinker now, a right brainer, everything needs to be done at once, or not at all. When the frontal lobe gets hindered, the brain loses the ability to follow steps, as well as execute a decision or action properly.

Stephanie longed for me to read her *The Cat in the Hat*, but she got lost in the maze of her Mommy's sickness. No small child deserves a parent longing for sleep, motivation, care, support, and more sleep. Stephanie ached to have her Mommy back, as I learned twenty years later, surprised, and sad. Without parents on the same page, who could offer her emotional support and understanding, she began to shut down, specifically in the classroom. As my patience with the children waned Jason began lashing out at the babysitter, throwing toys and temper tantrums. They mimicked my speech patterns as well, as I began speaking in literal, robotic tones, lacking emotion and drive. Just a short while ago had I feared leaving them orphaned, and now what? I asked God, guilt ridden. Who delegated me to be their mother in the first place?

God and Gordon got rid my seizures and cut the risks of graver damage later on, but what about my warmth and tenderness neutralizing? What happened to the fun, I asked the two Gs, of pushing my children on the swing and bike riding with them through the neighborhood? Why do they laugh alongside me? Why do they screech at me in one moment and hug me in the next? Friends and peers act courteous and humble, I told myself, holding the same neutrality as me, like a cashier behind the counter saying, "Thank you, have a nice day."

But my first cousins continued to burp in front of me, snore on the couch and crack insulting jokes. Jason and Stephanie still repeated, "I'm hungry, I'm bored, I love you, leave us alone, make the tv louder...."

So, my cracks in familiarity were bias, and the perceptual reversals were mine and mine alone! *

It was apparent that knowledge, perception and feeling all stem from various parts of the brain, and that I had just lost the ability to match them all up. Ironically, I realized over a decade later that even with its glaring faults, my brain still managed to unconsciously use the fake-it-till-you-make-it tactics of survival, relying more on the mind than on the brain itself.

While I was struggling to recover Steven lost job after job, and perhaps began to pop some pills here and there as well. My better mind pushed love and consistency to the best of its ability, but unfortunately Steven and his parents thought quite differently. I recall reaching out to Steven's father, Ron, many, many times after my surgery. From the onset of our marriage, Ron seemed to be a replacement for my father. When I met Ron and Steven's mother, Sam in 1990, I was living under the spell of the Lost Father Syndrome, silently longing for a father to replace my own. As an epileptic as well, and victim of childhood mental abuse, I was unconsciously yearning for a kind, nurturing father. I even called Ron "Dad" from onset, seeking his counsel like a biological daughter. Surrounded around codependency and enabling, and unable to care for myself financially or emotionally. Before I became a family burden, Ron afforded me emotional support, advice, gifts, and kindness, as if I was his biological daughter.

Just like Steven, I unconsciously longed for an extension of my childhood, and Ron, Sam and my mother provided this to both of us, giving us more money and luxuries than most people see in a lifetime. I followed everyone's overconsumption, as Steven and I built a large home from the ground up, drove the luxury cars he was accustomed to, took vacations, sent the kids to sleep away camps, ate at fine restaurants, golfed at private country clubs.... while failing to understand that money is not a replacement for love. Emotional support for Steven got substituted by bankrolling, brewing slowly into narcissism. But our diseases were denied early on, together with our rights to heal.

I continued subconsciously longing for Ron's warmth, since Sam was non-empathetic to begin with, superior and standoffish. She never bowed down to social interaction, small talk, and emotion. My left, irrational side wanted to take Ron's words as scripture, but my right intuitive side knew deep down not to. The lofty expectations and delusions exacerbated my prospects of healing and prolonged my journey of unmasking.

"I feel very depressed and anxiety-stricken again Dad," I cried out on the phone in acute depression. "I'm not doing very well."

I wanted to tell Ron that I lost my identity, my connections to my family, my heart, and my brain. I wanted to tell him I that hadn't gone to the bathroom for ten straight days, and that my stomach felt worse than giving birth. I needed a Daddy to take care me, since mine was utterly incapable.

"Your surgery is over Chrissy!" I heard again from Florida. "Give Steven a break!"

"It's not about our marriage," I replied. "I don't know why I'm crying so much."

"Stop always thinking about yourself! Ron said, "make more dinners for Steven. He started a new job for God's sake!"

Another new job, I told myself, and nobody sees the pattern, but me?

"With new medical insurance!" Ron shouted again.

"And who do you think has been paying for our family coverage every other month when it gets cancelled for nonpayment?" I asked him again years later, sitting on our deck in front of everyone. "It's not just you!" I shouted in front of everyone, while looking into Mom's eyes.

"You always start fights!" Sam said. "

"We don't wanna hear it," Ron yelled again. "We are here to spend time with the kids. You are going to lose everything if you keep this behavior up, including your own children!"

"She's nuts," Steven giggled, as I walked away covering my ears.

"Maybe they're right," I told Mom, following me from behind.

They failed to understand that gifts, money, vacations, country clubs and fancy cars do not supersede empathy, love, and truth. So, I must get my shit together, my left irrational side warned me again, when I hung up the phone with Ron.

Another night, bleeding in physical agony, I stood inside my walk-in closet trying to select a floral dress to pretty myself up, before serving Steven a homemade dinner. On that dreadful summer evening the hefty Thanksgiving meal was roasting in the oven, while I stuffed my fresh grief inside of the bird like a hypocrite.

*T*he first time Steven answered the phone, The New Christine heard an odd tone. Why does he say, Huuuulloooooo, as if he's sneaking up on an infant in a crib? I asked myself. "Steven, you sound condescending," I expressed.

Rather than a modest hello from adult to adult, he sounded patronizing. Then he giggled again like an infant. The smug tone and gestures reminded me of his reaction to Dad the week before in the hospital. "You sound like you're high and mighty," I snapped "Treat people how you want to be treated!"

"Shut up!" he shouted, squinting at me.

My right brain turned extraordinarily intuitive during those seven hours under the knife, I immediately discerned, insightful to people's mannerisms, temperament, and body language. I finally started challenging the condescending tones, fidgety body language and hyperbole. Over time I started challenging his parents' condescending gestures toward me as well, only me. At one point I went from calling them Mom and Dad to Ron and Sam. However, reading expressions exceptionally well from afar felt like only half of the solution to understanding them. In the beginning I didn't know that the other half requires a healthy left hemisphere, to allow us read between the lines and interpret people's underlying cues, motives, and connotative meanings behind their words.

I didn't know that our right hemisphere, holding our intuition, is far less civilized than the left, and more primitive like the animal. Yes, it's keen, bright, and perceptive, however it holds more trouble accumulating knowledge, contemplating outcomes, and thinking logically outside the box. Right brainers like us communicate mentally, physically, and empathetically through mime, sounds, gestures, and expressions, rather than words alone, specific to the human species.

In addition, the animal's frontal lobes are smaller than those of humans, and less developed like mine as well. Since we comprehend sentences through denotation rather than connotation, we often lose the underlying meanings and intentions behind them. This resulted in a pattern of men leveraging me, I learned the hard way years later, monetarily, sexually, and psychologically. Even with remarkable intuition, it became exceedingly difficult for me to keep abreast of people's intents, and to call them out on their bluffs.

On a beautiful September evening when I tried to reclaim the bond that never existed to begin with, I forced myself to grill steak on the grill for the family, with corn of the cob and a Caesar salad. Knowing that the woman from July could never get restored, I attempted to convince myself otherwise again. Knowing what Steven was all about, I still attempted to fix him as well, control him. I brought the condiments outside while the babysitter set the table on the deck with the kids. Fifteen minutes later Steven leisurely strolled in without a care in the world. I felt woodened and mechanical, but still reached out for a hug, trying to rewind our lives. Chrissy how are you feeling today? I waited for him ask. You look pretty tonight, I sought out.

I desired the unattainable while giving off the same. I waited for my husband to look at me directly in the eyes, rather than say hi to everyone, but to no one in particular. Just like Dad, Steven talks to the air, holding utter disregard for people around him. I had a hunch that gossip would proliferate, and sure enough he turned to the babysitter giggling, before asking her, "Do you want to hear the rumor in the office today?"

She was his part time receptionist as well. I saw Jason latching on to Dad's leg, pleading to be pushed on the swing, but rather than affording him attention, he sought attention from the outsider instead. Since his receptionist understood him, and perceived the distressing family dynamics, she simply ignored him. Narcissists listen to nobody, but themselves, and pursue admiration from anyone who would listen. So desperate to not get snubbed, and so clueless to as how they are truly perceived by others.

Everyone was ready to eat, but like usual, Steven rapidly excused himself and ran upstairs to the bathroom for a quick change of clothes. "You just can't overlook him," the babysitter whispered to me. "He always seeks attention, good, bad or indifferent. It's very distracting, and everyone is sick and tired of it!"

I'm certain that he sat on the toilet during his thirty-five-minute break, and called our landscaper and dear friend, Michael. I'm sure that he popped another pill or two up there as well. By the time he returned my neurological pain was fizzling like a fried egg. As I got up to wash the dishes, Michael happened to stroll in from the garage door. He saw my head and began to cry. "You're still not well, Chris?" he asked.

"Did you eat?" I asked. "There's still plenty of food outside."

But the garage the door had already slammed shut from the wind, and Steven darted in. "I ate already Chris," Michael replied, "but thanks anyway."

Aside from being best friends, Michael was our landscaper and Steven was his accountant. Sometimes they bartered, services for services. "Michael gestured Steven outside or vice versa, I'm uncertain," I told my therapist years later.

That night my dream therapy continued, and this time I witnessed Jeramiah's disobedience. I walked toward the pond, and behind the cat tails. I saw my luscious bullfrog smoking a pipe and splashing his peers with the yucky pond water for attention.

"There will be consequences for your actions," I screamed at Steven.

"There will be consequences for your actions," he screamed back at me.

"That's not like you to be smoking pot Jeramiah," I expressed.

"What are you talking about?" Jeremiah asked, innocently.

"Your brain is fuc... up!" Steven yelled.

Jeremiah instantly disappeared, snuck out for hours with the peculiar man who was trimming the hedges around Nana's pond.

My aged memories, decorated through dream content, were connecting to real time yet again, promoting further alterations in my brainwaves. Later that evening Jeremiah began playing tug of war with my fishes in the deep blue sea. "You don't belong in the sea!" I yelled.

"You belong with me Steven, not the landscaper, and you should sit beside me on a lily pad for an hour a day to reinforce our stability!"

It was Jeremiah's job to ward off the bad bugs in my brain and replace them with joy to you and me, but since they both failed me, the unremitting dreams continued paralyzing me, specifically during my REM stage of sleep when the brain's serotonin reduces. "Awakening from sleep full of anxiety," Dr. Schiffer notes, "signaling changes in hemispheric dominance."

My two lopsided hemispheres continued to shift their weight around and offset one another's assets and liabilities. Lightning striking maybe twice, I heard Stevie in the early morning. FOUR OR Five fish in a tree...How can that...? I wanted to know at the same time. My fish need water, I shouted from below, and I should have been a gypsy from the onset!

As an epileptic mother I loved my muskrats as high as the sky. No flattened emotions just yet, rather feelings like pride, love, gratitude, and attachment. I took them to tennis clinics, karate and music lessons, and every other activity that kids are too young to commit to or fully appreciate. They loved their bike rides around the duck pond and the rainy mornings inside watching Barney and Blues Clues alongside me.

Suddenly, poor little Stephanie began seeing her Mommy take five-hour afternoon naps, while teaching herself Blue's Clues on her computer. She felt more lost in the maze of Mommy's sickness than her brother. That summer they both began lashing out at the babysitter, throwing around toys and mimicking my literal tones and gestures.

Most times I felt like a dead body entombed in the ground of a cemetery. Most times I perceived family as bystanders. In fact, everyone appeared elusive to me. I continued to rub my eyes for clarity, knowing full well that the mother, daughter, wife, and friend that everyone loved died in the operating room.

Even feeling emotionally flattened, I struggled to utilize the fake-it-till-you-make-it strategies of survival. I attempted to recreate bonds with Jason and Stephanie and provide them some nourishment like before. I could barely take care of myself, but I forced my better mind to touch their faces, comb their hair, make them blueberry pancakes, and read them bedtime stores.

I cried for them in the operating room last week, I told myself, and now what? I asked God guilt ridden. Who delegated me to be their mother, and who delegated these innocent toddlers to be silently grieving? And what about my tulips, I wanted to know, representing undying love, eternal love, true love?

I was on a continuous search for prior attachment and association, persuading my better mind to take the driver's seat and play out the scenes of motherhood like a professional actor in a family sitcom. Over time, this better mind began silently uncovering various strategies to preserve their childhood the best way it could, the most imperative years of growth, learning, and development.

I also struggled to accept that I couldn't pick up exactly where I left off. It turns out that this has everything to do with me failing to acknowledge that a damaged brain needs to unlearn the idea it could get relied on the same way as before. Vital pieces of my brain gone, and the last thing it needed was pressure to move forward with higher expectations than before. Unlearning and unmasking require time, patience, security, therapy, emotional support, and repetition, because the brain needs ample time to say goodbye to its oldest networks, to provide space for the newer, healthier ones to develop. Dr. Doidge notes each trauma must unmask itself thousands and thousands of times, and the process can take nearly as long as the life of the tragedy itself! *

During this voyage, my two hemispheres were gradually redistributing themselves from past to present through the six stages of grief: shock, denial, anger, depression, and bargaining and acceptance. Each stage singled out. Each stage repeated themselves for years, overlapped, and even contradicted one another. Since the process in grieving one trauma is arduous in-itself, grieving two, three or more, can challenge your sanity.

It turns out that my original feelings of love, hate, betrayal, depression, immaturity, and disassociation from my early childhood needed ample time to be unlearned, and unfortunately these emotions do not reflect in our brains until much later in life, when our networks grow, alter, mature, and learn. It's later in life when we realize the wounds from our childhood upbringing cannot get ignored forever.

Unlike the heart, the brain undergoes chaos, regression and reconfiguration before recovery and restoration. A brain disorder is trickier to heal, because conceptually the heart fails in only so many ways. The cardiologist can restore the heart back to normal rhythm or restore the blood supply via a routine angioplasty. It is more straightforward. The brain, however, gets governed by chaos before accord, and the latter does not unveil until the prior demands get met.

Every day we undergo tragedies, including death, bankruptcy, divorce, deceit, theft, and physical or mental abuse, but the brain must embrace the hardships at a later point in order to facilitate the healing. When the brain develops unhealthy habits early on, such as enabling and codependency, it becomes more difficult to unlearn them later, because the habits entrench over time, and become familiar and self-sustaining.

When we come to our senses as adults, we can begin letting go of the tight grip that the past bequeathed on our minds and bodies. Again, neuroscientist Bach-y-Rita, known as The Father of Sensory Substitution, made powerful discoveries in neuroplasticity. Unmasking, he noted, is the principal way in which the brain reorganizes itself and promotes peace, especially those afflicted with later brain traumas, those that revert our minds back to the original scenes of the accident. *

A broken brain loses cohesion between its two divine hemispheres, the ability to function back and forth in accord. Normal brains are plastic, rather than elastic, meaning they are more resilient and modifiable to change. When life goes amiss, the brain finds new or alternative routes toward recovery, and this is the remarkable role of neuroplasticity. Neuro refers to brain cells, and plasticity refers to modifiable or changeable. The phenomenon of neuroplasticity once opposed the 20th century myth that the brain is elastic rather than plastic, meaning that when it makes a mistake, it will stretch back to its original shape all over again. It was scientifically believed that once early childhood developmental stages end, our critical learning periods begin to level off as well, and our brains are no longer subject to modification and adaptability.

Even in life's ever-changing environments, scientists believed our brains were hard wired, meaning they lacked precise, specialized functions. Finally, in the beginning of the 21st century, this theory of fixed and immutable brain condition got challenged by hundreds of findings about brain injured victims like me. Neuroplasticity started gaining popularity, and by the early 1960s, famous neurobiologist, Joseph Altman created the famous term: *adult neurogenesis*, which states that our neurons consistently grow and mature throughout our lives, until a ripe old age. Increased mental and physical exercise creates new brain cells as well, as proved in this book, which became easier to write and organize through time. Just like the body the brain craves exercise, and the lack of mental training triggers anxiety and depression. Yoga, walking stretching, and movement are just as important to the brain as reading, writing, and watching the news. When deprived of physical exercise, my brain feels like an inflated balloon ready to explode in midair.

Studies on mice prove the neurogenesis theory repeatedly. Groups of mice had their hippocampus removed. Some exercised regularly while others did not. Those on the running wheels all happened to grow twice as many neurons in the hippocampus than those in confinement. Those engaging in mental and physical exercise doubled their nerve cell growth as well. It was also believed that once gone, the hippocampus could never regenerate new cells. However, increased research proved differently; just another classic case of "use it or lose it.' Our brain is an organ requiring blood and energy from a limited supply of nutrients, so we must feed and nurture it in order to preserve its cortical real estate.

Dr. Alvero Pascual-Leone became the first doctor to state that "The system is plastic, not elastic," meaning that it's very resilient and modifiable to change. A normal brain stretches, changes shape, and learns, however a broken one remains more elastic like a rubber band. When it learns it stretches, but often reverts right back to its original shape without learning lessons from past mistakes. Normal molecules rearrange themselves and adapt to life's never-ending fluctuations. However, The Plastic Paradox does not promote or demote evenly, but renders vulnerability from outside influences, especially when making everyday decisions.

Outside influences often include false alarms, resulting in overthinking. It's why I found my brain having trouble deciding whether to make my annual mammography appointment on time or hit Starbucks beforehand and arrive late. My brain poised between urgency and lethargic, unable to discern all consequences. Decisions feel black or white to me, with little grey matter left for compromise and negotiation. The vast amount of white matter dissected from my brain is imperative in linking my neurons, as well as allowing them to send and retrieve messages back and forth effectively. These cuts make me feel either pressed for time or lackadaisical.

Dr. Frank Vertosick Jr. believes that we're all slaves to chaos, and this can depend upon miniscule variations in the "initial conditions" as well. In my case my birth defect, febrile convulsion and plunge down the staircase five years later all represented initial conditions. It's a butterfly effect, signaling that any slight change early on will promote bigger ones later.

I've read story after story of victims unable to shed light on their injuries. In 1848 a man Phineas Gage for example, sustained a traumatic brain injury in his frontal lobe from an explosion that drove a metal rod through his head. He dramatically altered from a calm, level-headed man to an emotionally unbalanced one. He became vulgar toward his loved ones, and his friends compared his behavior to that of an animal. Yet, unlike me, Gage failed to notice the changes in himself. Freud noted that our nervous system holds a distinct function of "I," making us aware of our "Self." However, the "I" holds little control over the rest of our nervous system. It is even unaware of what the nervous system is doing; that is until another party alerts them by saying, "Hey you've changed!"

It might seem bizarre to question Freud, but I knew both consciously and unconsciously, that I drastically changed and that I withered away in the operating room. Psychoanalyst Ruth Munroe wrote about Freud not conceiving the "unconscious mind" as a separate, unchangeable entity inhabiting our moral flesh. I agree with Freud in that we all hold behaviors and feelings that need to be repressed from conscious awareness, and that through time and unmasking some get exposed while others fail to. However, I agree to disagree that the unconsciousness is a process never thought of as an isolated entity, able to be studied independent from personality. Isn't this a major thesis in my book, detailing the distinctions between The Old Christine and The New One?

"Gross disturbances of organization of impressions of events and their sequence in time can be observed in patients. In consequence, however, they lose their integral experience of time and begin living in a world of isolated impressions, (and their

disorder) might spread backward in time....and in most serious cases...even to relatively distant events." Dr. Alexander Luria

One afternoon when I found Jason engrossed in a video game, another backflow of memory stacked in my basal ganglia and other surrounding areas in my limbic system, instantly ignited. I ran into his room asking,

"Knock, knock."

"Oh my God Mom! Who's there?" Jason asked.

"Cantaloupe."

"Cantaloupe who Mom?"

"Cantaloupe tonight, I don't have a car!" I said, cracking up aloud.

"Mom, go away!" Stephanie said, sitting near him.

They both failed to look up from the screen, but the joke continued sparking my right brain for many more years come. It lapsed back to a simpleton, who failed to give up its juvenile pleasures. That evening I saw Joey brushing his teeth and reading me the joke from a Dixie Riddle Cup back in the 1970s. I looked up into The Cumulous Clouds and saw his Pluto toothbrush again, his favorite Disney character. I reached my arms as high to the sky, in attempt to embrace him. I was trying to figure out how and why he got up there to begin with. He looked down at me in my dream, and smiled from ear to ear, before vanishing in the stars.

1966 / 1971

My first vaccine was at two months old in 1966. It triggered a 104-degree fever and febrile convulsion. Mom and Dad heard me bawling in my crib and gasping for air, but by the time they reached me I was already unconscious. They rushed me to the emergency room at New London Hospital.

"We ran every single stop sign and red light!" Mom told Dr. Levy in 1999, overcome with guilt.

I'm sure that Dad rode the brake the entire time well, I told myself, with his left foot on the brake and right on the throttle. Dad sadly mistook his two- pedal habit for safety, prompting vehicles to stop short from behind. But you can't teach an old dog a new trick. "Nobody knows the roads like me," he insisted. "People need to think and turn their little machines on!" I kept hearing again and again.

And the brain is just that, two-and-a-half pounds of machinery requiring steady refueling and care to function properly. Somehow Nana had arrived at the hospital before us. Nana never learned how to drive, but my post-surgical hallucinations conveyed differently. At thirty-three my bad brain rested on her shoulder, as she began rocking me back and forth again like long ago. Nana's warm, wrinkly skin felt soothing against mine, more so than my very own mothers did decades later in the kitchen. The Old Christine felt more intimate with Nana, than with her own husband and children. It turned out that nothing neurological transpired that day, and the neurologist told us I could go home. No! I cried out. I want to go to Nana's!" I insisted once again in 1999, lashing out to Dad. "My true home, where I always belonged!"

*F*ive years later. 1971. A fatal year indeed. That July morning Stuffed Pink Piglet was misbehaving, so I put him in the corner for a time out. Unlike normal though, she covered her mouth in panic. She always obeyed her time outs, whether through oinking, grunting, or burrowing between pillows, but this time around she squealed in fear. So, I walked over and kneeled beside her. I saw her pink ear tips paled and her curly tail tremble. I pecked her snout twice, before asking, "What's wrong honey?" We overheard Mom rambling in Italian.

"It's Nono's sister, Zia Melia from Naples," Stuffed Pig Piglet whispered in my ear.

"From Italy?" I asked.

"Yes."

Zia Melia, my Great Aunt visited the States each year for the month of July. A graceful Roman Catholic nun completely shielding her body with a starched black and white habit. She wore a white wimple around her head and rosary beads wrapped around her arm, granting her full access to prayer. Strangers marveled at her traditional habit. A devout nun from southern Italy who held high rankings. Admired indeed, but quite controversial on the inside as well, The New Christine realized years later. Narcissistic and cunning just like my husband. Even as a child I sensed a swelled head beneath her wimple. As a teacher in a convent or parochial school she was notorious for disciplining her novices by clapping her hands directly in their faces or banging on their desks with her wooden yardstick.

In public however, Zia Melia showed grace, poise, and refinement. She met Steven when we got engaged in 1990 and even the epileptic noticed two egos hiding behind the poise and brewing a witchy concoction behind everyone's backs. They had distinct religions, Steven and Her, distinct nationalities, and languages, but narcissism doesn't discriminate. The pair communicated through expression, gestural mutism, and silent approvals. Both impressed with the finer things in life, and Steven's wealth and self-love matched her high social stature and self-love. I noticed that Zia Melia was in awe of my six karat diamonds and home possessions, as I watched her delicately touching my furniture with her bare hands. The 1990s mauves and sea foams. The old-world stone credenza holding sterling silver flatware. While she touched, Steven trailed behind proudly, hands in his pockets.

During this one and only visit to New Jersey, we took her to a Spanish cuisine with her sister, Nono, and Mom. Steven pompously opened her passenger door to escort her inside the restaurant, while leaving the three of us behind. The mutual pride glowed right beside their agendas. Back then I wasn't cognizant that the evening was characterized around marital neglect and disrespect, both steadily worsening over time. "This behavior has always been Steven's pattern," Mom expressed to me decades later. "Nothing has changed Chris, except you, and you should be proud of yourself."

Most of my family sensed the red flags and read into the subtleties behind Zia Melia's angelic grace. But the restaurant patrons that evening were awestruck by what they saw. Her chastity, and complete obedience to God. But despite the underlying narcissism, she was indeed as a devout nun who dedicated her life to serving the church and humanity. People bowed down to her. She commanded the room.

Mom hung up the phone, trembling just like Stuffed Pink Piglet. It rang again, and this time it was Dad's stepsister, Aunt Rose. We heard rapid dialogue, half English half Italian. "Oh my God! Quest puo essere real!" (This can't be real) Mom exclaimed.

She slammed down the receiver before throwing us in the Buick Skylark and jetting over Mr. Bridge, back to New London Hospital. Too pressed for us to relish the morning hues reflecting along the water. *London Bridge is falling, falling....* trickling through my right hemisphere again, as I began noticing Mr. Bridge turning frail as well. Perhaps his death is coming soon, I thought, hearing *Iron bars will bend and break bend and break....* My aged database filled with implanted emotions felt new yet washed out. This sensory input was not self-intrusive, but self-perpetuating.

I played with my very special string toy in the hospital waiting room, my red, white, and black Dalmatian, as I noted in my dream reports that dated back decades before this publication. I saw myself pulling him on the leash again along the shiny floor, while the three of us were patiently waiting for Aunt Rose, Mom and Nana to pop out of the double doors so we could all go home and make mini meatballs for Belle. But years and years passed with more unmasking and embellishing, until finally Aunt Rose and Mom stepped out of the double doors sobbing. Not a word or turn. Just the music of *Wooden clay will wash away, wash away*, A brittle old lady with brown skin and silver hair placed her hand on my shoulder and kindly handed me some tissues. She didn't need to bend down because her hunchback did it for her. She held me, and lady's soft, dark skin felt soothing against mine.

*A*round three weeks later I found myself sprinting around that large foyer of the house again, a construction site in-progress. That morning Mom and Dad towed us along on a house hunt, and over four decades later I saw the dark wooden cabinetry lying on the kitchen floor for the very first time, right beside the piles of foam, insulation, and nails. The contractors were prepping the cabinets for installation, as I scurried past them and darted directly toward the imminent stairway.

This time around the sound of the drills were emanating from other parts of my temporal lobe, rather than just from my ears. The reverberation prompted by Gordon's surgical drill sounded piercing and intrusive. Yet, I also heard Joey behind me, paddling like a duck. The unfinished staircase was built in the shape of an L. The risers and railings not yet installed, so I came to a halt on the top stair. The basement smelled damp, raw, and musty. Rather than bending my body forward as I had done in 1971, The New Christine bent her body down to her knees and wrapped her arms around her head. This time around I will safeguard my skull, I hallucinated.

But next I glanced downward at Dad again, this time silently living through distress and fear. "Think and turn your little machine on!" I heard him repeat to me in real time.

Both Christines were undergoing terror, trauma, and helplessness once again. Finally, I heard Mom's petrified voice from behind me. My noradrenaline was increasing in my dreams, as Mom and Dad both witnessed me descend downward in the air from opposing directions, landing directly on my left skull.

The content was very vivid. The physical and mental impact of the cement floor was harrowing. My febrile convulsion at two months old was my first brain injury, and this was number two. I got rushed back to New London Hospital, to the same neurologist from five-years before, but this time with a bleeding brain. Nana had passed away in the same hospital just three weeks before, but The Old Christine craved the touch of her skin again. The last thing I recalled from that three-day hospital stay was a kind young man who bent down toward me before my discharge. I saw his sky-blue eyes and light blond hair again, as he gently placed a very special football helmet on my head, white with a blue horse logo on each side. "Aside from sleeping and bathing, keep this on at all times Little Lady," he expressed, before saying goodbye.

Dad rolled down the hill of our driveway, and Mom helped me out of the car. I swiftly let go of her and hopped along the sidewalk by myself, displaying my prize helmet to my black and orange orioles resting on the branches above. My semantic memories got activated during my dream recall again, interjecting with my implicit ones. "The oriole is the state bird of Maryland," The Little Man conveyed from deep within.

I was thirty-three years old and walking up the sidewalk in northern New Jersey with the cast on my head, but I was five years old as well, walking up the sidewalk of my childhood home in Connecticut with a cast on my head. Dreams hold no clear perception of time, space, or sequence. I plopped my delicate body down Indian Style on the wet cement and took a breather, before picking up a slimy worm and letting it crawl between my fingers. I saw other primitive earthworms crawling through the cracks of the dirty sidewalks of Broadway as well, while Glen Campbell sang "Rhinestone Cowboy" to me for the very first time in three decades.

I glanced upward again, directly through Carly's clouds in my coffee. Perhaps the owls were whoo-hooing in the bright of day. Perhaps the crickets were chirping in timbre with their front wings rubbing along the leaf blades. So many backflows of memory and perpetual noise generators, reminding me again of the Energizer Bunny that keeps going and going and….

Each creature vocalized very personal song elements, specific to my habitat. Well, it turns out that the basal ganglia, another piece of the limbic system, gets over-excited during the earliest stages of unmasking, notes Dr. Rodolfo Llinas, before acquiring association and meaning many years later.

"Don't do it you fool!" I heard Dad shouting from behind again, this time in my late thirties. "Think, and turn your little machine on," he shouted, ironically referring to my brain.

Instead, I savored the crumbs of my youth again, with the tasty chocolate ants in my mouth. I picked them up one at a time, savoring them like Raisinets.

At another point I must have conked out, because later that afternoon I awoke with piercing pain, thumps in my head. I followed the kind man's orders and placed the helmet on my head before rising. Mom handed me six chewable St. Joseph aspirins before preparing a peanut butter and Fluff on Wonder Bread for me. When I walked into the den, I saw Fluffy exactly like long ago, frolicking in the den with strings dangling from her fur.

Mom added peeled carrots and two cans of Coca Cola to my lunchbox, while I wanted to teach the world to sing all over again.

Only this time the song came from an unfamiliar place, rather than just the Coke commercial from 1972. Furnish it with... grow apple trees and ...As my pain slowly diffused, I grabbed the metal lunch box and skipped mindlessly out to the back yard. Stuffed Pink Piglet and I scurried down the hills toward the stream, singing honeybees and snow-white turtle doves. Mom pleaded with us to slow down, but before she caught up to us, we had already settled ourselves beneath a weeping willow by the swamp. I became ever so fond of the river and woods again, their lack of constraints and edges. I looked up at The Cumulous Clouds and heard The Carpenters silently echoing I'm on the on top of the sky looking down at the stream, and the love that I found ever since I've been around.... all while re-experiencing the freedom to walk the lands safely like a child again.

*I*t turns out my brain's left hemisphere had no choice but to compromise and find a place within the flow of the right hemisphere to continue existing. Brain surgery left this side no choice but to give up on the battle of my right hemispheric candor, providing a lower frequency of reality. It turns out that the left hemisphere perceives shorter wavelengths of light than the right, allowing the brain to delineate sharp separations, lines, and entities, but over time my left had no choice but to negotiate a deal with my right, the marvelous hemisphere that holds the freedom to explore the universe in entirety.

These two hemispheres process our various sorts of sensory information differently. Since our visual right is softer than our left and lacks edges, and focuses on one big corporation, rather than its individual entities. My personality followed the same pattern, going from inhibited and covered-up to free-spirted and lackadaisical, more comfortable barefoot and braless than fully dressed. This loss in left hemispheric boundaries created a wanderer navigating through her very own maze at her very own pace. Dr. Bolte Taylor notes that the last thing dominating this hemisphere's desire for boundaries is to share its limited cranial space with its open-minded right counterpart!*

We sat on our Donald Duck beach towel beneath the saggy branches and ate our sandwiches. After lunch we lied on our backs and relished the floppy branches dropping downward like tears, displaying shadows along the trickles below. Our massive willows provided our caterpillars with nutrients like nectar, juices, and pollen for their next stages of life. They were far from pests or infestation. No defoliating leaves or wreaking or havoc on the trees. The Old Christine stood up and picked one up with her bare fingers. Just like the worm, it joyfully crawled between them, before tingling up my arm. In-addition to its spinnerets, we noticed their thorax, abdomen, and three pairs of jointed legs, holding hooks at the ends. The gooey sap of the willow stuck to my fingers like maple syrup.

My brain turned so radically disorganized that it got blinded by the cascading, the re-categorizing, adorning, and camouflaging. When the picnic ended, we began moving the caterpillars one by one into mason jars, placing them on the deck in half sun, half shade. They had to vegetate before entering their next stage of growth, we knew. Stuffed Pink Piglet covered each jar loosely with Saran Wrap, and poked holes through it for air and water to seep through. Each day we fed them grass, insects, willow leaves and fennel. The rainwater afforded the host plants nourishment for them to feed on. We waited patiently for the baby jars and host plants to end their duties of harvest, so our caterpillars could grow out of their skin. Over time we watched their plumper bodies undergo a series of molts. My heightened peripheral vision noticed their layers of skin about to shed. They need more space, I told Stuffed Pink Piglet, and twigs to hang upside down on before they spin themselves into silky cocoons.

Dad built a small, wooden stoop for me to sit on while I colored. I spent most of my free time creating depictions on construction paper with colored pencils. Every day I sat on my stoop at the coffee table and fussed with my shades and sharpeners, while slyly developing into a right brainer, swayed by color and detail. Holly Hobby submerged between my hills and wildflowers again, with my tiger cat following behind. He was fat and brown, with orange and white stripes. My pair stood beside each other at the bottom of hilly valley. I saw my little red and brown barn house again as well, resting behind them from afar. My little barn atop the mini hills had three brown and white cows around it, with humped shoulders and long, straight snouts. They gracefully roamed the pastures beside my hairless, reddish pigs. My farm animals peacefully grazed the hays, below the blue sky and The Cumulous Clouds.

The Holly Hobbie sisters bore patchy rag-doll dresses flowing down to their ankles. Their heads garnished with fluffy bonnets and bows. They gazed at one another sideways, one carrying a basket of fresh fruit and the other three long-stemmed purple wildflowers. My depictions heightened this time around and extended beyond the page.

A couple of days later I plopped myself down on the stoop again to color. This time I placed my helmet on the floor beside me. Maybe I shouldn't do that, I thought decades later. Maybe I should have kept it on like the nice man at the hospital advised. But in the end, it did not matter. As I began illustrating more happy birds, happy cat tails, happy suns, happy bugs, and happy flowers, I rapidly fell sideways, landing on my left skull once again. I passed out unconscious as I experienced an epileptic seizure. The first of many to come. The beginning of my transcendent journey through Oz.

1970s / 1999 and Forward

I sipped my tart lime slushy at Frosty Treat in downtown Niantic beside Joey and my closest friend, Barbara Campo. Since they were one grade ahead of me each morning Mom and Dad instructed them to take turns walking me to kindergarten class, since my brain got insulted the month before. Barbara, my skinny, redhead bestie with pale skin, freckles, and dimples lived down the road from us in the cul-de-sac. I began hearing Bobby Vinton's "Roses Are Red" again from my hospital bed, while watching Joey devour his banana split. "Your father shouts at poor Joey, day in and day out Chris," Barbara expressed, "I feel so bad for him."

"What are you talking about!" I asked her mad, before I saw Dad from my bed with my very own eyes, downing his Schaefer Lights again, shirtless. He watched over Joey just like The Wicked Witch of the West. His broom always in tow, waiting for our crumbs to spill.

Barbara's family dynamics revolved around depression, alcoholism and lies as well, which is why she appeared and reappeared at our doorstep each day. She too was escaping her own rat-infested home and seeking comfort somewhere else. Her red-headed mother was the town gossip, and the chatterbox on the other end of the phone, never allowing Mom to get a word in edgewise. Verbose Mary in her cat-eye, pointy glasses smoked like a chimney

133

and drank like a fish, while her husband John held warm, quiet mannerisms. Barbara adored him. It turns out that John lusted for my mother, Barbara expressed at our reunion thirty-five-years later, my naïve, sheltered mother.

"Chris she was the emblem of perfection," Barbara said on that beautiful, early winter afternoon in Manhattan. "Your Mom cleaned, cooked, gardened, took ceramics, sewed clothes and even made dresses for you with her own bare hands. Everyone adored her."

When Barbara and I rekindled, it felt like no time had ever passed, and for me this was literal, after all, our early lives together in Niantic was the only past that I truly recall, feel, and identify with. It represents The Old Christine, my dream life, my unconsciousness. In 2021 I read something on TikTok that went like this: "Scary facts that will blow your mind…If you remember your dream when you wake up…. Then it wasn't a dream it was a message."

Most comments back were jokes, but all I thought about when I read this was the hundreds of dreams that ran through my brain and connected to waking life. On Sunday while scoffing down Mom's linguini with white clam sauce, Barbara saw me departing the kitchen again suddenly. I was having another seizure. As I left the room half unconscious, half conscious, I heard Dad emotionally mishandling Mom again. "Put more napkins on the table for these slobs and the salad needs more salt!"

Dad's taste was about quantity not quality. I was never a foodie like Barbara, since Mom raised Joey and I around heaps of delicious sustenance: garden vegetables, freshly caught crabs, baked bread, fresh pastas, fresh crushed tomato sauce in mason jars, and sausages hanging form the basement ceiling. At one point, I rebelled, and began despising cooking all together.

After my seizure we went outside to play. From my hospital bed I watched Barbara plop her frail body on the crabgrass again, right beside chunky Joey. Thunder happens when it rains, I heard Fleetwood Mac from somewhere deep in my limbic system, as well as from my Mickey Mouse record player coming out of my bedroom window. Poor-quality sound, but rich lyrics. I sat on our humongous rock, the black and burgundy boulder lying sedentary on the grass, sparkling from Mr. Sun. My heightened peripheral vision spotted the beautiful reflection of the sun's deposits along its shiny granite. "NOT TRUE BARBARA," I screamed. "PLAYERS DO NOT LOVE YOU ONLY WHEN THEY'RE PLAYING THE DRUMS!"

My unconscious mind stuck in the same groove. Rather than old, weightless, and incidental, I woke up to this brand-new 1977 hit. I wreaked in pain and starved for self-preservation. I dreamt of Dad's drum set and saw the snare and bass passed out drunk together in the back of his Volkswagen Bug Convertible. "The snare and bass are drunk," I shouted back at Barbara and Joey, "not Dad!"

"What's wrong Mommy?" Stephanie asked, shaking my body years later.

"He's a crazy drunk." Barbara lashed out.

"Well at least my Daddy's a professional jazz drummer!" I shouted at everyone, "so, stop giving him the short end of the stick all the time! Look at your father Barbara and yours Stephanie…they're no better!" I dreamt.

"You're scaring me again Mom," Stephie said.

"HE PLAYS IN A BAND!" I raged. "AND PLAYERS DON'T FUCKING ONLY LOVE YOU WHEN THEY'RE PLAYING DRUMS!" I shouted again.

"You're so stupid Chris." Joey said.

"That's not what the song means Chris." Barbara laughed.

"MY DADDY LOVES ME ALL THE TIME EVEN WITHOUT THE BEER AND DRUMS!" I shouted back, during another period of transference.

Sleepwalking again while carrying the heavy load of anger, fear, denial, and hatred. Next, I heard Dad stomping in the house at one am. Mom was fast asleep on my bedroom recliner. On Friday and Saturday nights we nervously waited for the hour-glass figure to dispense, for the sand to blow up and take away Dorothy's innocent life. Mom slept in my room on the weekends when Dad worked, I began recalling as an adult, in fear of the unknown. As a blind epileptic, co-dependent, and enabler, I thought this was normal, and I mastered the pattern early on.

I heard him stomping in after midnight like normal, slamming the doors behind him and sprouting wrath. I shouted back. Shouting was my only means of protection, my defense mechanism that I took into my marriage.

When the madness stopped, the three of us continued to listen to Rumors like novel. 1977 was real time. So, what was taking place in my brain? I asked myself years later. Well, it turns out that the contemporary lyrics of "Dreams" were floating somewhere between my basal ganglia and temporal lobe during this long stretch, between my limbic system and prefrontal cortex, and between my consciousness and unconsciousness. "Dreams" was happily resting right in the center of these pairs, and just like "You're So Vain," the song still floats midway and fails to reach real time!*

A life without memory is no life at all.   Oliver Sacks

Our earliest months and years are the most critical learning curves in memory development and emotional attachment. The caregiver is the driving force of the infant's emotions and social interactions, which we must learn, relearn, and ingrain into our memories hundreds and hundreds of times to create a distinct personality. Dr. Genova states that not only are attention, rehearsal, and elaboration all necessary to push our perceived information beyond our recent memory into our long-term memory for permanent storage, but the emotional significance of our events is necessary as well. Without all of this, our memories naturally discard over the passage of time.

Memories, commemorations, reminiscences, and feelings are what all tie family members together, as well as friendships, peers, classmates, and coworkers. Mood, personality, attachments, accomplishments, emotions, decision making.... all stem from life's events, and when memories get clogged, the brain can go haywire. Worst of all, the brain trips through life with neediness, codependency and enabling, all before detaching. Growing up I could not relish the same choices and liberties as Steven, my friends, peers, or even my children. As an epileptic I didn't enjoy sleep away camps in the Berkshires like Jason and Stephanie, college in Rhode Island or urban single living before marriage.

It didn't surprise me to learn that most of our explicit, conscious memories lie in our left hemisphere, whereas our implicit (unconscious) memories lie in the right. EEGS performed on brains with a history of neurological trauma prove that explicit memory contains more neutral memory as well, whereas implicit memory contains more traumatic memory.

The brain needs its entire cerebral cortex and limbic system to form, process and retain all forms of memory, and to mold them together over time into a solid structure, strengthening through growth, maturity, learning, development, and of course relentless neuroplastic changes. If one or two parts paralyze during the process, our memories will generalize and lose details, such as times, places, events, and emotions! So, I want to say to my friends that it is this very paralyzing effect that contributes to my dire need for solidarity.

Often while feeling like a tiny hermit crab on a vast, lonely beach, I ask myself, "Where do I stand on this colossal planet that we call Earth?"

Each stage of memory and attachment matures in different parts of the brain before integrating later on, and providing it with abstract reasoning, including rationality, negotiation, decision making, judgement, and critical thinking. Over time these healthy connections provide the brain with the ability to read between the lines and judge a good egg from a bad one. It turns out that abstract thinking is the last stage of memory development, which takes place between the ages of eleven to sixteen. This makes sense because I suffered through my mid-stages of epilepsy during this period.

Again, I wasn't aware of my abilities declining just yet, nor of the feeling of missing myself, since epilepsy was the only life that I knew. I didn't miss my earliest, most profound relationship with my brother yet, since I wasn't cognizant of detaching from him to begin with. But this all changed long after 1999, long after my third strike in the operating room.

Memory has everything to do with personality, mind, and self. One day a Sack's patient, Natasha K. walked into his clinic expressing a sudden euphoria. "A change," she expressed, as she suddenly found herself to be delightful, energetic, alive, and frisky. She appeared radiant, with a new lease on life, her friends first thought, before begging to differ and worrying about her personality change. "You were always so shy," one expressed, "and now you're a flirt."

Sacks wanted to know why the sudden extravagance. Something made her high and risky, lively, and impulsive, and she even began flirting with Sacks just after he sedated her lobes. He found lesions in her left frontal lobe and hippocampus. Her lack of verbal filter made her so high, she expressed, that she didn't want to seek treatment. The lesions stemmed from infections in these areas, which healed over time without long-term cerebral changes. But some of her quirkiness remained, and she felt delighted to have the best of both worlds.

This reminded me of another victim from back in 1981 who spoke and acted impulsively as well....so much that the important and trivial, true and false, serious and joking were all pouring out in a contributory stream, like a run-on sentence holding impoverished utterances. These two brain areas: frontal lobe and hippocampus, are pivotal for both tongue and emotion, and in what to embrace when speaking and what to discard. Our conversations come across as either overdone or dramatically reduced to monotone and indifference, lacking the pertinent grey in between.

This form of expressive aphasia, which made it difficult for me to produce speech, kicked in instantly and continued for well over five years. The New Christine was flirty at first as well, childlike, impulsive, and uninhibited.

At the beginning of the new millennium, I found my bratty adolescents mimicking my heavy breathing and lingering slurs. Years later after passing the road test, Jason pulled in the driveway at midnight like a big shot. So, I reprimanded the foul play and insisted that he obey the town curfews. With the point well taken, my mouth continued to gab haphazardly, which dissolved my main point all together. I was suffering from a major backflow in my speech, producing clutter, erratic rhythms, poor syntax, and grammar. The New Christine began adding groups of words or subjects to her speech, unrelated to the main point. My brain held poorer concentration, a lower attention span and ability to focus.

Once again, it was regressing before progressing, and gearing more toward childlike responses such as *stop* and *go away,* than toward adult speech. Sacks witnessed the exact reactions from his patients as well, and these speech delays and weak responses result from spending too much time decoding words. For years and years, I felt the words on the tip of my tongue, stuck somewhere and too tricky for me to access. So, between this and poor memory, I began avoiding collective engagements more and more. My self-confidence declined, and I began shutting down socially. I turned into an introvert. I may have turned impulsive and extraverted when I first awoke due to lack of hippocampal filtration, but over time the exact opposite transpired. I reverted right back to that introvert that I was before going under the knife, and I surround myself around reading, writing, yoga, plants, hiking and animals.

I find the ring of the phone jarring. I work on the phone all day, but the sound of my own makes me flinch. "State your plan or purpose via text," I express to the caller, "and if it warrants talking, I'll call you back at some point ok. But in the meantime, please don't call," I plead with everyone.

Autistics are sensitive to voices, rings, sounds and other forms of sensory input, specifically those that we cannot see. We prefer no abstract, sensory input. No planning, strategizing, understanding, or focusing on things that are not in front of us. Such deficits feel worse to the brain injured than to autistics, since we are fully mindful of what we cannot control.

If this isn't enough, I can hear the person saying hi before real time as well, and this intuition and high-speed processing raises others' intolerance of me. I come across as brief and curt, people tell me, rapidly soaking up the relevant while disposing the junk. This takes speed, Sack's notes, and speed is a crucial component of intelligence. For me to remember something, I need to hear what I want to hear, rather than all the jargon in between. The voice must be clear, the point concise, and coming from a firsthand source as well since memory forms from the original signal. I would much rather dream of taking a sip into Carly's Simon's cappuccino, smothered in white froth with a swirl of cinnamon, than socially interact with voices around me. I would much rather float beside Joey, atop of Carly clouds any day.

"Knock knock?" Joey asked me again from The Cumulous Clouds.

"Who's there?" I asked from below. "Hello...hello...who's there?"

We were seven and six years old. Or thirty-seven and thirty-six years old, but again dreams hold no sense of time. Joey moved to Atlanta, Georgia in his mid-twenties, when my memories were in full remission. He worked for Delta Airlines. Between our distance and my poor episodic memory, my dear brother faded away from my life. His knock, knock question faded for quite some time as well. Yet over time I recalled a specific phone call taking place during the winter of 2002. "Can you come see me on your drive back up to New Jersey?" he asked.

His voice sounded frail, I discerned years later, rather than deep and raspy like normal. Our family flew to Florida several times a year back then, however the day after Christmas, Steven and I usually took a road trip down to Jupiter to visit his parents, with the kids and dogs in tow. As lazy planners, we taught the kids how to "not pack in advance," rather throw their belongings into a suitcase at the last minute and take it from there. It was a twenty-three-hour straight drive along dreadful I-95, punctuated by roars of tractor trailers, traffic, sirens, pollution, and the smell of burnt rubber.

"Joey, I'm down at my in-laws on the east coast of Florida, and you're in Atlanta," I responded on the other end of the phone. "We can't drive west through the state of Florida with two small kids and two dogs in the back seat."

"It's fine Chris," he responded.

"I'm sorry," I said. "Are you ok?" I asked, unable to interpret his facial expressions through my visual cues, nor his deathlike atmosphere and plea for help.

"I'm ok Chris," he said. "I miss you and the kids that's all."

Speech requires focus, memory, muscle movement, and attention, notes Dr. Genova, as well as retention housed in our long-term memory.

"Another time," Joey expressed.

It took my brain too many years to reattach my feelings to the right people. It took too long for my brain to begin suffering through its buried grief, and when it finally began, it was already too late.

*M*y brain was living through my implicit memories as The Old Christine, *while* recalling bits and pieces of my explicit memories as The New Christine. It was tapping into its brilliance, drafting a book, and making new discoveries about the human brain along the way. Dr. Orrin Devinsky notes that, "The scientist's brain that makes the discoveries is extraordinary. They work on those whose brains are damaged, and it's rare that a person who makes and important discovery is the one with the defect."

I make important discoveries only when I am interested in something. Then I become obsessed. Sacks describes this as being stuck on subjects that we know something about, and many of my subjects were provided by The Little Man. He was tapping into my unconsciousness through selective memories and simultaneously matching them with real events in real time. This is a blessed clairvoyance I later learned, a temporal lobe sixth sense. * In addition, I was using the facts and trivia from The Little Man in my verbal dialogues as well, because like Sacks notes, such brains remain stuck on subjects it knows something about. The Little Man's tidbits turned into stepping-stones in my conversations, consistently building and widening over time. I'm fine with being literal and contextual since data adds variation to social dialogue.

Imagine watching a baseball game on television without the color analyst spurting out stats and history about the third baseman at bat. Savants and autistics with severed association skills soak up this material like a sponge. We come across as empty social simpletons because our brains are too busy storing a wealth of information unexchangeable through verbal dialogue.

The dialogue center of the brain is one of my favorite subjects in my book, because scientifically, so little known about *right hemispheric language.* * Language generates in the left hemisphere, specifically the Broca's and Wernicke's areas. Famous French physician Dr. Broca from the late 1800s revolutionized psychology by locating the motor center of the brain, lying solely in the left hemisphere. It's why this region of the frontal lobe gets officially labeled as the Broca's area. The second area of left hemispheric language development is the Wernicke's area. Our Broca's produces speech while the Wernicke's comprehends it. Our dominant left controls our verbal cues, activating the neurons and encoding them into language. When one or two neurons go faulty, then guess what happens? The domino effect ensues once again.

After four parts of my brain got eradicated, its remaining neurons did very different things. Some started repelling one another like oil and water. Others suddenly hit a cul-de-sac with nowhere left to go. Others simply died off. Others began blocking off others and forcing them to take secondary pathways to reach their point of destination, resulting in either shortcuts or delays in my thinking and speaking, either quick or graduated reactions.

Dr. Bach-y-Rita made an ideal analogy: *"If you are driving from here to Milwaukee and the main bridge goes out, first you are paralyzed, then you take old, secondary roads through the farmland, and then as you use these roads more, you find shorter paths to get where you want to go and begin arriving to your destination faster."*

Shorter detours include retrieving only what I seek in the present moment. This involves filtering out meaningless jargon, waffling through introductions and conclusions, desensitizing the irrelevant, and tightening up the conversations. Yet of course hearing before real time conveys urgency and rudeness as well, which Sacks refers to as "motor impatience" or "extreme restlessness."

An autistic child made an ideal analysis of a normal brain. She describes it as one big corporate building communicating through phones, texts, faxes, and messengers. But she lost the ability to convey her messages, as some go through while others turn distorted by fax jams, incorrect email addresses, or forgetting hit the save button. Her weak recognition and consistency-checking abilities meant her files needed perpetual rebooting.

It took eighteen years for me to notice another neuroplastic phenomenon, because this one snuck up on me from behind. * Walter Penfield noted that certain areas of the brain get committed to sensory and motor function at birth, while other parts get left blank for later purposes. The temporal lobes, he notes, are the blank, uncommitted areas, reserved for speech and perception when the child grows. Damages taking place between the ages of three to five years old cause the speech center to move to these uncommitted areas more rapidly. They transfer from the frontal lobes to the temporal lobes, and as more of these empty temporal regions got used, the less it became possible for my brain to establish and reestablish one major area responsible for language!

It is exceedingly rare for speech centers to reestablish themselves like this, and that day, the realization changed my life. In one moment in time, I felt an instant, unconscious, permanent shift in my speech, transferring from the west side of my corpus coliseum to the east, from left to right.

This rapid swing involved zero tug of war, zero pain, zero planning, and zero persistence. A silent bombshell occurred instantly, where my right hemisphere took on a unique form of speech of its very own, very different from standard left hemispheric verbal speech. This area of neuroscience remains under researched, and even unheard of. By now my readers know that the left speaks, and the right is mute. Yet, one day out of nowhere my right formed a rapid acquisition of language.

My left stopped struggling to string together words into sentences, as my right took over, stringing together sentences into paragraphs, and paragraphs into stories as swiftly as a net kills a fly.

I not only read in entirety, but I speak, think, and perceive in entirety as well. I can feel my speech deriving from a different place in my brain than before. This new lexicon of language holds mostly principles, concepts, and facts, but again this is fine. What's not fine however is that this ideographic form of speech often sounds like a mannequin, lacking elasticity and flexibility. It' because it stems from a very unfamiliar place in my mind, a faraway, semi-conscious place in my right hemisphere. I feel in a semi-conscious state when I speak.

I convey tongue through what Soviet psychologist Dr. Vygotsky labels as the power of "inner speech," and this inner right hemispheric speech he notes, "Remains on the other side of the moon!"

Well, it turns out that my two hemispheres were convening in silence for nearly eighteen years before I made this discovery. My mute right was listening intently to my talking left the entire time, I later learned, and in fact, it got overworked and undervalued throughout my life as well. It covertly lingered and strengthened over time, until one day my left finally gave up, and succumbed to the inhibitions of the right, instantly stealing the ball on the court, shooting a three pointer, and winning the series. In the exact moment my left surrendered, it celebrated in glee as well. It was done fighting. This is the only rare time when the right can be the "good" Broca's area, Sacks said, too powerful for the left to resist! *

Sacks had a patient with heightened cues after her brain operation as well. As she watched her brother lighting his pipe, she became startled by the way he followed regular time and sequence. To her the process felt slow and elongated. She held uncanny ability to see the match strike before her brother's hand even touched it. She watched the match moving up to the pipe a few milliseconds of a second before real time, which can feel like hours to us. She saw the pipe entering his mouth a frame too soon, then the pipe lighting before the match even touched it.

It takes a long time for visual information to travel to the visual cortex from the retina, so why such speedy access? She wanted to know. Well, this gift of extracting an outcome before real time entails heavy unconscious reasoning, as well gut instinct in the right lobes. We notice cues, signs, possibilities, and predictions effortlessly, and out of our explicit, conscious control. This cognitive talent results from dopamine neurons in the emotional right brain able to subtly and unconsciously perceive reality before real time.

Just like speech, Dr. Doidge notes such superior right hemispheric registration can develop slowly over our lifetime as well, without revealing itself until much later, if-and-when the brain gets struck again from a later trauma! Again, this implies that my savant syndrome was slyly emerging in my right hemisphere over time, once again resulting in little or no remaining left hemisphere left to inhibit it.

Only mentalists hold these right hemispheric abilities to dispose of old habits that slow us down. A fine example is reading with your lips rather than your eyes, reading word for word rather than sentence by sentence. The latter just happens to improve our comprehension by twenty-five percent, since the brain sees a bigger picture, before contextualizing it into pieces. When I did research for this book, I perused through articles and grasped their entirety first-and-foremost. I swiftly and unconsciously desensitized unwanted information and fixated on only what I was looking for. It's why speed reading increases the brain's fixation zone. It's best to read in sentences or paragraphs in a single eye movement without stopping. Right brainers read ideas rather than words and breaking the flow with excess wastes our time.

Speed reading is a fine example of the brain taking shorter paths to reach its destination, faster and more efficiently. However, in other cases, it's not all it's cracked up to be. Shortcuts can fail you as much as bless you. For example, my right hemisphere begins uncovering the end of the movie before everyone else in the room, before the plot unravels and unfolds. I impress people. "Yay!" they say to my speedy access and sixth sense.

However what good is forecasting the ending before real time when my grey matter surrounding my cerebrum, the thinking part of the brain pertinent in processing and integrating our sensory signals, fails on working properly. This thinking part of the brain slowly draws conclusions about the plot and characters very early on as well. It often exaggerates or minimizes the importance of a single event. You can't make a broad interpretation with only a few events to back it up.

When I try to follow the plot of a movie or a long joke, I fail at paying attention to the waffle in between, which carries the main plot of the joke or storyline. * Grasping in entirety does not work in these cases. Understanding a movie requires a healthy frontal lobe to follow the narrative, understand the underlying intents, assimilate the descriptive passages, and see the characters developing through time. When abstract thinking becomes camouflaged, the brain loses the storyline, which is why savants and brain-injured persons gear more toward nonfiction like science, history, and autobiographies.

So, in the end my path to Milwaukee is bittersweet indeed. "*Alas,*" I say, as The Plastic Paradox reveals itself once again. In this paradox, Dr. Doidge notes that "*The same neuro-plastic properties that allow us to change our brains and produce more flexible*

*behaviors, can also allow us to produce more rigid ones… and the
challenge lies in finding a healthy balance."*

One Christmas I unwrapped my Lite-Brite again, the
magnificent toy marketed by Hasbro in the late 1960s. I unwrapped
another Hasbro game as well, Battleship, produced in 1967. The
toys felt fresh and contemporary, as I fit the tiny, colorful,
translucent, plastic pegs into the holes again, recreating my
marvelous creatures of the Earth. I couldn't wait to plug it in and
watch my brown bear and blue lake colorfully illuminate before me.
"Lite-Brite holds just eight colors of peg," The Little Man said.

I had the Milton Bradley version of Battleship and started
placing the plastic chips along the different ships again, in their
various lengths and sizes. Dad and I competed that afternoon, while
listening to Elvis's "White Christmas," and sipping eggnog with a
splash of anisette. He was trying to sink my fleet of five ships, until
the very end when I heard "You sunk my battleship?!" in my dream,
like a demeaning question.

As Joey unwrapped his Matchbox cars beside our fresh
evergreen tree, Fluffy was amusing herself with the wrapping paper
and cardboard boxes. I watched Dad assembling Mom's new
electric knife, before manipulating his model electric train around
the tree with just one button. Before my epilepsy hit its sleepy
period in the early 1980s, Mom and Dad loved the celebration of

Christmas. The night before on Christmas Eve before Joey and I went to bed, we placed Oreos and milk on the countertop for Santa. Joey removed the ornaments around the fireplace as well, in-order to provide ample room for Him to slide down the chimney for a safe landing.

As I looked up to my brother again beside the fireplace, I couldn't even imagine that our unity could one day vanish behind my disease and surgery. I couldn't fathom cutting his toenails and creaming his feet with pleasure. I couldn't imagine potty training a brother eleven months my senior, nor Dad happily cutting an evergreen and joyfully decorating it with green and red blinking lights, before topping them off with silver tinsel and snow spray. Dad had some decent traits, especially around the holidays.

But Dad was an alcoholic, and unlike Joey observing the pattern clearly and later trailing behind, I remained a blind epileptic, I discerned as an adult, living in a plastic bubble surrounded around my happy chipmunk Little Chip and my happy mouse, Silver Sylvia.

Uncle Louie and his second wife Aunt Vicki reappeared on Christmas morning as well. For the very first time I noticed bourbon and anisette bottles on the breakfast table, rather than just orange juice and coffee. By noon the bottles were replaced by vodka and beer. "Mom you're the biggest fuc…. enabler," I screamed from bed, "So gullible!"

Living in time travel with a brain unmasking more mayhem, all while shouting, laughing, sweating, balling, re-transcribing, and learning. For the very first time, I noticed Uncle Louie's fancy gold rope chain and over-sized gold pinky ring. I saw his button-down silk shirt and tight pants, and he looked like a sex trafficker! Aunt Vicki's long black hair parted straight down the middle looked glamorous on the outside, but she was very seductive and sexual as well, which was how they made their money, The New Christine figured out years later.

Dad's drinking, ignorance, neglect, and rages caused my poor brother Joey to become a victim to childhood torment as well. My failure to recognize the pattern as a child provoked so much guilt later as an adult. Too many years later. My Irish Twin kept his needs and feelings stifled, repressed, and Dr. Sarno notes that "Repression does not involve a conscious effort to put aside emotional pain."

My final point relates to the condition and age of the secondary roads that I use each day to function. I take right hemispheric detours in almost everything I do, since my left hemisphere is worn-out, emptier, and cracked. The right is more neurologically primitive than the newer, younger left, holding more modern technology. Of course, detours take us where we don't want to go, further and out of the way.

I continued to hear Dad calling me "Bitch, bitch, bitch," again. I was silently hankering for a stress relief valve, and sure enough, my childhood charm resting deeply in the remains of my limbic system, re-appeared, and her name was Silver Silvia. My little mouse was wearing the same round reading spectacles I created with my colored pencils very long ago, with the identical crystal beaded chain around her neck. Silver Sylvia snubbed Dad and Uncle Louie, and instead started parading around the Christmas tree in her puffy, white baker's hat and pink and white striped bowtie. It turns out that I was an incredible young artist back then, with magnified visual cues. Surprisingly, my gifts of asymmetry were astutely kicking in during my epileptic inertness as well. I saw Silver Sylvia's tiny, pointy nose again, long pink ears, and hairless tail.

We heard him shout "Bitch" again, so we scurried out of the house and hid under our enormous mushroom down by the stream. I screamed for Joey, but I could not find him. It turns out that I created the mushroom as a child with my colored pencils, but as an adult it was used to shelter our frail bodies and minds from the upheaval taking place inside our house. This depiction represented another unconscious transference taking place in my mind, used to deny my brain from reality, and my heart from the pain and abandonment. This defense mechanism was used to protect my fragile ego as well.

After we calmed down beneath our mushroom cap Silver Sylvia leaned up against the trunk and began reading her tiny book on fine cheeses. I attached a tiny telephone to the tiny trunk of the mushroom as well, just in case we needed to call 911. This time around my new occipital lobes responsible for sight saw a boxier pay phone than before, with dangled, vintage coiled wire. I saw Sliver Silvia's book of fine cheeses and the pay phone collectively as well, as my brain learned how to diverge *and* converge its visions simultaneously, allowing each eye to focus on two different things at once. I'm gifted with spectacularly striking stereoscopic illusions now, and dimensions beyond the normal eye.

I was undergoing transference again by sprucing up my memories a bit differently every time. For many years our mushroom remained a haven, shielding our bodies and minds from the rain, wind and cold. It buffered Silver Sylvia and I from life's adversities and contamination, like Dad peeking out the window and spying on us with his broom in tow. "He's probably prowling around the house," Silver Sylvia said, "sweeping his narcissistic, drunken crumbs under the rug again."

"Yeah, and his empty cans of Schaefer Lights brewed in Milwaukee." I replied.

The chronic dreams failed to contain themselves. They usually involved one of God's creatures of the Earth; and ironically, animals appear in forty percent of children's dreams, note Zadra and Stickgold, but only in about five percent of adult dreams! This proves where my brain stood in time. My critters represented chameleons, altering, and blending into various patterns to suit my present needs. Yet, their powers were a tremendous aid, helping me think outside of the box, and teaching me valuable lessons for later on. They dated back decades, yet always managed to re-attach themselves to real time.

Quenton Skinner, a British historian and writer notes that the brain prunes unnecessary synaptic connections during sleep, which is when the strongest emotional experiences reappear. When the unconsciousness awakens and the consciousness shuts down, logic, reasoning and inhibition all take a back seat from intuition and imagination, which house our visual and auditory memories. These were the precise moments when my body and brain were living in fear, threat and upset, and these feelings felt like quicksand, the more I avoided them the deeper my brain sank to denial.

*F*ear, threat, upset, fight-or-flight responses. How and why did they get so pumped up when I awoke, The New Christine started asking herself, in my dreams, recollections, and present experiences? In addition, why did these fight-or-flight responses seem to reverse themselves sometimes as well, promoting worry in my brain when there was no need to worry, and no worry when there was a dire need for it?

Again, eradicating the epilepsy took precedence over all else, but the procedure ingeniously provoked severe emotional distress and worry on my brain as well, specifically my right hemisphere. The operation removed my entire left hippocampus in my limbic system, but what about the neighbor to this seahorse living right next door? I began asking myself. But, what about the pear-shaped amygdala responsible not only for fight-or-flight responses but for controlling our fear, aggression, anxiety, and anger? As if my external alarms with Steven weren't enough, I was having internal false alarms as well, threatening to overturn my life. I was also getting suspicious.

So, I Googled, and Googled more, only to learn that our amygdala controls our memory's emotional processing while our hippocampus helps us organize and store memories. In addition, the seahorse-figure helps *regulate* our stress responses in the pear-shaped figure as well. In other words, our amygdala and hippocampus work together hand in hand in just about everything we do.

I knew my hippocampus was slowly shriveling up over time from a ripe grape to a dried-up raisin, as the seizures kept pounding against it. However, as a guinea pig I can attest that there lived some healthy cells inside my grape as well, helping my brain ward off normal, everyday stress and anxiety; helping me travel from point A to point B without getting lost; helping me recall more explicit memories; and helping me articulate words into sentences. But the surgery meant removing all or nothing, and the damages outweighed the benefits. More, importantly the seizures would have destroyed my entire hippocampus all together, so removal was a "no brainer."

And back to the amygdala. I've lived around addicts, narcissists, gas-lighters, and mental abusers, but I didn't know that these trepid circumstances can literally destroy healthy cells in the victims' hippocampus and amygdala., and that my brain had been undergoing yet another double whammy. * I had another gut instinct, but I needed the medical backup. So finally in March 2021, overcome by curiosity and fear of truth, I delved into my twenty-two-year-old medical records.

It turned out that my instinct was right all along, and that my poor amygdala was not only severed, but it was dissected in the operating room as well, right alongside its neighbor! Why in God's name wasn't I informed of this, I asked myself enraged over two decades later. Informed of losing yet another survival mechanism, suitably reacting to real danger rather than everyday menial stress?

I read four papers, all dated July 7, 1999. One read like this: *"Specimen is received fixed in formalin in a container labeled the" "amygdala"* and *"consists of a single piece of soft, white, tan tissue measuring..."* *

*S*oon enough I looked out my bedroom window again to observe where the noise and stench were coming from. It was dark outside, loud, and smelly. Another summer pool party, I told myself in my onesie pajamas. The cigarette smoke proliferated upward, right through my bedroom window. Joey heard the reckless noise, laughter, screams as well. He walked into my room, and we saw a crowd of grown-ups splashing in our pool and being bad. I ran back to bed and covered my face with my quilt. Joey closed the window for me and put on the television. He came into my bed and together we watched a rerun of *Room 222,* where Pete talked to his students about the city planning to cut down trees in his neighborhood to widen the streets. They all began staging a protest, but the fumes and commotion were coming from outside my window instead. I was all too much for me to bare, and I had another seizure, right beside Joey. I woke up and found my head resting on his right shoulder.

Years later I got up again in the middle of the night and walked toward my window again. This time however, The Old Christine heard her robins chirping, soothing her brain from the archaic white noise. Robins chirp throughout the entire night and early morning, I knew, when there's less commotion otherwise drowning their pleasing sounds.

But when sunrise hit the birds stopped chirping and Dad started seething again. He found a tiny silver beer tab along the bottom pool lining and went ballistic. Joey entered my room again and walked along my freshly raked shag rug and toward the window. I watched him shake his head back and forth in dismay.

"The sharp metal could have ripped plastic lining!" We heard Dad shout from below. The metal tabs not attached to the beer cans back then, I suddenly recalled.

"And the gallons of chlorine could have flooded the whole damn yard and killed the grass!" he shouted.

People need to think and turn their little machine on! I heard again as an adult.

"Joey, get down here," he raged "and dive in the pool to pick up the metal!"

If only he knew that his children's little machines, specifically their amygdalas, were cunningly rotting over time from his intensifying threats and rages.

My aged right hemisphere often elicited joy during the unmasking process as well. One day Mom and I were skimming through some old, cardboard boxes in the unfinished part of my basement, when I spotted some Kodak instant photos from long ago in Connecticut. After decades of frontal lobe dementia, I saw Fluffy again, sporting her colored threads. The back of the photo read 1972. I began cracking up, living through reminiscence again. "She looks so fat," I expressed to Mom from the basement in real time, before rewinding back again to that incredibly special morning.

I found my body walking downstairs to our basement again in Niantic to pay a visit to my furry friends. I saw Fluffy resting contently in my gigantic baby carriage!

An enormous, rectangular carriage, I vividly noticed, in maroon and white. With my gifted binocular lenses, I saw the four large wagon wheels, and the canopy hood pulling up and over the carriage. "Mom she sought comfort in my baby carriage!" I shouted once again, "to deliver her six, tiny miracles!" *

Her baby kittens were resting peacefully around her, all on top of Nana's crochet blanket, black and lime green. "Oh, that's why she looked so fat." Mom said dumbfounded to me.

"You mean nobody knew Fluffy was pregnant?" The New Christine exclaimed.

I discovered something else. "You were a seamstress Mom," I said, "sewing in the den every day, and ironing our clothes on Friday nights while Joey and I were watching *The Brady Bunch* and *The Partridge Family*. That's where Fluffy threads came from!" I shouted to Mom, as she bore them gracefully before me once again.

"I think you're right Chris," Mom replied uninterested.

Apparently, Mom and Dad were just as lax with Marshmallow, too lax in fact, even for a bunny cage. On Easter Uncle Louie surprised Joey and I with an Easter Basket, and inside was Marshmallow, a white rabbit with pink ears. Like Fluffy, Marshmallow had free rein of the house, freedom to frolic without barriers or restraints. One morning I had another big fight with Steven about not waking up on time for work. While he stayed in bed suffering from withdrawal symptoms, I walked downstairs to chop carrots and celery sticks for my powdery puffball. But when I brought them to her in the basement, she failed to hop her normal hop, in fact, she wasn't hopping at all. "Get up and go to work!" I screamed, in the chilling basement atmosphere. It was cold and damp. My heart raced again as my body sunk in quicksand. No hippocampus or amygdala used to ward off my fears. However, this time around I looked at poor Marshmallow, adamant that she did not die from overeating like Dad expressed long ago. Instead, someone accidentally left the basement door open the night before, I recalled, and she escaped. I touched her chalky, white body again, lying cold and stiff on the cement. I blew her kisses, while recalling that my powdery puffball gorged on the grass fertilized the day before.

When Dr. Gerald M. Edelman speaks of *"the remembered present"* he states that we all hold detailed memories of how things looked and sounded long ago, and as these memories recall, they blend a bit differently than before. *"Every act of perception,"* Edelman notes, *is to some degree an act of creation, and every act of memory is to some degree an act of imagination."*

When brain functions become limited, Edelman notes, significant reconstruction in their functions will follow. Much of what seemed irretrievably lost for a long period-of- time will become available again in large measures, with richness, resonance, emotion, and recreation.

*I*t took me a very long time to realize that Steven mirrored Dad's behaviors, and that they commingled together in my waking life. It took me a very long time to realize that Silver Silvia and I felt most comfortable shaded beneath our white buttoned home. Over time our wonderful mushroom was growing fleshy gills beneath the cap, which further protected us from the stormy weather inside the house. I loved tickling Silver Sylvia's whiskers, sprouting outward from her nose. I loved hearing the soft musical pitches behind her squeaks like a child again. Later that afternoon when the house noise ceased, we began sipping our sweet, pink lemonade again, through our tiny straws. Silver Sylvia picked up the paperback, Curious George. We loved silently reading. The unspoken pleasure felt mutually comforting. "Mice, chipmunks, birds, dogs and worms relate better to us than any human possible could," I expressed.

"Yea, because we don't judge by size, color, shape or disability like humans, poisoning our lives with fungus," she squeaked back to me in mouse language.

1980s / 1999 and Forward

"You must begin to lose your memory, if only in bits and pieces, to realize that memory is what makes our lives. Life without memory is not life at all...our memory is our coherence, our reason, our feeling, even our actions...Without it we are nothing."
Louis Bunuel

It was the beginning of the new millennium, and I knew that my narrative was long gone, so I continued to ask myself the same question: Where do I stand on this vast planet Earth? My cynical left hemisphere existed in 2002 with explicit knowledge of real time, but my genuine right hemisphere still lives in late 1960s and early 1970s, I knew, beside Nana and the gypsy movement. My brain functions in real time, but my perception remains within the frame of my two childhood traumas, The New Christine discovered, between my febrile convulsion and subsequent fall down the stairs on to the cement floor.

This led me to more questions: Where do I truly belong, in Connecticut, New York or New Jersey? The New York metropolitan area puzzles a brain that lacks boundaries and requires definitive lines of separation. The Tri-State Area, the most densely populated part of the country, includes Manhattan, Stamford, Trenton, Newark, Bridgeport, and parts of Long Island. Although Stamford and Newark separate by a bridge Stamford and Bridgeport do not. I crave borders, the feeling of placing one foot in each state! These populous regions encompass the highest ethnical diversity in the country as well, the melting pot consumed with sundry industries including art, finance, media, biotechnology, business, hospitals, tech, international trade.... One byproduct of this density calls for urban dwellers in Manhattan and Queens to interact with strangers peacefully. Facts, concepts, landmarks, strangers, and borders often distract me and add to my personal storyline.

This is because our events inextricably tie to our explicit memories, including times, places, boundaries, and sequences. They maintain the continuity of our personal history and self-awareness, so we learn lessons from mistakes, make better decisions, locate where we stand in the present moment, and who we strive to become in the future.

The limbic system gets labeled as the reptilian brain and the emotional brain, as it lacks the sophisticated abilities to run on its own without help from the higher cortical real estate, the dominant cerebral cortex. Dr. Bolte Taylor notes that these higher brain cells in the thinking mind provide the brain with the ability to take "new pictures" of the present moment, and then compare this new information with that of the limbic mind. This conjoining gives the brain the ability to continue evaluating its present circumstances and make proper judgements each time. However, when the brain gets traumatized at an early age, the limbic mind remains immature, and our memories rewind into an endless loop. A damaged hippocampus or lack thereof gives the brain trouble perceiving real time, and a damaged amygdala or lack thereof triggers impulsive rather than logical behavior. Without aid and cooperation between these two entities, the brain gets sucked into time travel!

*D*uring this time, The Old Christine began raking her long, shaggy rug again with her indoor plastic rake. I raked it once a week to keep it plush. Afterword I plopped myself down on my orange rug beside Fluffy, and two of her kittens. I rested on my tangerine bean bag chair, but this time my new set of eyes noticed the tiny, plastic pellets surfacing from wear and tear. When I turned toward the kittens, I saw my rotary telephone again, the retro donut-shaped phone with a curly chord. Next, I saw my Mickey Mouse record player, with Stuffed Pink Piglet napping on the plastic cover of the turntable.

Next, we heard a knock on the bedroom window. Stuffed Pink Piglet flinched. We both got up to peek out, and there he was again right before our very eyes, our marvelous Little Chip from childhood with his elongated whiskers and tiny upright ears. Little Chip melted my heart again, just like that little girl that I once was. Little Chip was hibernating the entire time alongside us, right outside beneath the ground. Like us, he held the innate ability of homing, of navigating back to his original birthplace in Niantic after being far away for so long.

Our sharp instincts and intuition matched. He sensed my pleasures and pains just like long ago, as our childhood melancholy began blending with our fear and anxiety all over again. Stuffed Pink Piglet and I opened the window and jumped out, landing on the grass covered with moist spring dew. She gently picked up Little Chip and placed his furry body on her palm. She pecked his tiny wet nose, stubby legs, and whiskers. Then I ran my fingers along his bushy tail. When he closed his big brown eyes, his long eyelashes whipped in glee.

The three of us sat on the moist grass again, and my magnified occipital lobe noticed each speck of dew condensing along each blade of grass. This close perception showed that, on one hand, the operation had severed my peripheral vision, but on-the-other-hand it magnified it like a microscope as well. Just another example of the brain's asymmetry. Nature's wonderful acorns, maple leaves, grass seed and berries surrounded us again. Stuffed Pink Piglet's diamond-shaped pink ears and Little Chip's glossy eyes set on each side of his head hypnotized me. My scrumptious little critter held the identical reddish-brown streaks across his backside, as well as the set of plump cheeks used to stuff his acorns and berries for winter hibernation.

Later that day we rested in the shade beneath the weeping willow trees again. All my humble delights began flourishing along the sacred lands, to help me disassociate from the verbal cruelty boiling inside of both houses, in Connecticut and New Jersey.

Over time these backdrops dawdling in my limbic system artfully made their way to my temporal lobe, my consciousness. During these endless stages of unmasking and transference, Dad's rants were commingling together with Steven's, as my past and present continued to interact. I wanted nothing more than for these two to disappear, rather than just loiter between my cerebral cortex and limbic system like freeloaders. This prompted my brain to play out the role of private detective again, unscrambling dribs and drabs of its remaining explicit memory, and filling in the blanks through its dreams, cues, emotions, embellishments, and intuition.

I got up from the blanket to collect some berries and acorns for Little Chip to make a stockpile for him for winter use. Afterwards the three of us embarked on an excursion. We stepped on our wooden raft and navigated down the wavy stream of flowing, shallow water. I saw colorful grave through the transparent water, and dragonflies with transparent wings. Little Chip and Stuffed Pink Piglet paddled while I enjoyed the wonderful ecosystem filled with living creatures and nonliving particles. Dr. Sacks describes such scenes as reminiscence, waking up from the past housing some conscious memories, while decorating others to fill in the gaps.

A wounded brain can be keen and insightful like an animal, while simultaneously, unable to think logically and outside the box. When two dogs living together have a fight, they may snarl for a moment before reverting to pals in the next. The brain thinks problems through using logic and can create reasonable opinions all while detaching from emotion. When human association gets torn, the brain loses the vital differentiation between anger and love, feelings and decisions, forgiveness and denunciation, recognition and emotion, and mistakes and consequences. I never denied Steven's deceptions and overspending, yet I forgave, forgot, believed, and failed to learn lessons from my mistakes. Knowing and feeling are far from the same.

The left brain is one of the finest tools in the universe, Bolte Taylor noted, more modern, civilized and savvy than its primitive counterparts. It houses a sort of critical censor as well, whereas our right brain manages data and situations with more neutral behaviors. This is the reason why I treat the corporate president the exact way as the janitor. Like an autistic, I can't perceive differences in gender, age, race, or status, and while world should be more like me, unfortunately, it's not. In the beginning, my humanity and goodwill made my peers question my authenticity.

Although this sounds great, it comes with grave consequences, including over trust, failure to read underlying intentions, and failure to set healthy boundaries for myself. It's not always best to treat a boss like a coworker or an acquaintance like a relative. Again, this all stems from a dearth in memory and a grounded sense of Self. So, it makes sense to me why my brain pines for boundaries like a kid in a candy store. It needs to know exactly how many licks it takes to the to the center of a Tootsie Pop! Years later I discovered another irony. This selective analogy popping out of my unconsciousness was far from coincidental, since the first commercial for that candy aired in 1970. Since my licks go on to eternity, "The world may never know."

The 1980s held little relevance in my unmasking process. I was a full-blown epileptic during this decade, holding latent, inactive memories. However, these few explicit/episodic memories stored held very important messages, lessons for me to learn much later on. Much later on implies that these forms of memory are the last to resurface after brain injury, the last to get recalled.

By 1980 we had already lived in Long Island, where Mom's parents, brothers and sisters all resided. Dad, the New Englander at heart dreaded leaving the rolling hills in Niantic and New London for the flat grids in southwestern Long Island, the multiple-lane turnpikes, traffic, and lights or stop signs at every intersection. But Mom insisted on cohabitating beside her family, five families all enveloped within a five-mile radius in The Five Towns. They sit right alongside the massive borough of Queens, The New Christine discovered in her thirties after residing there for over fifteen years. Out of nowhere the tiny, dilapidated sign along The Nassau Expressway impressed me as well. It reads: "Welcome to Queens." The sign still feeds my hefty information system.

The Five Towns is an asylum of sorts, unattached to a major throughway to get in and out of The Island. On one hand, it's an urban, overpopulated region, but on the flip side, it provides dwellers with suburban comfort as well. It's funny that anything beyond these towns can feel foreign to these dwellers. These towns sitting in the most obscure part of Nassau County, get historically dubbed as both sheltered and privileged. Residents are so tied up with being in the suburbs and "Being Not in the City" that they believe their suburb is real, when geographically it's not! The Five Towners think that the physical boundary along The Nassau Expressway screams across the landscape, but who are they fooling? I began asking myself. The boundary is just an illusion!

Rather than recalling the celebration of my high school graduation, I remember the blaring noise and turbulence of the jets flying above my us. They made the house rattle. The 747s never considered respecting the residents and communities back then. They failed to delay their departures and landings for the next tv commercial, so my remote remained at arm's length. I turned the volume up or down exactly every two minutes and shouted to be heard. It took time for me to acclimate to the staggering jets flying just five hundred feet above me, but eventually, I became deaf to them.

Dad's job troubles and drinking habits traveled right along us to New York, I recalled through my unmasking process. As Mom moved closer to her family, she began neglecting his narcissistic needs as well. On our very first New York Christmas, Dad's blue spruce got replaced by an artificial green tree. "A fake New York tree" he shouted at me. It held Nono's shoddy, plastic ornaments, and chipped metal balls. The silver tinsel still hung along the plastic branches from the year before. From this point on Dad's joy and tenderness in decorating got replaced with a lack of exertion and excitement. I watched him finish the chore with a can of powdered snow, saying, "Fake like New Yorkers!"

We lived with Nono and Papa for over ten years, the same period when I began to increasingly disconnect from others. I loved them both the same, Mom told me later on, but unlike Nana, my memories of Nono and Papa remain scarce. I recall knitting blankets with her while watching Dynasty and Falcon Crest. I recall Dad and Billy, my boyfriend, downing beers outside on the patio like buddies, and Nono serving them Entenmann's crumb cake like an altruistic, and cans of beer like an enabler.

I recall Grandpa Angelo often sitting on the porch step of the shoe repair shop around the corner, holding a whisky bottle in a paper bag. I recall Nana finding the empty bottles every so often in the dilapidated shed. Neither of my grammas ever entertained the idea of walking away. There was no wealth of information in cyberspace to enlighten them about Alcoholics Anonymous, enabling or codependency.

Rather than recalling anything about The Italian Club that I belonged to in high school, The New Christine recalled the navy bumper sticker on Mom's maroon Buick Skylark instead. It read: Yankees ready for the eighties! A sedentary decade for sure, not just for me, but I think for the team as well. My fondest Yankee memories still dawdle in the 1970s, around my favorite player of all time as well, number 14, left fielder Lou Piniella. As much as I loved Looooouuuuu, Mom's love for Thurman Munson went unmatched. She was baking bread with Aunt Christina in Cedarhurst when my cousin Maria and I heard the devastating news on AM Radio. "Thurman died in a plane crash," I went to tell Mom.

I saw her drop the cookie sheet, before placing her hands over her ears and circling, crying. "A burned body and broken neck?" we learned weeks or months later, as Mom mourned. She felt wronged and betrayed, and the tears represented her body's release valve.

Growing up as an avid Yankee fan, my recollections should be far from scattered and segmented, but unfortunately, they are. Of course, they stem from the 1970s as well, and the selective players include: Catfish Hunter, Mickey Rivers, Bobby Murcer, Sparky Lyle, Willie Randolph, and Reggie Jackson. Then my memories went blank, at least until the days of Derek Jeter and Bernie Williams. I had crushes on a few third basemen as well, specifically, Wade Boggs, Scott Brosius and Alex Rodriguez. Certainly, the dividing line in New Haven between the red and blue teams remains very prevalent to me. Finally, I started recalling collecting baseball cards as a child, and the metal coins that came the packages. I organized them alphabetically in a shoe box by team and player. I failed to understand those that read "Traded," so I filed them in the back, together with those reading, "All Star."

*T*he thirteen-year-old started avoiding The Big Lifeguard with the Frog Tattoo again. In 1999, she refused to have anyone grip her body from behind, nor admit that she was battling a rippling current at Atlantic Beach in Long Island. But the water stung my body and the waves felt harsher than those I got acclimated to growing up. No more mobile New England water encased within The Sound, I dreamt. Joey and I can swim very well, I shouted out, fighting the undertow, unaware of the technique of maneuvering my body parallel to the shoreline during the heavy riptide.

Who knew that the Long Island current holding no enclosed sanctuary of inclusion can be dangerous? I later asked myself. Sure, the Connecticut shore eventually affixes to the vast, open sea, The Little Man may have reminded me, however much further east, and by the way of the Rhode Island Sound. I never gave a hoot about the transition between lake and ocean seawater before, I told myself nor of the stonier gravel along the Niantic beaches, which were nearly impossible to walk on.

Years later I latched on to his shoulders, or perhaps to his rope or rescue can. The Big Lifeguard with the Frog Tattoo began swimming parallel to the water drifts and lugged me back to shore safely. He talked to me gently throughout the rescue. "How old are you?" he asked.

"Forty-one," I answered in real time.

"You will be ok," The Big Lifeguard with the Frog Tattoo assured me.

In no time he gently placed my body along the smooth, wet sand, no rocks or gravel like Niantic. As I rubbed my eyes from the stinging salt water, I overheard him calmy explain the scenario to Aunt Sina. From the corner of my new set of eyes, I saw her bend down on her hands and knees again, sobbing. She kissed my forehead like long ago, before thanking The Big Lifeguard with the Frog Tattoo for saving my life. As I woke up from another sudden seizure, I heard people clapping in the background, at someone or something, not knowing what.

The New Christine later recalled morsels of Junior high school, some bitter chocolate, some sweet chocolate. My science teacher, Mr. P. leaned against the front if his desk, and asked the class, "What's stomata?"

"Nothing's the matter," the students replied.

"What's stomata?" he asked again, this time getting up and spreading out his arms.

"Nothing!" The class responded again, baffled.

After decades of disassociation, I failed to understand why this random, explicit memory was stored safely for a later recap, but as the years passed, it began making sense. It turns out that stomata is a plant structure on the outer skin layer known as the epidermis. Stomata means mouth in Greek, and it provides communication between the plant's internal and external environments. Stomata allows carbon dioxide, water vapor, and oxygen to move in and out of the leaf. The stomata found on leaves, stems and flower petals, The Little Man expressed, make the plant more colorful, healthy, and vibrant.

As a horticulturist at heart, I used an analogy between stomata and the human brain, to set future goals for myself. My hemispheres still had trouble communicating back and forth, alongside my internal and external chaos. Moving forward was a struggle, but the memory of that teacher defining stomata to me over-and-over again felt inspirational. He gave me motivation to employ my neuroplasticity to its maximum potential, and someday bloom after overcoming so many hurdles. My right hemisphere has ample space to flee the vast, open sea with creativity and imagination, but I still lack those few safety measures to protect me. So, I still struggled to keep abreast of where I stood on the vast planet as one, single person in one, single moment in time, physically, mentally, and spiritually. The term stomata floated in my brain for a very long time, weightless yet solid. It represented communication between my two opposing hemispheres. Dr. Taylor notes that the last thing dominating the left's desire for boundaries is to share its limited cranial space with its open-minded right counterpart! *

*Random high school events started popping out much later on, which is when I discovered that Dad's dispirit of Christmas went unnoticed by my friends. In fact, they all looked forward to celebrating the holidays with my family. Decades later through

Facebook, I learned my Jewish friends Dawn and Amy fancied our seven fishes on Christmas Eve. Out of nowhere The New Christine wondered why The Old One never felt worthy of Dad's love on Easter. He didn't treat me like his little princess, the way my uncles treated their daughters, my two close cousins. My uncles proudly boasted about Maria and Angela's accomplishments and spoiled them like angels. I wanted so desperately to unwrap a pretty, pink Easter basket just like them, filled with chocolate bunnies, sugared marshmallows, and plastic eggs holding five-dollar bills. My Dad never whisked me to church in bright Easter bonnets, gay ribbons, and bows. In fact, his brain held minimum space for anything positive, and Joey and I followed the path of worthlessness.

My friends and I spent summer days at Point Lookout Beach, baking in the rays with our reflecting mirrors and covered with Johnson's Baby Oil. 1988 was our last summer of leisure before entering the workforce. Dawn and Amy sang along to "Don't Worry Be Happy" and "Pour Some Sugar on Me," as we blasted our symbolic battery-operated boombox and competed with the other beachgoers. Every boombox clashed and held the need to connect to the world through their high and low frequency speakers and impressive modern technology. My sultry figure carved out with a defined midline, but unlike my friends sporting bikinis, I concealed my body with a conventional one-piece suit from L. L. Bean.

Most of my friends kept kosher homes, and the first thing I learned as a Five Town dweller is that kosher diets do no not mix meat with dairy, so cheeseburgers and chicken parmesan are out of the question, just not at my house. They devoured Nono's shrimp parmesan, and Italian sausage hung on strings from the basement ceiling. I quickly turned into their family tool as well, spending two Friday nights a month at Amy's. As a gentile I flicked the television and light switches on for them, since strict Orthodox Jews refrain from using electricity during Shabbat.

At another point The New Christine recalled watching a romantic comedy with Amy's brother called *Crossing Delancey,* where actor Amy Irving turns enamored with the intellectual world, the world far away from her traditional Jewish roots and upbringing on The Lower East Side of Manhattan. She turned into a snob, setting her sights on The New York intelligentsia turning out to be a pompous prick. Of course, in the end her grandma Bubbie hired a matchmaker and set her up with the local Jewish pickle man, Peter Reigert, and the rest is history.

Before watching the movie, we lit Shabbat candles and ate Matzo Ball soup, followed by kosher poultry and some casserole dish that I never really cared for. Presented on their Saturday morning breakfast table was a cold, white fish with a bubbling eye glaring up at me from the plate. I had trouble looking at the freshly ground and deboned gefilte fish as well, minced fatty fishes drowning in sedimentary water. Amy loved the food and rituals, and

I loved being a part of them, especially Sukkot, The Fall Harvest that followed me into adulthood.

I contacted more high school friends through Facebook, and a few years later in 2009, some of us attended our twenty-fifth high school reunion. That evening I felt like a trespasser embraced around warm hugs and forgotten memories. The Capgras Syndrome, my visual problems with face recognition and emotional attachment shone right through the entire evening. As old peers and friends approached me, I failed to recall their names, and barely even recognized them. So, I used alternative matching strategies like voice, posture, gestures, as well as silently speeding through the alphabet in-order to locate the first letter of his/her name. This usually worked, but when it failed, I poked my select friends for reminders or details of how the relationship developed. I continued to use more fake-it-till-you-make-it strategies as well.

Apparently, I got called "The Social Butterfly" in high school, flying around the cafeteria from table to table and chatting among various cliques. Since I failed to recall my boyfriends, prom, or graduation, my friend Maria helped me by going on a Facebook binge, posting click of seven. Dressed in balloon pants, striped shirts, and Minnetonka Moccasins, we all stood in the school hall hunched forward like a football tackle. "I wasn't in that picture," Abby commented, "Because Dr. Cole brought me to his office!"

I can't recall the year, the pose, or even Dr. Cole, the high school principal for that matter. Another day Maria brought me back to my first boyfriend in high school through another Facebook post on a Throwback Thursday. It displayed my arms reaching up and around his shoulders in high-waist pants with gold zippers and polyester striped top. The picture lacked memory, emotion, and familiarity. The only feature that stood out to me were his eyebrows, and for the first time they bothered me. Jimmie, my boyfriend had one eyebrow growing in a straight line above his eyes. "Don't you remember Chris?" Elyce posted. "His nickname was Unibrow!"

My only recollection of my sweet sixteen is dancing with an Italian stud, Carman Curra, to "Our Lips Are Sealed" by the Go-Go's. In 1982 this first all-woman rock band that wrote their own music and played their own instruments topped the charts in U.S. The pictures display me wearing a shiny-gold metallic pants that ballooned on top and tapered along the bottom. My hairstyle matched figure skater Dorothy Hamill's wedge bob, I saw in a photo, and I held a Gear clutch, molded like bubbles on a rubber bathmat.

Without reminders and photos, my memories had not much to fall back on, and this life of dotted lines sparked my baffling reactions toward my children. I was in awe of them, of how they laughed at their elementary school music teacher, Mr. M. for scolding the kids in the cafeteria by blowing a whistle, before having them wheel the garbage can to collect trash. Even in college they continued to mock the nerdy teacher, who lived with his parents and came into school each day with a peanut butter and jelly sandwich in a brown bag. I heard them laugh about how his toupee blew off on one windy afternoon, and laugh about his "Five on Lines," each time he made the kids stand on-line for five minutes when recess ended. "Five-on-line is not five dollars, it's free, so get going!" Stephanie laughed.

Jason cracked up as well, while I stood there perplexed, not about the joke, rather the solidarity and continuity between them. As a brain injured mother, I still admire them from afar. I mourn my empty shell. I ponder the possibility that I might have been able to save my brother Joey from alcoholism, if I didn't undergo loss of memory and dormancy. It's a nightmare when I think about all the lives that got drastically altered due to one person's inadequacies.

Freud notes that the first thing the brain needs to maintain relationships is a clear autobiographical self, which requires explicit, episodic memories. But my seizures launched a waterfall, leading to a series of steep drops. This brings me to another favorite part of my book, the distinctions between personality and self and between the mind and brain. *

It turns out that science uses various measures to differentiate among all of them. Most discovered about one hundred years ago from tests on persons with frontal lobe injuries like mine. Yet, the differences remain somewhat vague in psychiatry because personality and self each hold unique motivations, preferences, and behaviors, while they overlap and integrate as well.

Losing your personality implies losing the psychological characteristics that develop and change over time, including our motivations, behaviors, and preferences. Losing your self implies losing part of your original identity. I will begin with personality, which continuously changes based on life's experiences and growth. Our personality matures over time as we break old habits, learn from mistakes, unmask our experiences, and live out new ones. Mine altered so many times over in response to the febrile convulsion, fall down the staircase, seizures, brain inactivity, family upheaval, and two adult brain surgeries. It's scientifically proven that mental abuse shrinks the hippocampus and amygdala over time, damaging our fight-or-flight responses as well. Weaning off meds provides the brain clearer lenses as well, to observe life through a new set of eyes. Seizures evaporate. Inactivity activates. All of this transformed my personality over time.

Our sense of Self is far more mind boggling because it turns out that the frontal lobe shapes our identity and being, all while the hippocampus keeps the brain grounded in real time. While all four lobes are imperative for survival, the frontal lobe remains the most crucial lobe, assigning every person and individual character. It represents the essence of humanity.

I started considering that my original sense of self originating in 1966 remained unhinged, buried in the ground for decades like a dormant bulb in the dead of winter, patiently awaiting spring bloom. Then suddenly, my limbic system provoked, and Stevie's lightning bolt struck the ground thirty-three years later. My bulbs instantly bloomed, right beside the bohemian that God created in the first place, before her disease transpired. It is why I was gifted with the pleasures of cornrows and beads, bandanas, and ponchos, all of which I was too young to revel in and enjoy as a child to begin with.

Freud noted that the unconsciousness contains three united systems: the id, ego, and superego. The id is our unconscious primitive drive, instinct, and emotion. It includes impulse, sexual regression and instant gratification. The id makes the demands. The superego represents our moral consciousness adding ethical codes to our actions. Finally, the ego is realistic, as it mediates between these two desires. It bases itself on reality. However, Freud was never clear or concise on the boundaries between our conscious and unconscious parts of the ego, nor of the relationships between them. Dr. Sarino notes that, "One cannot experience something, that by definition, one is not aware of."

I have always sensed that my id got sparked in 1999, opening the oldest can of worms lying dormant in my limbic system without intention. And for years, my brain was "Reluctant to open the floodgates," Dr. Sarno notes, in fear of them being empowered by my emotions.

The internal floods, filled with overwhelming childhood despair, contained themselves throughout my stages of denial, anger, shock, depression, bargaining, and transference…before releasing after surgery. In addition, the external floods, filled with gaslighting, lying, theft, co-dependency, enabling, and addiction, all contained themselves as well, before releasing themselves like a sloth. My life felt like quicksand, unable to escape. Other than Mommy, who provided with me water, fertilizer and sun for growth, the others continued to pollute me with paranoia, anxiety, and most prevalent, a lack of self-worth. The stages of shock, denial and anger overlapped for years and years, and trust me, anger is the easiest stage to endure, since it tampers down our emotions, which are often too much for the brain to manage. The three initial steps of grief were all originally designed to protect us from the painful emotions we would otherwise be experiencing.

Unlike Steven's passive aggressive behavior, my anger sat in plain sight, my screaming and assault. I was defending my rights as his parents witnessed my wraths and refused to acknowledge the source. This triggered more defense mechanisms in my brain, and the cycle continued, both conscious and unconscious. Dr. Sarno states that, "We live in a world of the conscious, and most of us think it is our only world. We acknowledge only what we are aware of, what we feel consciously."

For me this is not true, as my unconsciousness became just as imperative as my consciousness. In addition, when the brain gets rejected and battered time and time again, it begins unconsciously perceiving the world as a very painful place as well. It begins building walls to block its emotions; it begins creating a safe place to retreat; it begins writing people off easily. And these painful dynamics "begin" sooner than we think. In fact, they originate in our childhood, when we slowly begin building walls, as I did with Silver Sylvia and Little Chip.

Famous Swiss psychologist Carl Jung notes that dreams and hallucinations play a vital role in developing one's personality as well, presenting it with even more unconscious material that needs someday to get recognized, and integrated to form a more balanced sense of self. So, we don't just live in just the world of consciousness like most presume, nor acknowledge only what we are aware of in present.

Various dream studies were performed in attempt to match dream elements to waking life and find newer sources or interpretations of old memory. But there were very few successes, limited matches in locations between dream life and waking life, times, characters. There was little or no reactivation of old memories, reprocessed, re-transcribed, and recalled, for anyone to write about them. This is where the neurological guinea pig comes into play again.

During REM sleep the hippocampus shuts down right along with our explicit memories. A shutdown of a neurotransmitter called noradrenaline during REM sleep occurs as well, which works with adrenaline when the brain feels threatened, and prepares for fight or flight. Together they protect the brain from outside distractions and irrelevant sensations. But we need a healthy amygdala and hippocampus for this all to work normally. We need our neurotransmitters to shut down during REM as well, in-order to search for older and weaker dream memories.

Since my brain fails at a lot of this, my dream recollection is outstanding and profound. Brains with PTSD experience increases in noradrenaline during sleep as well, rather than decreases. This inability to suppress things results from my lack of normal REM sleep, which then triggers replays of old episodic memories. My dreams cascading around past events from long ago always tie to real-life events. They repeat the joys and traumas in unusual ways, which was another reason it took my brain so much longer to fight off its PTSD and move past its traumas. This failure alone, Zandra and Stickhold note, ironically defines the very development of PTSD as well!

My abnormal responses to fight-or-flight have to do with a separate part of the limbic system than I mentioned before, the *cingulate gyrus*, as well as a separate part of the prefrontal cortex, the *orbital cortex*. In normal brains these parts offset each other and help regulate our behavior and process our emotions. The orbital cortexes, also known as eyes sockets on each side of the prefrontal cortex, receive visual information involved in our decision-making and cognitive abilities. An overactive or damaged orbital cortex promotes 'brain lock,' releasing false signals of worry even after mistakes corrected.

*L*ying right along the distinction between self and personality lies the distinction between the brain and mind. The brain holds billions of neurons and individual cells that generate our emotions, thoughts, and perceptions. They guide and regulate our behaviors, choices, and opinions. They direct and execute our actions. Further, the conscious brain is responsible to bring the unconscious mind into awareness, to eventually separate the sorrow and collect up all the…. just like "The Candy Man" from "1972"!

I'm ending the differences between personality and self, and brain and mind, with some questions Dr. Fredrick Schiffer asks in his book *OF TWO MINDS*: "What instructs our unconsciousness whether to repress or censor its ideas? Is there a pattern? What part of the brain decides? If the unconsciousness decides or opposes the consciousness, then why can't it get studied in isolation? How can analysts describe the unconsciousness, tell us it was primitive or childlike, had wishes, memories, fantasies, yet say it did not exist, but existed only as processes?

I'm proud of myself for staying on top of my game by writing dream-notes throughout the unmasking process, for tracking and reporting each unconscious dream and hallucination before they dissipated. This higher right hemispheric mind maintaining dream reports helped my weaker left hemisphere fill in the missing pieces of my life, draw inferences and conclusions, and clear my past doubts.

In 2013 I got friended on Facebook by a man named Brian Long, and since the name sounded somewhat familiar, I responded, asking him how he knew me. He immediately replied:

"Christine-It's kind of sad in a funny sort of way that you don't remember me. You were one of my most memorable breakups, but you don't remember me at all. We dated for a month during your senior year of high school and then you went back to Connecticut to visit your old school. I drove with your brother to pick you up, and as soon as we got there, I knew something was wrong. You gave me a note you had been writing the first three days you were there, and I kind-of figured out what happened when I got to the last line of the note, which read, "I just saw my ex-boyfriend." I hope this brings back at least a vague memory of how we know each other. Two days later, on Easter morning, just before we were going to work a nine our shift together at Beefsteak Charlie's, you dumped me. I don't want you to think any of this as bitter, because honestly it isn't any more. I have very fond memories of you. I have always wished you nothing but the best, but I never actually got around to writing to tell you that. Now I am glad I didn't because it probably would have confused you since you didn't remember me and maybe still don't. Anyway, I hope life has given you nothing but reasons to smile, and that you are as happy as you deserve to be. If you still don't remember me and you want to unfriend me, I'm not the type of person who holds grudges, but if you wouldn't mind, please write to let me know that you are doing so. Thanks Brian."

Another relationship that took place in the 1980s, not housed safely in my long-term memory. I just discarded the memory of him through time.

I responded: "Wow, I just read your message now, and I cried. How are you? I have two kids. One in the first year of college, and the other in the second. And U? I don't remember much of my past. Long story. We can catch up if you like. My AOL is_____."

He's Irish and worked as a busboy at Beefsteak Charlies where I was a host. Tall and thin, I recalled, with light blond hair and a young Irish baby face. He said I love you to me, too many times as well, which is likely why I shunned him. I hold no recollections of intimacy, of him meeting my brother, of my boyfriend in Connecticut, or of breaking his heart. But as I began writing about him, I finally came to realize just how many men I've broken up for getting too close to me.

Of course, our fear of intimacy originates in our childhood developmental years, and as adults we unconsciously search for the same prototype. Brian was not one of them, but Billy was. I got accustomed to the drinking, cursing and neglect, so I searched for these traits not knowing any better. I met Billy in my senior year of high school. It was my first day of work at Beefsteak Charlie's, a low-end steak house in Lawrence. Very tall and ruggedly handsome, I recall, with thick, blond hair. Twenty-one years old, much older than me. I walked in to drop off my employment application, but nobody was at the concierge. I walked into the lounge and saw him stack glasses behind the bar. He turned his head around, and we locked eyes. This moment of passion instigated a four-year tumultuous relationship. The New Christine discerned over two decades later.

Billy was not coy like Steven, nor monetarily hungry, rich, and spoiled. He was moody and temperamental with a noticeably short fuse like Dad. Follow me please, I said to the customers regularly, before walking them to their tables.

"I'll follow you anywhere," repellent Billy repeated, "the boobs, the legs, the hair, the hostess with the mostest!"

Billy and I spent my last summer weekends after college graduation and before entering the workforce at Point Lookout Beach. We ate prime rib and lobster tails on Saturday nights and drank Tanqueray and Tonics with a wedge of lime. I shouldn't have mixed alcohol with medications, but I could not resist the dry London gin that tasted like fresh cedar evergreens. "Chris, you're entitled to some pleasure," Billy insisted. "You managed nailing three interviews with three different CPA firms before graduating from college!" he said, envious. "Better than me going to Nassau Community, and besides, I can drive your car home. At least you have a sports car," he mocked.

I failed to notice the envy or mockery, the high fuse resulting from his low self-esteem and envy. Billy was disdainful of me like Dad, The New Christine later discerned, always in need of control, and using his body size as an intimidating factor as well. By this point I'd accepted an offer as junior auditor at a C.P.A. firm in Manhattan, and deep down I couldn't wait for summer to end. After four years of dating Billy, I knew I was ready to begin a new chapter in my life. Although I have no recollections of having seizures around Billy, I am sure that I did. I have no recollection of driving Mom's Buick to college the afternoon my Firebird went into service, but apparently, I crashed into a telephone pole in Garden City, close to Adelphi University, where I attended. Later, The New Christine heard the police sirens in her sleep, over-stimulating my damaged temporal lobes. I covered my ears with my hands again and bent forward on the steering wheel. I felt bruising on my forehead. I overheard Dad tell Mom that he could fix the car himself and save on the labor. "You're an accountant now," I heard Billy shout in the same dream. "An auditor, studying for the C.P.A. exam, and soon you'll be dismissing the small people like me."

My brain spent, but my altruistic mother tried to convince me otherwise. "I'm not marrying him Mom!" I shouted at her.

Toward the end of my unmasking process when my explicit memories were hitting the forefront of my brain, I recalled the August evening when Billy drove my car recklessly once again. He adamantly insisted on driving my Firebird rather than his worn-out Chrysler, and the arrogance and persistence represented red flags that my poor abstract thinking failed to recognize. That evening after downing too many Tanqueray and Tonics, he slammed the gas pedal on the Southern State Parkway. Van Halen's "Jump" was blasting on the radio, and he knew I was not fond of hard rock or heavy metal. My neck jerked. I lowered the radio, before kindly asking him to slow down. But he raised the volume up again and sped faster. I shut off my radio. "If you're going to drive over the speed limit drunk, then take your own damn car and do it without me!" I shouted. "My father would never approve of you driving my car in the first place, never mind, drunk!"

"Mine's old and falling apart!" he raged back.

"Then I'll drive," I said, "pull over."

Even with his disease, Dad played by the rules. He paid every bill before the due dates, netted every leaf from the pool, swept the floors day and night, and made sure that all the gas tanks remained full. "Amoco premium," he insisted, "no regular, premium gets better gas mileage and running, and higher fuel efficiency!"

Each time our gages read a half a tank, Joey and I found yellow stickies on the steering wheels reading, "GET GAS, AMOCO PREMIUM!"

"And nobody drives the car but you," he insisted. "I'm the one making the payments."

But just like with cooking, I rebelled. My gas gage goes in the red before I hit a gas station. Sure enough, Billy crashed into a stop sign that evening and shattered the passenger-side window. I recalled the glass bursting inside my car and the shard penetrating through my right arm. It bled in dots. I was more scared of his rage than I was about my own safety. Rather than help me wipe the blood off my right arm, he demanded I switch seats with him, to avoid Dad's wrath. Rather than feeling angry and disappointed in Billy, I cried in fear instead, in fear of him and my father. "Your Dad's an auto body professional who fixes broken windows for a living!" he shouted. "So, get in the driver's seat, it's not a big deal!"

I drove home sobbing, bleeding, and suppressing my anger in fear of his reaction. I lied right in Dad's face to protect Billy, but he immediately noticed the passenger side window cracked. He looked at Billy right arm and raged. "You're a disrespectful son of a ___!" I heard, wiping my bleeding right arm with my shirt, fully acclimated to his alcoholic tendencies. But his did not mean that I liked them.

I never intended for Billy to meet my future co-workers and bosses three weeks before my starting date, I told myself in 2015, when he appeared on Facebook as a friend request. I did too much internalizing back then as an epileptic, The New Christine told herself, and accepted people who wronged me on so many levels. Why in God's name did I invite the aggressive drunk that I despised to my company picnic? I asked myself when my decision-making process was finally improving.

The left brain tells us how to act upon our feelings based on our prior experiences. This hemisphere creates hierarchies of past events and people, including those we trust and those we don't, to later act on lessons learned, and accesses alternatives if or when needed. Remember what I wrote about the ACC in my presurgical chapter? The ACC connects to both the cognitive prefrontal cortex and the emotional limbic system. A damaged ACC monitors predictions exceptionally well, but with an asymmetrical brain, it comes with a cost.

The ACC helps us remember what our dopamine cells just learned, so we won't make the same mistakes over-and-over again. When lessons cannot fully internalize, such as Billy smashing my car and demanding that I lie to my father, then future predictions fail to revise themselves. Once again, all of this requires memory and emotion. Jonathon Lehrer explained that "If we can't incorporate the lessons of the past into our future decisions, then we're destined endlessly repeat our mistakes. The brain doesn't exist in a vacuum, and all decisions are made in the context of the real world."

Throughout centuries of evolution civilization continues racing forward and influenced increasingly by modern culture. The once seemingly simple choices became more difficult to make, because the brain was not originally designed to choose among so many choices and variables. Our culture, technology and vast array of possibilities often overwhelm our decision-making process, and yet when cut off from round-the-clock cyberspace, we become impatient and bored. Plato gives the finest analogy on decision-making by comparing the charioteer to the horse. What appears as a simple decision, he noted, such as the charioteer deciding whether-or-not to follow the lead requires ample reasoning, master, and skill, reason, and foresight. The injured brain feels perfectly fine going off course and making its own rules, since it lacks guilt and fear in the amygdala. Unfortunately, our emotions impact our decisions, and when lethargic, impulse often prevails over common sense.

Plato divided the mind into two conflicting spheres: Reason and Emotion, both imperative in deciding what to do next, but paradoxically, they function in accord as well. Our reasoning is a byproduct of our rationality, he notes, our common sense and choices. In a normal brain reasoning overpowers emotion, and reasoning includes weighing pros and cons, compromising, understanding greys, expressive language, and cognition. On one hand, an injured left becomes inflexible, holding trouble deciding, planning, and setting realistic future goals, all while the right feels a newfound sense of freedom, joy, and liberty. This is another fine example of The Plastic Paradox.

The reason an autistic, savant or brain impaired have trouble understanding broken promises, is because a promise is literally just that: a promise, matchless. One part of the massive cerebral cortex deciphers the motives and intentions behind our actions, while another processes them, while another rationalizes them, while another implements them. If these routes get cut off, then confusion prevails over common sense.

The autistic, savant, and brain impaired are geniuses at detecting liars, but another downside of our asymmetry lies in the inability to interpret their ultimate motives and to tie our emotion with our actions. This combination provokes narcissism. It provokes the illusion-of-truth effect as well, where everyone is telling the truth. Like, narcissism, the illusion-of-truth effect founded my Michael Dregni, gets embedded in the brain early on as well, so any mere possibility of dishonesty got erased from our dictionary long ago. Then again, the human brain is "Built to default to truth," notes Dregni, "and the side effect is being easily deceived by the occasional sociopath!"

Billy and Steven congregated just that one time at the firm's annual picnic and softball game. After dating for four years, I expected him to make a good impression before my peers and bosses, and on the mound as well. When the managing partners saw him, they started composing a last-minute plot, I later learned, to back up the field as he approached the mound. Good for a homer or at least a double, people thought.

"A real slugger," Steven later mocked.

After nine innings with two pitchers throwing cutters and knuckleballs, Billy made a dismal performance, striking out four times at bat. The poor loser, unable to deliver on the challenge, threw a harrowing tantrum in front of everyone, and left. Back then his temper was not just a frivolous noise, I later learned, the wah-wah voice of Ms. Othmar in Charlie Brown. Only The New Christine learned Billy was a child that never learned how to leave the schoolyard, and another parasite of more to come, one undercutting people through smugness, contempt, and inner self-loath.

*T*he day after Labor Day finally approached, beside my aspiring hopes and seizures. On my first day at the accounting firm, Jay Ash, the oldest senior partner that hired me, welcomed me into his office. He appeared aloof again just as he had during the spring interview, but even more ripe and ready for retirement. I recall his hunchback, white hair, dark suit, and cane. He asked me about my goals and desires, before rambling about his six grandchildren. I tilted my head to the right and smiled back, pretending to be interested.

Next, the founding partner staggered off with his cane on a beaten path, and as an inconsequential junior accountant I shadowed him from behind. He plopped his fat, short body on a chair to take a breather, before glancing upward at the first passerby. "This is?" he asked.

"Steven," he replied.

"Chrissy, right?" Ash asked me, glancing upward.

He had hired Christine, but not Chrissy was ok. I failed to recall Steven from the picnic, but he certainly recalled Billy and I, and relished on his grim performance. His cocky demeanor felt potent and familiar. When we shook hands, he lacked grip and eye contact, The New Christine discerned decades later, and held farce entitlement. I am not worth eye contact just yet, I told myself, but maybe I will earn it soon, I considered, as he scanned elsewhere for someone better to come along.

Everyone else recognized the cocky behavior as a sign of underlying low self-esteem, The New Christine discovered, but I took it as confidence. I credited his patronizing attitude as a sign of care. Steven was obsessed with me. He followed every audit and every colleague that I communicated with. That day his polished appearance included an impeccably tailored, pinstriped suit accessorized with a rich, burgundy tie. Brooks Brothers suits during the week, I soon discovered, and button-down Oxfords or collared Lacoste's on the weekends. He seemed to be a one-hundred-and-eighty-degree-circle from Dad's JC Penney nylon slacks and Billy's rolled up jeans. A northeastern university type, I thought, before learning he graduated from a famous Boston college.

My clothing appeared somber and undistinguishable, yet still managed alluring a handful of accountants of all ages, levels, and religions. A man's imagination sees beneath the apparel, I learned quickly.

While the seniors worked in cubicles, the insignificant juniors like me worked on countertop workspaces in a large, dim room, windowless and smack in the center of the 19th floor. However, Steven, still a junior, managed manipulating his way into a higher-up cubicle, stationed just outside the room of doom and gloom. It was a stereotypical, water-cooler-area, where gossip proliferated and rapidly seeped through the walls. No emails or texts to communicate back then, just rumors unfolding through whispers and notes.

Mr. Ash placed me on a bankruptcy case, and he even escorted me down to the seventeenth floor, covered with old boxes and dusty files of dissolved companies. "You have a very important job to do," he expressed, "and that's taking inventory of them."

Photocopying and check marking the yellow, stale paper was all about hourly billing rather than humiliation. A dark-skinned woman named Davonte chatted up a storm about her wedding, as she swung her arms up and down and complained about a typo on her invitations. The New Christine recalled her out of nowhere, probably because she lived in Astoria, another town in the vast borough of Queens that I still fail to define to this day. "It's your very first audit!" Ash expressed proudly, before leaving me desolate for the following six weeks.

But I was far from deserted, because the men flocked south regularly, to help me photocopy and learn how to use the adding machine. Mathew trained my fingers to add and subtract on the Cannon, fast and furious like him. Larry helped me compile the lignin, paper turned yellow. A heavy Queens accent, chunky waist, mass of red hair, I recall, as well as the buck teeth of a chipmunk. He appeared at my doorstep on the weekends, and I was not sure why. It took brain surgery, as well as years of unmasking these 1980s scarce episodic memories for me to discern my gullibility and over altruism. Although I disallowed any romance to materialize, my brain lacked the boundaries that would have prevented the visit from occurring in the first place.

My kindness illustrated both fear of commitment and over-altruism, inducing me to take care of others before myself. This ran in my family as well, I later learned, and links to poor self-esteem. I minimized other people's exploitation of me because I loathed myself, and over time the inferiority complex was silently breeding inner shame. Trust me, shame can feel like quicksand; the heavier it becomes, the deeper we sink and the more elusive our self-forgiveness becomes.

The final contestant was Weinstein from Brooklyn, who managed bolting out of the office like lightening every Friday before sundown for Shabbat, the Jews' day of rest and atonement. People respected this no-doubt and worked late Friday nights and Saturdays throughout tax season as well, to catch up from the lack of staff. But nobody respected him when he jolted out at 5:00 pm in mid-June, July, and August as well.

I can't recall allowing Weinstein to frequent my home during Shabbat, but the more I began recalling selective memories, the more I learned about my poor rationality and the more I wanted to bang my rotted head against a brick wall. Was he breaking his customs for his self-serving needs? The New Christine asked herself. And why did I provide him my address in the first place?

I recalled Dad answering the door one Saturday shirtless. "The boy from Brooklyn is here again Chris!" he yelled out.

Weinstein had a dark mustache and thick, black waves. That day, The New Christine recalled him sitting on the edge of my bed. What was this stupid epileptic thinking? I asked myself in rage. She allowed him to scratch her back and shoulders on her bed with her grandmother in the next room watching mass on channel thirteen.

"No, Steven," I expressed. "We're just friends."

"I think you're so beautiful Chris?" he replied.

And it would not surprise me if I replied with a thank you, and besides, living with Mom and Nono certainly did not help. In fact, Mom offered him a cheeseburger later in the afternoon, already knowing that the Orthodox do not mix meat with dairy. Gladwell's illusion-of-truth went into effect again: the tendency to believe false information and mannerisms, repeated so often that it embeds in the brain through time. *

"The Elton John tickets at Madison Square Garden got sold out in six minutes," I told Stefani, working beside me. The following morning Steven presented two tickets to me, with the date and time. We chuckled together in mutual flattery. He lived in northern New Jersey, and that evening he picked me up in Long Island, before we headed back into Manhattan. I heard a double honk, but when I peeked out of the front door, I failed to see his Ford Explorer. He bragged about his new black Explorer at work, the Eddie Bauer version. I noticed the beeping coming from a silver Porsche, so I went back inside.

"My truck is for my weekend off- roading," he chuckled moments later. "This one is for fun!"

The seat felt low to the ground. When he sped up, I feared my rear end would burn on the asphalt. As he raced off, he commented on the parked car lying sedentary in my driveway. "My first car, the Firebird was not my choice," I expressed to him in defense, "but this car was, and I'm responsible to make the payments," I said proudly. "It's my dream car."

"Why Chris, why?" Steven asked, shaking his head back and forth in dismay.

"You had a decent price to work with," he said. "You could have gotten a 1988 Toyota Celica, front-wheel drive with hidden popped-up headlamps retracting on the hood!"

"My car feels youthful and sporty to me," I replied. "I love the aerodynamic appearance."

It was a 1988 Mercury Sable in pearl white. "Stop saying it's a grandmother car," I told him. "It has a great new feature, embodying modern, future technology!" I said, proudly.

"Intermittent wipers are old features Chris," he replied.

"I guess the tv commercial sold me," I replied. A *new style of success ready and waiting, enabling tomorrow's technology today...*

We laughed. And even more water-cooler gossip proliferated after he took it for a spin. "The steering sucks!" he whined, "the transmission sucks and the power sucks!"

There was heavy traffic on the Grand Central Parkway, but it provided more time for him to boast, and more time for me to feed his bragging rights. I looked at his profile. "You look very cute tonight, Steven," I expressed like a child, blushing.

I caressed the back of his neck with my left hand, and he relished it like a puppy. Two adult bodies holding adolescent brains, The New Christine discerned, giggly, lovey-dovey codependents and enablers. After valet parking, we walked toward The Garden, weaving through thousands of pedestrians. We saw the same vendors we passed during the work week, roasting peanuts, and selling scarves. Yet that evening felt more colorful than most others. We proceeded past a jewelry store window as well, which displayed a remarkable pearl-cluster necklace and matching bracelet. "Oh my God!" I expressed, "gorgeous!"

From that point forward, Steven impersonated the "OOOHHH MYYY GODDD" repeatedly over the next thirty years. Imitation is the sincerest form of flattery, at least until it develops into jealousy, envy, and rage. We darted toward The Garden in mutual admiration. With his hand in his jean pocket, I wrapped my arm through his. My favorite song was, and remains "Your Song," and we danced our first dance to this our wedding three years later.

The following weekend, he sat on my kitchen chair and met Mom. He placed the lustrous pearl necklace and bracelet from the window in front of me at the table, wrapped in blue and white ribbon.

*U*nfortunately, the man behind the adorable face and generosity got intrigued by my disease as well, I learned three decades later, and the control he may someday obtain. One afternoon at work, I stopped at an ATM before lunch, and back in the late1980s, account balances got displayed right on the screen for anyone to see. It was an insane lack of privacy. "Ooooh, you got some money in there Chrissy," he chuckled from behind me.

Chrissy, I thought, rather than Chris or Christine. I turned around, disappointed about the prying. Everyone at work knew Steven was a snoop, I later discerned.

"Not nearly as much as me though," he said, laughing.

But I had no time to roll my eyes at him in disgust, because my body and brain already started descending. Struck by another aura, I started shuffling my fingers and pursing my lips. I know he felt inclined to help me like any Good Samaritan. I did not know that my seizure provided him with a sudden rush of endorphins as well. During my dizzy sense of nothing, I continued with my transaction powerlessly, half conscious and half unconscious, I would have never guessed in a million years that decades later I would overhear Steven on the telephone with my first editor, expressing, "The seizures seduced me, and I relished the control. Plus, I had my own demons to contend with, so her seizures were an entertaining distraction."

1990s / 1999 and Forward

*A*s a sheltered epileptic tied up in The Five Towns, I had multiple fears about driving to New Jersey. I scribbled the directions down on notebook paper and precisely followed them, without knowledge that the hippocampus is heavily involved navigation, maps, and spatial skills, together with the temporal lobe. When I reached the sign midway along The George Washington Bridge reading New Jersey, my brain went from heavy concentration to exhilaration. Again, I desired to step out and place one foot in each state. But fifteen minutes later when I reached exit 172 along The Garden State Parkway, I was utterly perplexed. It read Park Ridge, the last exit in New Jersey.

I pulled over at Dunkin Donuts to call Steven. "How could I have left New York for New Jersey, and enter New York again?"

"Chrissy," he lectured, "states don't get configured in perfect squares and division the way you think. You're ten minutes away, just follow the directions!"

Sure enough, I entered the quaint town of Park Ridge within minutes, nestled in a valley with narrow roads and winding hills. I passed just one traffic light before reaching his house. In addition, I never drove up and down such steep, tapered hills, nor had to release the gas pedal going downhill with my right foot. I predicted protective swamps and wetlands in the area, and sure enough, I passed a little scenic farm on my right, with an indoor and outdoor nursery. At the bottom of the hill rested two lonely tractor trailers. I imagined the tractors transporting families with pumpkins up and down the hills in October. I imagined savoring fresh apple cider with Steven and touching various textures of orange gourdes. Perhaps purple crocuses, the first spring flower, budded in March, followed by red fringe tulips in early May.

Unfortunately, a lot of Long Islanders perceive New Jersey as nothing more than an ugly stretch of industry along The Turnpike on their way to Atlantic City. It is far from the truth, I discovered, in fact it's one of the richest states in the country, so closed minds should come with closed mouths.

I pulled into Steven's gated development and the security guard raised his voice at me. "Turn your high-beams off! You're driving in dense fog!"

He buzzed Steven's unit and I heard a feminine voice telling him to let me in. When I walked up the driveway, I heard a high-pitched screech emanating from inside. A pretty, young man answered the door, holding a scrawny little Yorkie. "Hullo dolling," he expressed, as if we knew each other well.

"Cutie vocalizes loudly," the man said. "He's a Red Lord Amazon. Come in darlin."

He placed Ginger on the floor, and she suddenly peed right in front of us. "Another brat!" the man said, just before Steven popped out of the elevator.

"Hi Steven," the man said.

I waited for a formal introduction, but Steven lacked manners, so the gentleman walked away. He was a famous interior decorator who had flown in from Dallas Texas with his business and personal partner to remodel Steven's parent's brand-new condominium, 5,100 square feet of luxurious space. We rode the elevator up to Steven's bedroom, his fourth-floor sanctuary, a plush finished attic extending the entire length of the condominium. Fully equipped with a wet bar, pool table, sauna, water- bed, and any other amenity imaginable for a twenty something year old young man.

We plopped down on the waterbed together, chatted and kissed, before studying together for the C.P.A exam. We were two identical peas in a pod dressed as if we were attending a golf outing. The album *Tango in the Night* blasted out of his high-fidelity stereo system. It might be why The New Christine continued to hear speak a little louder, and even shout years later during Steven's drug withdrawals. The magnified temporal lobe provided me absolute pitch again, as Steven took control of my destiny. I will be with you everywhere, Christine McVie unconsciously expressed, as Sacks' theory came into play once again, asserting that past events get fed to us literally, precisely, but in the wrong order.

I loved to watch Steven study; he ripped through the audit questions rapidly and precisely. I admired his memory recall, especially since I sensed my own worsening. He thrived when applying himself. I am not sure exactly when this ended, or how much I had to do with it since narcissists never stop blaming victims for their failures. He recently told me that I was too stupid to ever become a CPA. It turns out that I passed all four parts of the exam, but I never got the license due to lapsed time and a lapsing memory. "You're a user and a loser," he recently wrote, "a slut, user, abuser and ugly bitch! You will never get your alimony or life insurance. I'll die first!"

I already noticed my explicit memories fading gradually, but I didn't understand why. My brain excelled with speed and precision in the long computational problems that require complex math skills and little episodic memory. It was memorizing facts and exceptions that gave me trouble with the exam.

A few hours later we ran down the four flights of stairs into the finished basement and heard the pretty gentleman whistling "The Star Bangled Banner." This time I formally introduced myself, while Steven ignored them and began fiddling with a remote for the theatre size television screen on the wall. Ginger barked, Cutie squawked, the men whistled, and I stared at Steven in awe. He was kind and warm to me back then, but very immature for his age as well. I wanted to be his caregiver, and he wanted to be mine. We sought parenthood and attention. That evening we made love all night in the basement bedroom. I hadn't met his parents just yet, as they had taken their yacht down to Florida just a few days before.

A few months after surgery The New Christine had her post-surgical visits with Levy and Gordon. My feelings and perceptions transposed. My brain fueled by contradiction, undergoing shock, anger, and denial and perplexity. Somehow, I forced my gratitude to prevail, and sent two bouquets of flowers to New York Presbyterian Hospital, one addressed to Dr. Gordon on the 10th floor and the other to Dr. Levy on the seventh. I attached warm thank-you-notes adorned with XX's and OO's. My left was cognizant of the death of my disease while my right wailed for food like a hungry newborn baby.

Gordon was the genius that removed spoiled pieces of the pie with his own bare hands, I knew, but my weightless mind felt like a ton of bricks. It is funny how I feel so much, Sarah McLachlan sang from far away, but I'm unable to say a word. Her musical nuances replaced my seizures timely, the same way as Stevie and Carly. I screamed at Gordon from deep inside, failing to get heard, as Sarah's lyrics targeted my over-sensitive auditory cortex and amplified my hallucinations. Such musical ironies get compared to deaf musical masterminds, such as Stevie Wonder, whose abnormal auditory input admixes with a heightened musical perception and imagination.

Adam was in a league of his own, presenting himself to me as a psychiatric, optical, temporal illusion. With my illusions set aside, I felt that Dr. Adam Levy cared more about my well-being than my husband Steven ever did. I felt like a crippled, newborn baby beginning a new life and bonding with my primary caretaker. It felt real, and some bond felt better than no bond at all. I began a new life as somebody else that I even failed to connect with, and Adam's patience, gestures, compassion, and belief in me seemed to keep me alive. Plus, other than Mom, everyone from my previous life turned overly critical and judgmental, and desired instant remedies.

When I shared the first eighteen pages of my book with Adam and Steven in 1999, my husband never gave me the honor of reading it in full. "Good luck getting this published," he chuckled, while Adam responded with praise. This proved again that The Old Christine had never seen her husband for who he really was. This is the evil power behind narcissism.

The New Christine missed her first 9:00 appointment with Dr. Levy, and without a worry in the world, I casually strolled in at 9:30 instead. He waited for me, while surrounded around a handful of fatigued interns. I felt flattered yet guilty, and I apologized for my tardiness.

"It's ok Chris, but why are you alone?" he asked me, "and how did you get here?"

"Forget the driving!" I replied to Steven's double. "My seizures are gone now Dr. I drove to CVS to pick up my prescriptions last week, and besides, driving isn't on my list of tribulations right now," I exclaimed.

"But I told you not to drive for six months," he replied, "and thank you for the flowers."

My mind is screaming inside Dr. Levy....my limbic system shouted beside Sarah, but it cannot be heard. The limited rays of sunshine remained muddled behind the dark clouds, ready to submerge into another downpour at any point in time, I wanted to tell Levy, while clinging to a past that failed to let me choose.

"You're welcome, Dr. Levy," I replied, ashamed to share my love for him just yet. My brain needed more medical research to back up its claims, proof that my wires crisscrossed to the wrong people.

"Why do I suddenly feel apathetic toward my two children?" I asked him out of nowhere.

"Maybe it's depression," he replied warmly.

That is only part of it, I thought. "Why am so I robotic, and when will my feelings return?" I asked, expecting immediate answers, after-all, he had a reputation to uphold, and I had an identity to salvage.

"I'm putting you on Zoloft, and make sure you take them accordingly this time, ok? You have a habit of making your own rules."

So, I started the antidepressant knowing full well that a pill lacks the ability to reclaim an identity. Granted the antidepressant provided calming effects and eased some symptoms of my depression, but certainly not the reasons behind them. It is because depression is not a disorder within itself, but an expression of symptoms behind the disorder, including poor environment and grief. Anti-depressants would only barely sugarcoat the turmoil, I knew.

"I promise I'll listen this time," I replied, "and follow the scripts."

"You have my email so stay in touch," he said, "and I'll see you in three months or even less."

Adam, I am seeing double, I emailed him one Sunday evening less than three months later. I am dizzy, I am shaking, and my vision is blurry.

"Ok Chris come by tomorrow at 5:30. I'll be finished with my patients then," he quickly responded.

"I dread going through another E.E.G or M.R.I. Dr. Levy," I said.

He diagnosed the problem within two minutes. "Chris you're overdosing on your meds," he calmly said. "Go home and read the labels on your bottles."

His wisdom, I thought, his solution to another quandary. Sure enough, I had taken eighty rather than forty milligrams of my meds over the past eight days. Either way, I was love struck again, and this time around, I ordered a box of chocolate cookies online created in the shape of a human brain. I had them delivered to his office the following week. Years later when another similar dilemma took place, I just happened to spot a small wooden box in a gift store, engraved with a side angle of the human brain. The arrows directed toward the frontal lobe, temporal lobe, occipital lobe, parietal lobe, and hippocampus. Never enough gifts for Dr. Levy, I thought.

We hold three major structures in our brain, which I will refer to as continents: The Brain Stem, Cerebellum, and Cerebrum. The brain stem was the first to develop over five hundred million years ago, and this primitive area manages basic life support like breathing, heartbeat, reflexes, and digestion. This stem is highly functional in our social behavior and emotion, including how we react to incoming sensory information. On one hand my brain stem works faster when processing information. I feel a shorter circuitry. Yet, it feels slower in other ways as well. It became oversensitive and overstimulated. A musician can have a sensitive brain stem as well, with the ability to hear and foresee milliseconds before real time. The brain stem also mirrors that of a modern reptile, primate and Homosapien. Plato states humans are part animal; we are primitive beasts riddled with primitive desires. Sure, a reptilian's brain is dependable, but unfortunately, it gears toward rigidity and compulsion as well.

The cerebellum commonly called the "little brain," developed around four hundred million years ago, and the human's is remarkably like that of other mammals. The cerebellum controls our posture, balance, and movement. It transmits vital information to other areas of the brain via the brain stem as well. It judges distance when we drive, walk, and run so we can perform rapid, alternating movements and without tripping on our own feet, like me.

Our cerebrum is the largest, most prominent part of the brain, filled with the white and grey matter that I discussed earlier my book. The grey matter lying in the cerebrum is our cerebral cortex, containing the largest, most modern brain areas. This evolutionary part of the brain, developing around two hundred million years ago, holds our four lobes, as well as our corpus callosum connecting our two hemispheres. Remember this helps transfer our motor, sensory, and cognitive skills from one side to the other, our information, feelings, and agendas. Without a healthy corpus callosum, we often contradict ourselves like oil and water.

My temporal lobe processing turned hearing and sound into a seesaw as well, as I can hear the sprinklers hitting the trunks of the trees at 5:30 in the morning and the cat meowing at midnight from two floors below in the basement. Yet, I often scream when I speak because I cannot hear my own voice. I cringe from auditory overstimulation. The spatial processing in my parietal lobe often fails as well, as I became a curbside driver. I have trouble navigating around my own neighborhood, while easily finding my way through foreign places. When I visited Niantic again as an adult, I navigated around the town with a bizarre sense of familiarity. Unlike my present neighborhood, I failed to get lost. This proves again that my aged networks from the early 1970s got targeted again in1999. *

Every day I place a cup of water along what I think is the edge of the counter, before watching it fall off and spill right before me. My occipital lobe, in charge of sight, weakened as well. My vision turned into an enigma, as sizes, structures, shapes, and colors all intensified, with richer detail and element, while I see the roads as narrowed due to tunnel vision.

Doidge noted that two researchers in neuroplasticity, Helen Neville and Donald Lawson proved that deaf persons with defects in their temporal lobes intensify their hearing through the peripheral vision in the occipital lobes! I even read about a woman whose vision turned three dimensional when looking at her gardens. Gifted with the proficiency to see every single blade of grass standing out of a massive field. Don't get me wrong these visual and auditory disparities aren't nearly as mature for the blind or deaf, but stem from what's being transmitted between the two eyes instead, just like my auditory and temporal disparities of the deaf, which stems from being transmitted between the two ears.

My brain often diverges and converges simultaneously, allowing each eye or ear to focus on two different things at once. My stereotypical illusions of sound, depth, hues, contours, and illustrations turned so exaggerated that nothing seems to break through the camouflage.

Finally, the marvelous frontal lobe performs the highest mental functions in the human brain including, memorizing, interpreting, reasoning, decision-making, speaking, judgement, comprehending...

It provides the brain with willpower, as well as the divine gift of rationality. At first The New Christine worried more about running out of laundry detergent than about arriving to her annual mammography on time, knowing full well that my mother is a breast cancer survivor. One day I had a training session at 9:30. The clock read 8:55. I was cognizant of the time strain, but I lingered in bed until 9:10 without worry. When my body and brain finally agreed that I should get up, I threw on my gym clothes and brushed my teeth simultaneously, knowing full well I had to leave the house. But I made myself a cup of coffee and removed some clothes from the dryer. Sipped a few sips, folded a few articles, put on my sneakers like slippers and left the house. Then when I was just a half a mile away from the gym, I made a split decision to U turn and run into ShopRite for laundry detergent, making me late for my prepaid session. And don't forget that the frontal lobe assigns distinct traits and characteristics to each person, making one subdued and another comical. This gatekeeper to our emotions represents who we are as individuals on the cosmic planet Earth.

*E*very single day I grapple with neuropsychiatry, the link connecting neurology to psychiatry. They each revolve around the human brain, work homogeneously together as one, and represent the autonomy of the mind. I guess I expected clearer consensuses from the doctors, more long-term control studies and risk/benefit ratios behind the complex procedure. Maybe I would not have been 'four-square' in favor of the idea of brain surgery, and I had the right to be warned of the ramifications. This made me wonder whether neurologists and neurosurgeons know more than they share, or perhaps they lack interest in post behavioral problems like depression, mood swings, changes in personality and even suicidal thoughts. Neurology doesn't just pertain to seizures, but to the underlying issues behind removing them as well, which shouldn't get limited to the psychiatrist's domain. It is necessary to categorize neurosurgery, neurology, and psychiatry, however not bridging them together reduces vital benefits.

Thank God for doctors like Oliver Sacks and Norman Doidge, who both note that events and sufferings can be so deep and extraordinary that it becomes impossible for patients to communicate everything to their doctors. Sacks got challenged by science and the media for delving into the mind of the ill, not just with vast, knowledge, but with acquaintance, creativity, and expression as well, which makes me feel as if he lived as one of us. Dr. Alexander Luria wrote Sacks a letter stating that while he was sure that a good clinical description of a patient's case plays a leading role in medicine, especially neurology and psychiatry, unfortunately, the ability to describe this gets lost, because mechanical and electrical devices cannot replace the study of personality.

The tense evening finally arrived. After work Steven and I took New Jersey Transit to Jersey City, before driving north to see his parents. He wore a posh double-breasted suit with broad shoulders, and I wore a wool cowl-neck dress in charcoal grey. We met his parents at Valentino's, a stuffy Italian restaurant nestled in the valley of northern New Jersey. I recognized his father, Steven's replica from the moment we walked in. He looked like his handsome older brother, but taller and more sophisticated looking. Unlike Steven he stood up gracefully to shake my hand and looked directly into my eyes. Once again, Steven displayed his lack of manners by failing to introduce me to either parent.

Ron was tall, thin, bright, and charming, but Sam's mannerisms replicated Steven's to the tee. She stood up to kiss her son, before sitting back down in a hunchback position and placing her elbows on the table with a gloomy facial expression. I learned quickly that whether she was happy, sad, or indifferent, the aloofness always remained. She avoided looking at me through dinner by addressing her conversations directly to Ron or Steven. Steven's smugness mirrored hers, but I failed to read red flags back then.

Ron and Sam remained exclusive in social settings, providing one another 110 percent attention and focus, as if nobody else was in the room. I envied their mutual affection, but the narcissistic brain lacks the capability to love and maintain other healthy long-term relationships. The over self-attentiveness made others uncomfortable as well. They acted as if nobody else was in the room, functioning as a unit, rather than as individuals first and foremost. If Ron said the sky was purple and I said the sky was blue, Sam would insist that the sky was purple. I was always wrong no matter how hard I tried, and when The New Christine began challenging them and standing up for herself years later, their mutual smugness shone through.

Although The Old Christine was able to determine everyone's underlying narcissism, she enabled it due from her own insecurities. Before 1999 she babied Steven and allowed him to behave like a long-lost child in front of his parents and our children. Narcissists are whining, immature brats, exaggerators, instigators, and paupers. Our parents watched me commend these behaviors though pats on the belly and pecks on the eyes. He was mildly arrogant like his parents, but giggly, lazy, and monetarily and emotionally needy as well. Both sets of parents worked and earned their own way. Even now at the ripe age of seventy-nine, Mom still insists on driving herself to work to tailor clothes. She says that she works to keep her brain active and spirit young.

Although Ron and Sam retired by fifty years old, they did so by selling their multi-million-dollar business that they built themselves. They paid Steven's way through college and spoiled him with multiple cars and vacations, all before helping us build our home from the ground up..... at the cost of half a million dollars back in 1995. Everyone behaved spoiled for quite some time, but unlike the other brains, mine knew when to halt the spending. Mine knew when Steven's disease worsened. Narcissists and addicts are known to steal credit cards and social security numbers. They are known to overspend and become bankrupt.

Why are victims blamed for addiction? I asked myself. What about the addict's earliest childhood years with parental enabling and denial? What about their failures in insisting that their child learns to stand on his/her own two feet?

We began to plan our engagement, before his cold feet kicked him in the ass. His parents disapproved of me for multiple reasons. I was his first girlfriend and not of Jewish descent or similar culture. On a drive back from their yacht, harbored at a marina in Orient Point on the southeastern fork of Long Island, I started sensing atypical behavior in Steven, detachment. "It's funny that Orient Point holds a ferry for cars, trucks and passengers," I expressed, "crossing over The Sound to New London Connecticut, right where my Nana lived!" I laughed.

But Steven was far gone and unresponsive. We failed to speak on the rest of the ride home. Rather than going back to New Jersey together, I asked him to drop me off at my parent's house. I never turned back.

My old writing states this: We broke up in 1990 toward the end of the summer. He felt out of reach to me that afternoon, and I had a hunch that I had fallen from grace somehow. So, I made it easy for him, by saying, "Go explore options and find the woman that will make your parents proud."

Even the epileptic Christine sensed nothing truly worth fighting for. Perhaps she felt a little disgusted by the clinginess at the onset of our relationship, as well as Steven's insecurities and dire need to stand out in social settings. He acted like a middle school child, rather than a grown adult during table conversations. Unlike decades later when the addiction heightened and the blame got directed at me, I still wasn't convinced that I had done anything wrong, nor that I was trying to recapture a role. I wasn't in emotional limbo like years later or fighting to understand what I did wrong. I was not paranoid, or guilt ridden just yet. My world was not collapsing in front of me. These deceptive emotions launched much later when Steven's narcissism and gaslighting exacerbated. Finally, my gut knew that Steven would return. If it's meant to be then it will be, I wrote in my first draft long ago.

The breakup felt calming, but back then I failed to fully understand why. I spent a lot of time with Joey as well, my story read, although I have no recollection of this time-period. Apparently, he kept asking me, "Have you called him yet?" I later learned.

Unlike The New Christine, my old brain was adamant about following the no-contact rule. Sure, enough nine months later, in March 1991, Mom and I heard the phone ring. No caller ID back then either. The narcissist on the other end said hi, while fishing for bait and asking for forgiveness. I took the role of Chrissy again, I later learned, the enabler and codependent, and we thrived together for years to come.

Before considering marriage, we had to agree on how to raise our children. For me, as a Catholic and future mother the decision was another "no brainer," and besides, Judaism states the child is what the mother is. But Steven and his family failed to yield, which was a major reason behind our break-up to begin with. After careful consideration, I agreed to raise our children Jewish upon one condition: Steven and his family help to teach and celebrate the culture of Judaism with our children someday.

Ron and Sam threw us a lavish engagement party, a wedding before the wedding. They were the most financially giving parents and in-laws on the planet, I told myself. The photos display my shoulder-length, chestnut-brown perm, and tiny body frame covered in a gold linen suit. It's sad and ironic that The New Christine can only recall one snippet of the entire event. Sam's friend looked at my enormous rock. "Congratulations Christine, it's beautiful," she kindly expressed.

"Thank you," I replied looking down, "I'm not worthy I know." I replied.

Nine months later we got married on December 7, 1991. A Hollywood wedding, at The Sands Country Club on Long Island. Hundreds of red roses surrounding the tables. A priest, rabbi, and breaking of the glass. Stefani, a work peer who had married the year before, offered to lend me her wedding dress. I could never in a million years have imagined wearing such an extravagant, elegant dress. A size zero that fit me to the tee. The wedding was even more elaborate than our engagement party, but unfortunately, I can only remember two small recollections of the massive celebration. I helped hand out our party favors at two am on Sunday morning, which comprised of bagels, cream cheese, and lox for every guest, together with The Sunday New York Times. I can't recall the ceremony, guests, dances, food, vows, speeches, as my memories vanished almost as soon as they got created. Yet many, many years later, one more event revealed itself from my old brain, inconsequential and playful perhaps, but it fastened to my brain like super-glue.

"Do you know what else today is, Chrissy?" Ron asked me on the dance floor.

"No," I replied, "what?"

"It's December 7th," he joked. "The day the Japanese bombed Pearl Harbor.

"Huh?" I replied.

"Yeah, the beginning of the end!" he chuckled.

We lived extremely comfortably for young newlyweds in a luxurious three-bedroom condominium just over the George Washington Bridge on the New Jersey side. Steven was a successful CPA steadily moving up the socioeconomic ladder, people believed, as I began losing one accounting job after another, due from seizures and memory deprivation. I had seizures in my office, as well as Grand Central Station, Penn Station, and while walking to work along Broadway.

Steven was a hard-core racquetball player as well, competing in matches two, three times a week in Saddle River, The New Christine began recalling, and limping in between 9:30 and 10pm in pain. He excelled at the sport and won ninety percent of his matches, as I tendered his pain and massaged his ego. But his moans and groans swelled over time, and each evening by 9:30, I found my body resting sideways in bed, with the baby kicking inside me. We waited patiently for Steven to stroll in with a Greek chicken gyro and a bag of Lay's Potato Chips. He made his presence known by stomping up the stairs and moaning and groaning. I coddled it his pains with TLC and downed the gyros and chips as he bragged about his pain rights, before darting directly toward the bathroom medicine cabinet.

I noticed he had developed a habit of exploring other people's medicine cabinets, Mom's. Marc's, Michele's, Glenn's. "Why are you going through people's private bathroom cabinets and drawers?" The Old Christine yelled. "Get out of John's medicine cabinet!" I screamed as both The Old Christine and The New One, and my rages began getting noticed.

"You're a paranoid lunatic!" he shouted back.

Addicts are professional gas-lighters as well. The term gaslighting originated from the 1944 American thriller, *Gaslight,* about a woman who was mentally tormented and manipulated by her husband to the point she believed she was going insane. Their tactics revolve around lying, constantly changing stories, manipulation, as well as denying what was just said the minute before, so much so that they began losing track of their own lies. These wretched geniuses tricked me regularly by attempting to alter my broken memories and perceptions, deepening my paranoia and madness. My biggest liabilities were Steven's biggest assets, as he had learned very young how to spin and omit information to suit his present needs. "Can I have fifteen-grand for business this week?" he asked his parents regularly, before money got wired.

We were two adults with adolescent minds living in a plastic bubble of wealth and fueled by toxic love. Steven is an honest man, I continued to lie to myself, holding grandiose dreams, hopes and promises. I watched him earn heaps of money, but every high seemed to be followed by a low, and upon each low, his parents bankrolled him to make up the difference.

As years pass narcissists continue to borrow, steal, lie and manipulate, and in plain English, its financial infidelity. Yet the victims want to believe their successes. We don't fully comprehend that addicts, narcissists and gas lighters relish control and false entitlement. We don't want to believe that they break the laws and make up their own, and usually wind up broke, alone, or even jailed. Their ideas of planning for the future gets tossed out the window.

He followed his parents' path of spending, but rather than spectacular mansions, fifty-foot yachts, private country clubs, and two-bedroom R.V.s, I found Harley Davidson motorcycles, BMWs, and pills in the garage. I spent money on landscaping our property, since the lands fail to speak and accuse me of insanity. Narcissists are shysters, filled with shenanigans, embellishments, and desires to impress others. During a therapy session in 2012, another random memory elicited and struck the wrong chord. We were dining at an upscale steakhouse right along the Hudson River in Fort Lee, I expressed to the therapist, while in the-midst of building a new home. That night Mom and I listened intently to another one of Steven's concoctions, this one about raking in tens of thousands of dollars on another new venture. "I am working on a colossal deal," he exclaimed proudly, as Mom and I nodded our heads up and down in praise. "Stop worrying so much about the bills, Chrissy, got them all in the bag now."

While the epileptic Christine didn't essentially believe him, she gained some comfort in the decorated stories. I perceived the belittling and patronizing as care, familiarity, and comfort. Steven held a timid personality back then, passive aggressive, but controlling as well, and I failed to decipher the differences. "I think I'll go to law school Chrissy," he said, while enjoying his Kettle One and Club.

"Alcohol was never my drug of choice," I heard him saying years later over the phone.

"The ability of abstract thinking and deduction would have helped me along the way," I said in therapy. "Mom and I were two altruistic souls that listened to his gift of gab and continuous projections of an ideal life. That evening we were two credulous devotees watching him order New York strip steaks for the table, and garlic creamed spinach."

"Lots of dough is coming in." he continued, as he avoided looking either of us directly in the eyes.

"Mom and I gripped on to propaganda like a never-ending loop," I said in therapy a decade later. "Steven and I each found the ideal partners to fill in our years of early emotional abandonment as well."

During therapy I began recalling my volatility as well, not only stemming from narcissistic behavior, but from my epileptic outbursts as well. One evening I raged at him for taking too long in the bathroom before dinner. Nearly forty-five minutes later, he walked past the dinner table and plopped himself on the couch to watch Seinfeld. By this point, the kids finished dinner, and were outside the swing set, as I began washing the dishes. "You never sit at the table for dinner, because you spend too much time on the damned toilet!" I raged. "I've never seen a person spend so much time in the bathroom!"

But that evening my volatility directed at Steven had to do with my epileptic flare-ups on a bad day as well, specifically, my brain losing oxygen before a seizure erupted. These outbursts occurring before a blackout all derive from odd temporal and frontal lobe activity. They are not goal directed, nor channeled at anyone in particular. In fact, it is best to ignore them until they seize, and Mom and Steven did very well with this. They never channeled the epileptic rages back at me. Yet Dad often retaliated, and his anger exacerbated my head and tension.

I continued therapy, and as the years passed, I began discretely undergoing Free Association. Besides dreams and memories and standard therapy, this psychoanalytic treatment founded by Freud helped me to unmask my memories as well. Free Association takes place when we began speaking with the therapist and telling our stories without conflict, interruption, outside ideas or suggestions. The brain silently works through aged heaps of happiness and anguish by expressing anything that comes to mind in the present moment, rather than relying on outside advice and censorship, or parroting the therapist's suggestions.

This buried conflict began arbitrarily unmasking itself without effort or exertion. Free association also helped me to differentiate between my dream's reported content and latent content, to locate the connections between them much later on. Our brain is like a vehicle, not just requiring fuel to run, but upkeep as well, to reduce its daily wear and tear, and the distortions created in our brains. Maintenance, time, and repetition are all essential in tracing past unconscious conflicts, to discard them later. Imagine a failed brain over-saturated with information and distortion, and failing to let go? Again, it results from overthinking, poor decision-making, and lack of self-control.

In therapy I learned that the brain must understand the fine balance between being active versus being reflective. Lehrer notes that when the injured mind overthinks in the wrong moment, it cuts off the wisdom of our emotions. As a right brainer, I relax, ponder, nap, and take a few days off before trying to write again. This reflection time is when my gut instinct and insight kick in, which takes place just before my left hemisphere promptly executes the action.

Simultaneously, we need the left hemisphere to make everyday decisions as well, and Dr. Jeffrey Schwartz explains this perfectly. "It's not what you feel while applying the technique that counts. It is what you do. The struggle is not to make the feeling go away; the struggle is not to give in to the feeling."

Throughout therapy in the new millennium, Schwartz was freeing me from pity and wrongful pardons by reminding my brain to regulate its emotions by allowing the horse to rein over the charioteer. This helped improve my judgment and ability to read silent cues, which in turn, helped my brain to regulate its emotions.

Another evening while we were still living as newlyweds, I picked up the phone at around nine p.m. "I just ripped my left Achilles tendon on the court," Steven expressed, "and I'm on my way home."

"You didn't call 911?" I asked, "how are you driving?"

"It's the left side, so I'm fine to drive. Meet me in the driveway in twenty minutes."

I threw on maternity wear from Pea in the Pod and dashed outside at the sound of his triple honk. Even with a broken Achilles tendon he failed to give up the driver's seat. He raced northwest to Englewood Hospital, screeching in pain, while our baby was kicking me in the abdomen. "I'm the single best driver on the road," he proclaimed, "and the safest."

But he exploded with road-rage as well. He rubbernecked, tailgated, cut off other drivers, and stopped short. "These fucking idiots can't drive the fucking speed limit!" he ranted. "Slow driving is not safe!"

The cursing made me cringe, so I rubbed the back of his neck with my fingers like usual, trying to calm his nerves. I had various car accidents over the years, pre-and post-surgery, while Steven had never hit another car, so I had no right to judge. Even with a ripped Achilles he still managed turning his head sideways on Route 9 W in Englewood Cliffs to fixate on the Porsche dealership. A spitting image of his parents, I knew, who would not think twice about breaking a car lease and dishing out thousands in fees to satisfy their impulses. His head swerved in temptation just as the baby kicked my abdomen again. I changed the subject. "If it's a boy, he will be Jason." I blurted out.

"No way," he replied laughing.

"And if it's a girl, she will be Stephanie with a ph rather than an f, and with an ie rather than an i."

"Chrissy, ph is Catholic, and f is Jewish," He expressed puzzled.

"Nope." I replied, "I'm naming her after Stevie Nicks, and by the way her real name is Stephanie!"

This proved my love for Stevie Nicks even during my epileptic inertia, just in a more conventional way. Her gypsy flair, willowy chiffons, and never-ending determination to preserve her identity did not hit the plane until five years later. Steven's insistence on driving turned out to be a blessing in disguise, because as he pulled into the hospital, I had another seizure. I fell unconscious. It could have cost three lives.

Over time Steven ripped his right Achilles Tendon on the court as well, before suffering four or five herniated disks. I remain uncertain about when the fictitious pain replaced the actual pain, and when dependence on OxyContin and Percocet morphed into addiction. I knew various doctors continued to prescribe pain killers, and that pharmacies failed to monitor one another's dosages back then as well. "They're a rich-man's pills," I overheard him on the phone one evening, after I had become diamond-free. Back then I never guessed that addiction does not discriminate between plentiful wealth or lack thereof, between the haves and have nots.

The OBGYN carefully monitored my high-risk status during both pregnancies, decreasing my doses of Tegretol and Dilantin. "My major concern is low baby weight and need for incubation," Dr. Friedman expressed.

I experienced multiple seizures throughout both pregnancies and thanked God they failed to harm the fetuses growing inside of me. After nine hours of painstaking labor, Jason was born at five pounds, just missing the threshold for incubation. Stephanie's delivery was rapid and painless. She popped out after within twenty minutes of labor and two pushes. A six-pound beauty born in 1995, just over a year after Jason, with blond hair and large blue eyes. Strangers on the street often mistook her for an Olson twin. "Are you Mary-Kate or Ashley?" people asked.

*T*wo months after brain surgery and struggling with fake-it-till-you-make-it tactics, Jason and Stephanie's new Mommy walked them to their first day of school. Jason entered kindergarten and Stephanie pre-school. With a shaven scalp and odd sense of disassociation, I spotted some neighbors and friends through my twisted perception, but I struggled to match names with faces. Everyone felt like a mere passerby, sharing little if no history with me.

Jason adapted to kindergarten well, but Stephanie's brain endured some underlying troubles. She failed to speak in the classroom throughout preschool and up to the second half of first grade. She chatted on the playgrounds and during play dates and yet remained silent in the classroom. I was too ill to consider that perhaps Steven and I had started her in preschool too early, at just four years old. She was always the youngest in her grade, just making the cutoff by one day. We never considered that she was undergoing profound grief as well, mourning the loss of her Mommy. Looking back all these years later, I feel as if I threw her into preschool selfishly, to provide me with more time to sleep and recover.

"She will grow out of this," her kindergarten teacher expressed the following year. "She does very well with ABCs and 1,2,3s so she will certainly advance to first grade. If the mutism continues next year, I suggest you take her to a child psychiatrist," she said.

Yet nothing changed the following year. In fact, Stephanie talked excessively at home to offset the anxiety and mutism that she exhibited in the classroom. By the middle of first grade when nothing had changed, I decided intervening and becoming the class mom. Steven and I also took Stephanie to a psychiatrist who specialized in this rare social anxiety disorder. It's called selective mutism, when children remain silent in certain areas, specifically the classroom, even when the consequences of their silence include internal shame and punishment. The specialist prescribed a small dose of Zoloft for her. In addition, I appeared in school three times a week to read to the class, cut and paste, organize holiday celebrations, and most important, socialize with all the children without treating Stephanie differently.

As a mother I struggled inside of her silence beside her, but as class mom I treated her just like everyone else. I had the notion that if I continued the pattern, the built-up anxiety would slowly wane, and her emotions may even explode like a volcano. Over the following three weeks she began to loosen up, laugh, and use hand gestures and facial expressions to communicate, before suddenly boom, she spoke before everyone in the classroom!

Her entire elementary school from first to fifth grade including students and faculty all celebrated Stephanie's extraordinary accomplishment, with tight hugs, explosive laughter, and balloons. In addition, she had selected two classroom friends to confide in during her trying times before breaking her silence, I later learned, Ross and Kelly. Years later I asked why she chose Ross and Kelly, to confide in, since they never stood out to me as being her close friends "I picked them because they never held high expectations of me, Mom, they never judged me."

Ironically, her years of suppression shifted to excessive talking and classroom interruptions, her teacher informed me. It took another three weeks for her brain to cut loose, let out the steam and finally reach normalcy. However, Steven and I failed to find the root of her social withdrawal, and each time we asked her, she failed to answer. Besides childhood anxiety, I was unaware of the deeper underlying reasons behind her selective mutism. All I knew was that my fake-it-till-make-it tactics were working, and that my right hemispheric hunch helped me put my foot in the door and temporarily relieve the problem.

It turns out that even with Capgras Syndrome and false perceptions, I must have loved my children anyhow. This implied that feelings indeed existed beneath the delusions. I began working on stimulating and restimulating my lost memories and associations as well, by relying heavily on my scrapbooking albums. Jason and Stephanie's pictures got surrounded around my tulip stickers in the spring and white roses in the summer. Die cuts of pigs, chipmunks, dogs, and turtles surrounded their school photos, beside my chrysanthemums in the fall and snowflakes in the winter. T

Their birthday parties, Christmases and graduations once holding an epitome of novel and quintessence began slowly rebooting in my brain through recollection and repetition. I committed myself to one image at a time and sustained it before moving to the next. Jason's first birthday party read: February 1995, and apparently, we celebrated alongside Barney and Friends during a wicked eight-inch snowstorm. The die cuts of snowflakes and icy hills triggered my grief as well, the underlying pain of losing that old part of me.

Over time I learned new mechanisms of survival as well, fighting for the relationships worth fighting for, including those with my mother and children. My brain went on automatic pilot, ready, willing, and able to do anything to prevent the kids from succumbing to generational patterns of family addiction that they witnessed early on. I was getting ready to battle Steven and his parents' blame game as well.

In a later therapy session, another morsel of memory elicited through Free Association. I recalled February 5, 1994. Shortly after giving birth to Jason, Sam whisked him away in a flash, and whisked him away again and again in my dreams as well. As she headed down the long corridor without asking, my five-pound muskrat disappeared, right alongside my first memory of holding him beside Steven. So, my first memory of touching my son vanished, I expressed to my therapist, while Sam's controlling behavior got stored for later recall. This proved that control and dominance are unhealthy, self-serving mannerisms that intimidate the victims and make them feel guilty and insecure. They are major characteristics of narcissism as well that later haunt the brain.

Before the new millennium, terms like codependency, enabling, narcissism and gaslighting were not universal common language flooding the media and cyberspace as they do today. Unlike addiction, the brain isn't genetically prone to these behaviors, since they develop during early childhood development, the most pertinent years of growth and maturity. They all stem from either a lack of love, warmth, parenthood, and attention or too much pampering, indulging, and spoiling, neglect, and over-entitlement.

Sigmund Freud depicted narcissism in pathological terms, but it wasn't until the early 1980s that mental health professionals in the United States started agreeing, labeling narcissism as a true medical disorder: narcissistic personality disorder, (NPD). NPD associates with codependency, enabling, and gaslighting, however codependency and enabling alone associates with over-altruism. My maternal grandmothers, Mom and I held these traits, and they impinge on close relatives, partners, and friends of the chronically ill and mentally disturbed. Codependency is a vague term that professionals label as a "normal reaction to abnormal people."

Without unmasking childhood demons through therapy, the brain will continue to walk the fine line between delusion and reality to the point of no return. It will never, and I repeat never get cured. As narcissism worsens over time, it overlaps with bipolar disorder, depression, substance abuse and pedophilia. Addicts, narcissists, drug abusers and pedophiles hold zero empathy and self- esteem. Their false, inflated egos fixate on gaining attention and admiration of any form from anyone, since they lacked them growing up.

When the child gets physically harmed, emotionally neglected, or over-saturated with attention and monetary objects, he/she remains on an endless hunt for the perfect partner, dumping every victim along the never-ending path. There will always be a better catch. Narcissism and impulse go hand in hand, specifically regarding overspending. Spending to impress others fills in their emotional voids, so much so, that the pattern can lead to bankruptcy, foreclosures, and life-time debt, not just for the narcissist, but for the entire family. When faced with legal challenges, they turn into parasites, fully conscious of their inner mendacity and desire to disregard judges and break laws. But eventually the law catches up with everyone.

Selective Mutism, Capgras Syndrome, entitlement, narcissism, enabling, codependency, gaslighting, over-altruism, Lost Father Syndrome, Illusion-of-Truth-Effect, inferiority complex...It was too much for any brain to contend with, never mind an underdeveloped one. We already know that the limbic system cannot fully mature on its own without help from the more advanced areas in the cerebellum and brainstem. It became clear my seizures targeted these immature areas as well, prohibiting my brain from moving forward past its unresolved childhood issues, threats, and upsets. All these demises not only deteriorate the prefrontal cortex, but they shrink the hippocampus and amygdala as well. So, between the seizures and external forces, many areas of my brain were waning.

Childhood is when we are most vulnerable and least capable of protecting ourselves. Dr. Schiffer notes that children with underdeveloped brains are even more vulnerable, holding fewer rights of protection. They need adults to look after their needs and fears. They perceive ridicule and bullying as mental torture. Depression stems from a sense of defeat, Schiffer notes, and anxiety from a sense of threat. An immature limbic system causes a permanent delay in childhood development, and the last thing it needs is adult upheaval.

So, my present left hemispheric upheaval combined with my past right hemispheric upheaval. "Move your legs so I can sweep the crumbs from under the table," I heard Dad screaming at my brother Joey again, in the backdrops of real time.

I was grasping on tighter to Joey's childhood innocence as well. He never deserved Dad's mishandling and anger, nor his sister's slow dismissal. "I'm trying to sweep up your old crumbs now Dad!" I shouted back at him in my dreams after it was too late to save Joey. "Your pitiful broom represents nothing more than The Wicked Witch of the West's manipulation and a false control!"

The brazen narcissism is not genetic or predetermined, rather learned over time, and spread over generations.

I was not at all surprised to learn that the pieces in the limbic system act as a consolidation process as well, calculating the emotional significance of our events to the lost period in our lives! This staggering discovery led to me to another. In the back of my mind, I wondered for years why my love for Nana reignited sooner than that with my mother and children. Why did my aged, implicit memories unmask immediately, I kept asking myself, and my explicit, later memories so much later? Why were my explicit memories ambiguous and hazy, and some spared? Why did I recall Weinstein from Brooklyn visiting my house on the weekends?

Well cyberspace finally led me to Dr. Harry Scheinin from the University of Turku in Finland, who placed his subjects under anesthesia to test their memories. When the sedation wore off, their primitive memories resumed before their present and later ones! * It turns out that this initial emergence stems from the limbic system, the oldest, most primitive parts of the brain. Dr. Scheinin was taken aback, since it used to be believed that the outer, more modern parts of the brain get restored first. However, his research suggested that the primitive state of mind needs to be restored before the higher orders become conscious! Primitive represented my weeping willows, Silver Sylvia, Nana, Mr. Sun, Stuffed Pink Piglet, Belle, The Cumulus Clouds, and not to mention Stevie and Carly. Primitive represented digging into the earth with my bare hands again, dreaming of the worms crawling between the dirty sidewalks of Niantic. Primitive just happened to represent the period between my two childhood brain injuries, the febrile convulsion and fall down the staircase.

A limbic system that fails connecting normally to the cerebral cortex triggers over or under trust. I over-trusted the narcissistic behaviors and promoted other people's welfare at the cost of my own. When narcissism exists beside altruism, it turns into pathological altruism, signifying good intentions gone awry. In addition, dogma has it that our four 'big boss' lobes teach us to play by the rules. It is our basal ganglia in the limbic system that identifies them; before training the cerebral cortex to absorb them, follow them and learn from them! *

Narcissism stems from permissive parenting, causing adult decisions to bare little or no boundaries, consequences, or emotions. This leads to attachment issues later in life. My adult decisions stemmed from pathological altruism, a selfless concern for other people's welfare, rather than for my very own. After my divorce I still went grocery shopping for my boyfriends before work and cooked for them after work. I served them dinner and dessert, and cleaned up, without physical, emotional, or monetary reciprocation.

I waited for them to change the same way I waited for Steven to. Both narcissism and pathological altruism spread like wildfire, and lead to rage, low self-esteem and a cry for attention of any form. Ironically, just like Steven, this led me to attachment issues later in life as well. *

The brain will continue protecting itself by disallowing anything beyond an arms-length relationship, which allows the vulnerability back in. Even five years post-divorce, it remains difficult for me to connect with a man for a lengthy period. To me connection represents neediness and co-dependency, when in fact it plays the biggest role in maintaining healthy relationships. My right to be intimate, happy, and cared for still gets overridden by guilt. See guilt is one of those intolerable feelings in the primitive mind, unconsciously amassing over time with inferiority and self-depreciation. Long-term relationships entail trust, asking for help, and compromising, but each time a boyfriend offered to carry a heavy water case upstairs for me, I grabbed it back. I carried it upstairs by myself. Independence is certainly admirable, however fierce independence sabotages intimacy, as well as the partner's ego.

It was exceedingly difficult for me to understand impulsive, delinquent behaviors, numb of consequence and guilt. These behaviors derive from upbringing, Dr. Lachmann notes, leaving the child feeling forgotten and unimportant later in life, as well as unaccountable to others, including family members This led to me to believe that drug addiction and its glaring components may sever the brain deeper than removing actual pieces of it.

Can long-term therapy and Free Association help the addict and narcissist unmask their long-term habits as well, I asked myself, and set them free? Wouldn't therapy allow more space for their morally intelligent brain cells to transpire and strengthen like mine? How much of this is neuroplasticity, I ask myself, and how much is outright choice? Walking out on Steven and long-term therapy helped me unmask my old lifelong habits and eventually set them free. This allowed more space for the morally intelligent brain cells to transpire and strengthen.

*O*n a brighter note, Ron and Sam treated their grandchildren very well, providing them with affection, clothes, toys, consistency, knowledge...Although they never cared for me, their generosity was over the top for my children. But they wanted to parent them as well, even if it meant disagreeing with me in front of everyone. Steven did the same. According to them I am uneducated, abusive, aggressive, demanding...... To them Steven was always right, and I took a lot of heat for it. "Steven what are you doing about the tax audit," I asked calmly for the third time.

"Shut up, stop making up stories...You are nuts!"

"Stop yelling, I don't want your parents to hear our business," I replied, before he left the room in rage.

"Leave Steven alone!" I heard his parents say again. "We are here to spend time with the kids! He worked hard today, and this is what he gets!?"

My kids. During the new millennium, my photo albums pulled me from one recollection to another, so the bonds with my children were slowly redeveloping. My die cut machines, trimmers, cardstock, stickers were all organized to scrapbook my family photos into various albums for each birthday, graduation, and holiday. The kids and I giggled at my right hemispheric creativity and immaturity, my animals, birthday hats, grumpy faces, and happy flowers adorning each page the same way as my drawings from my childhood had done.

We used to play basketball in the driveway, I saw in photos, and over time Stephanie turned into a great point guard, I began recalling, at just five feet tall. Her high IQ allowed her to set up plays and consistently shoot threes and swishes. Jason drove his sister around in his fire-engine red Jeep, circling around my glorious purple and white petunias. I snapped another shot of Stephanie, plopped on the enormous pumpkin that Michael dropped every October, and holding our puppy Lily on her lap. "The lollypop inside of your mouth looks like a cigarette!" I exclaimed.

Mom stood beside me as my prompter, continuously feeding me memories of the love and adoration I displayed to both children during their adolescence while I was undergoing dissociation and separation. My fake-it-till-you-make-it strategies became easier over time, even as my depression stemming from a sense of defeat took over, right beside my anxiety stemming from a sense of threat. No more amygdala or hippocampus to manage the brain's normal fight-or-flight responses, nor to camouflage the false fears. My two hemispheres battled for a place to call home, and coveted peace, hope, love, and stability, rather than lies and neglect.

It became apparent that I held feelings, buried feelings, perplexed feelings, dismantled feelings. Five years later I finally stumbled upon information about my rare condition, Capgras Syndrome, and I diagnosed myself, before sharing it with Dr. Levy. Capgras Syndrome is an atypical disorder that mixes the brain's senses of familiarity and unfamiliarity, together with knowing and feeling. My familiarity and feelings were directed at strangers, while I knew full well that they weren't bona fide. It turns out that these misperceptions result from clips in the occipital lobe, responsible for sight and perception, crisscrossing over to wrong side.

The massive bundle of connections in the corpus callosum got cut during surgery as well, before reconnecting to the wrong places and transmitting impulses and feelings to the wrong people! *

Although Steven's doppelganger never heard of Capgras Syndrome back then, he supported me, nonetheless. He never questioned me. Studies show that while one site of damage in the occipital lobe affects the emotional connections to people's faces, the other site affects our brain's consistency checking abilities! Face recognition alone is a complex process that includes association, consistency, and attachment. The hippocampus and amygdala maintain the memory needed to sustain them, and to preserve healthy, long-term relationships.

The attachments swapped from family and friends to virtual strangers, which is why my brain had to reboot its sense of familiarity each time I encountered family members. During this decade-long syndrome, I continued to ask myself, how can I associate with family members when I feel disassociated from my very own self? Austria scientist Dr. Eric Kandel noted that, there are indeed parts of ourselves that can become radically disassociated and cut off from the rest of us. Sacks describes such disassociation as being carried away by an illness like a swimmer gets sucked out by the tide.

It turns out that face recognition is based on knowledge and familiarity; and knowledge and familiarity are based on feelings. Everything emerges, escalates, and matures from individual parts of the brain, before conjoining collectively and harmoniously. In addition, the brain holds two distinct paths of face recognition: conscious and unconscious. The first site affects our emotional connection to people's faces while the second affects our brain's consistency-checking abilities! *

It's why I started approaching peers and counterparts, asking, "Where do I know you from?"

"Christine, we've known each other since kindergarten. I'm Kyle's mom," Helen replied. "Our kids are in high school, and you still ask the same question! Are you kidding me, Chris?"

The contrary to false localization is hyper-familiarity, where the brain approaches strangers, asking, "Who do people say you look like?"

Sacks labels this a super-recognizer, where every single face holds a replica of somebody else, a twin!

"I get Paul Ryan all the time," The man at the restaurant responded to me, smiling.

"Close but no!" I replied, clenching my bottom lip in deep thought

"In fact, you look just like Matthew Morrison from Glee."

"Better than the Speaker of the House!" the stranger replied blushing.

Over time my friends mimicked my charade, which spread into a giggly funfest. "Who does she look like? OMG it's on the tip of my tongue.... Yes.... yes.... yes! He looks like Barack Obama...the President!" my friend Barbara shouted out at a local pub.

Imagine creating a detailed, convoluted spreadsheet on Microsoft Excel that took weeks to layout, design and complete. Imagine years ago, before auto-save, forgetting to click the save button and losing the entire file. Trouble accessing your memory bank means starting from scratch, feelings included. It is this shortfall, this detachment from mind and body that leads to a life of derealization, lacking emotional coloring and depth.

I grew up around twelve first cousins, my flesh and blood, yet I failed to perceive them the same way as before, because upon every encounter I found myself asking Jason or Stephanie the same question: "Do you remember my cousin Angela? Aunt Rose's middle child?"

She puzzled me. I stared through her with my mouth wide open. "Mom, we've known them our entire lives, so stop introducing us each time we see them. It's annoying!" Stephie repeated.

Over the following ten years I still wanted to make a good first impression on my first cousins that I grew up around and danced together to "Staying Alive." We have a massive bundle of connections in our corpus callosum and when they're severed, they transmit different impulses and feelings to different people. "They're your first cousins, Mom!" Stephie repeated for years, "so who are you trying to impress?"

Angela is indeed my first cousin, I repeated to myself like a broken record, two years my junior, and the only cousin who knew where I hid my Hershey Bars with almonds when I had my period. The people sitting beside me at The Cheesecake Factory are undeniably strangers, I repeated to myself one evening, who do not hold true ties to me. I must stop chatting to strangers on the street, I told myself, because I have plagiarized perceptions.

I came across a story of a wife referring to her husband as Another Alan. While Alan suffered from traumatic brain injury, she watched a different person emerge in recovery. Her husband's new lack of inhibition provided a general entertainment value, she expressed to his neurologist Dr. Andy, who also got a rise from Al's latest shenanigans. Alan felt better exhibiting his newfound inhibition rather than remaining in withdrawal. The article written by three renowned neurologists: Scott E. Lipson, Oliver Sacks, and Orrin Devinsky. The 46-year-old man underwent a right temporal lobectomy, not a left, yet experienced changes in perception strikingly familiar to mine. Alan began acting jovially toward people who were only slightly familiar to him, such as strangers in the supermarket, laundromat, and shoe store. He stopped kissing his wife like before and even became alienated from his family. Like me, he felt content alone. His wife described him as, "The happiest man in the world on his own island."

Before the operation they spent all their time together, his wife expressed, but overnight the relationship ended. His flat affect got erased with strangers, specifically his doctor, as he began treating him like a lifelong best friend! "His neurosurgeon is like a God.... It's over the line!" his wife explained. The doctor got hugs while she did not. Alan repeated how wonderful it was to see him. He even clasped his doctor's hands for over a minute right in front of her.

Unlike Alan, my brain understood that Dr. Levy was a false mirage, an optical illusion of Steven. In addition, it is medically noted that healing from Capgras is extremely rare, if not impossible. "There is currently no cure," I read.

But my brain never fails to surprise me. It turned fully capable of altering over time, improving, and strengthening in many areas all due to employing its remarkable gift of neuroplasticity. Unfortunately, Alan's never did.

<u>2000 / 2010</u>

*T*hinking in wholes versus piecemeal is another hefty skill of the right brain, making our decisions speedier and more efficient. Today, my brain never attempts to become an expert at any one thing, rather it tries to know a little about a lot. Sure, it can create a detailed spreadsheet on Microsoft Excel like a leftie, however, grasping numbers in entirety and translating them into useful knowledge is more important to me than detail. These insights unconsciously tap into our senses without the ability to explain how.

In a fabulous article titled The Mad Genius Mystery, Kajal Perina discussed the brain's right hemispheric power and broad spectrum of intelligence, holding two distinct styles of thinking: Mechanistic Cognition vs Mentalistic Cognition, which work together to balance our perceptions and reasoning. * This is another favorite part of my book, and by now my readers can discern that my brain gears more toward the medical than the personal. Our Mechanistic Cognition gravitates toward math, science, tech, and literal concepts. It bottoms-up and begins with specifics before gravitating toward the general. It focuses on the laws of nature. Two of my good friends Liz and Debbie, use this form of cognition to operate successfully in their businesses.

But there lies Mentalistic Cognition as well: a brain like mine that gravitates towards decoding, and engaging more broadly with the minds of others, holistically, humanistically, and interpersonally. We top-down and focus on a larger scale before breaking it down into smaller, more manageable pieces. This brain flourishes through risk management, relishes on its original ideas, holding degrees of uncertainty and unfinished business. Those darn lefties that seek to complete, tidy up, and fix the loose ends, before taking the next step forward drive me crazy. "Did you make the reservation Chris…maybe we should make it for later…and if it rains…we need a backup….and let me check if it's a bring your own…."

Blah, blah, blah. I wrote this fabulous neuroscientific-personal memoir flooded around papers, books, folders, binders, articles…but each time I sought a specific subject, I knew exactly where to find the material pertaining to it. An exceptional writer grapples with writer's-block throughout daylight hours as well, because our creativity soars during owl time. Envisioning and philosophizing in wholes supports my lifetime adoration of the giraffe, the spectacular beast high above that visualizes the world in entirety and from afar. I am struck by their symbolic grace, and elongated necks, commanding respect from all the other living animals below. Their high-reaching, wide-angled vision is extraordinary as well, as it holds the ability to spot any moving creature from a mile away without distraction. A giraffe sees in color like the human, yet its wide-angled vision allows them to see behind their own bodies as well! This marvelous creature holds the highest visual acuity of any African big game animal in the world. From a global viewpoint, it represents a totem of sorts, a messenger encouraging us to heighten our goals, elongate our desires and rise to challenges with grace and dignity.

As a global thinker philosophy comes across to me as ethical, general, and abstract, more or less the way I envision life. I came across a term that tightens the gap between my two dividing hemispheres, my left conscious brain and right, unconscious mind. It's called Existentialism. It's a philosophical approach to life, emphasizing individual existence as free, and responsible for determining one's development through acts of will, despite the irrationality surrounding it. Famous philosopher, Jean-Paul Sartre, expressed existentialists feel deeply committed to truth and investigation, but may simply fail in finding all of it. In his piece, BEING AND NOTHINGNESS, he states that "I" the human, am free, I can make up my mind about my acts. What I will BE, he states, is what I make for myself. Thus, my acts are not trivial, but definitive of my Self.

"Who am I?" asked another philosopher, professor Ambrosia. The question feels near and dear to me. "*My experience always comes in individual little 'packages,*" he noted, *more or less disconnected, bits of knowledge or understanding of here and there, desires and fears, needs and hopes of diverse, often conflicting sorts. We speak of the person as divided into a body and soul,*" he says, "*and the soul as divided into reason, will, and passions. Where does the wholeness or oneness, the integrity of these many experiences and parts lie, which I call my "'self?'"* he asks.

One of Dr. Doidge's patients describes his life as like living in a fog, in a world that feels no more solid than cotton candy. Another oxymoron, since I sometimes feel no more solid than cotton candy, while other times the intangibility accompanies my unconscious humanity and benevolence. It provides rewards like dreams and hallucinations, unfolding into lessons learned. This humanistic right side allows me to philosophize and theorize, without left rationalization, reasoning, and judgment. So, weightless cotton candy is a metaphor, centering on freedom, insight, and creativity. Like I said before, socks and bras constrict me, and expensive brand names represent mere objects of vanity. Fancy zip codes are meaningless to a drifter, drifting back and forth between resolution and uncertainty. In fact, I laughed at a study that stated lefties accept and adjust to new environments just fine. They operate from a normal sense of fear, which drives their decision making, and they adhere to rules and exceptions adequately, whereas righties often try to modify them, and we cannot change because people want us to change. It would be like teaching a fish to fly.

Every healthy mind lies somewhere within a diametric cognitive spectrum, and as Perina notes, general intelligence lies somewhere in along this spectrum. General intelligence holds the ability to master both rule-based activities and abstract thinking and link them together with interpersonal skills. Yet, when one side of the spectrum, one hemisphere, gets dialed up too high as it does in the brain of a savant, it results in either mental illness or off-the-charts intelligence. It is either an overshoot in mechanistic cognition (autism) or an overshoot in mentalistic cognition (genius). *

Ironically, autism and genius can go hand in hand. On one hand, this paradox states that highly creative, imaginative types like artists, writers, and musicians are prone to develop mental illnesses like bipolar disorder or schizophrenia, whereas non-creative types like lawyers and stock traders hold more general intelligence. So, there is a very thin line between insanity and genius, creativity, and madness. Look at Vincent Van Gogh and Michael Jackson for instance.

Alexander Grothendieck, a phenomenal 20th century mathematician believes that this broad spectrum of intelligence indeed represents both unparalleled creativity and off-the-chart intelligence. The genius lives in this rarified space, he notes, but an overshoot to either pole or to both may, engender mental illness. Over time this genius-madness debate widened and believed unlikely for creative individuals to be at greater risk of carrying a mental illness than their noncreative peers. In fact, creative individuals are more mentally stable than noncreative types. But Grothendieck believes that it all depends on the degree-of-giftedness.

As it this were not confusing enough, there's yet another fact to consider: The correlation may reverse itself in the presence of exceptional creativity! Dr. Keith Simonton, professor of psychiatry at the University of California noted that exceptional creative individuals and savants are more likely to exhibit psychopathology than the non-creative ones, and he dubs this as the Mad Genius Paradox! *

I will allow my readers to decide if I fit into the category of a mad genius. But what I know, however, is that I hold many of its characteristics. You see those exhibiting the Mad Genius Paradox hold an inability to exclude every single alternative that runs through the mind when it makes a choice. When my brain rests it over-rummages through trivia and nonsense. Look at my memoir, incorporating medical with personal, and often going astray, changing subjects, and taking detours, but those the detours also illustrate my ingenuity. Perinia notes that this state of mind known as reduced latent inhibition, allows excess information to reach our awareness, which in-turn fosters association between related and unrelated concepts. Both high intelligence and cognitive control needed to be present for me manage the cascade of information running through my mind that I used to write this book. *

Harvard psychologist Shelly Carlson believes people like me initially remain protected from our illness, not through our brilliance but through our drive to be creative. Dr. Badcock writes in The Imprinted Brain that: "True geniuses in any field of endeavor (may rely on) a mind that is not merely more or less balanced between brilliant and psychotic, but actually represents an overdevelopment of both."

When there is no specific goal or deadline for me to meet, my creative, mentalistic thinking takes over by default. Imaging studies show unusual connections between persons with highly creative minds and those who are psychotic. It represents a dynamic tension between the brain's executive networks and default networks, which ironically are both a hallmark of mental health and a high IQ! As readers, it isn't difficult to notice my average left hemispheric skill when writing about my personal life, versus the extraordinary high right hemispheric intelligence when I write about neuroscience and the human brain. I wrote this book all by myself, which is the finest example of a split brain.

And if this isn't boggling enough, my very own ah-ha moments usually occur when these two opponents work in unison, usually during the middle of the night! Neuroscientist Anthony Jack notes that genius comes from engaging with both sides of the spectrum, then blending them together while maintaining stability.

The kids got older before I could even turn around. Soon they were twelve and thirteen: time for me to begin planning two large celebrations, their Bar and Bat Mitzvahs. Since Jason's Bar Mitzvah in 2007 subsided from my memory as fast as the five-hour event itself had done. I relied on my photo albums once again. If I never spent my spare time scrapbooking, then this thirteen-year milestone would have evaporated like clouds over a warm body of water. Jason selected the Las Vegas theme for his party, the dazzle behind

Sin City. The colossal red-and-black picture remained suspended above his bed for the next decade, reading, "What Happens Here Stays Here!"

That evening the Sin City décor showed black and red tablecloths, black dice, and red tokens. By this point Steven's gaslighting, drugs, lies and financial infidelity overshadowed my feelings of pride and joy in the celebration. I wanted to savor my son's accomplishments, but in no time, my right to be happy got violated again, along with my mother's right to be happy as well. After Steven left for rehabilitation a few years later, I began unmasking my memories of the event through Free Association therapy, and my rage escalated when recalling my mother's contribution. I recalled the three-way telephone conversation that took place just before Jason's big event, and a similar three-way telephone conversation the following year just before Stephanie's.

The first one took place between Steven, his mother Sam, and I. The memory of his scathing remarks, combined with her grand expectations instigated my rage once more.

That evening, I suggested we hold a B'nai Mitzvah for both children at once, a joint service and celebration to commemorate Jason and Stephanie's first steps into adulthood. A B'nai Mitzvah is a celebration for siblings born a year or less apart. In Jewish tradition, a boy's Bar Mitzvah transpires at thirteen and a girl's Bat Mitzvah can transpire at either twelve or thirteen, and the option lies with the parents. As a proud Mom and Irish Twin, I wanted their spirit and celebrations to conjoin, and Jason and Stephanie both agreed, after all they shared the same camps, temple, sports, peers, and college, I said to my therapist, all while each maintained a distinct individuality as well. They each built a solid foundation for themselves, and yet incorporated their lives around similar values, interests, and friends. "They should celebrate together!" I expressed during the three-way telephone conversation as well.

"They get one party each!" Sam insisted from Florida, before Steven chuckled.

"And who's paying for two celebrations?" I asked them, "at fifty-thousand dollars each."

"No worries, Chrissy, that part will work itself out," he said, pitying me and laughing as if money was never an issue.

"Two celebrations!" my mother-in-law Sam insisted loudly again.

We do not have the means for this, I dreamt that evening. We cannot afford to double down on dresses, suits, party favors, themes, DJs, invitations…I saw Dorothy, Toto and their three pals finally reaching The Land of Oz, after their long journey of hope and despair, only to encounter further dismay. The wizard that I married back in 1991 isn't so grand after all, I dreamt, in fact he is a fraud. I began sweating, as I got out of bed and sleep-walked again. I bumped into the stair railing and woke up. Then I must have fallen back to sleep again, I told my therapist, because I dreamed watched myself turn into the Tin Man, from The Wizard of Oz, in search of a new brain, a different brain, one that Steven and his parents would approve of and grow to love.

During the two-decade journey down my version of The Yellow Brick Road, I later learned, I crossed allegories and metaphors, scary images, and magnificent scenes, all while waiting to pin down the evasive Wizard himself, who hid behind his façade of smoke and mirrors, just to protect his weak ego.

By this point I was living with a full-blown addict. I cannot recall the exact time the addiction commenced, but I am certain that by this point, he was in a very poor state. So, like a normal victim of drug abuse and narcissism, part of my brain fed into the illusion-of-truth effect again, convincing itself that Steven and Sam had everyone's best interests in mind. However, my better brain noticed the financial infidelity worsening.

At various points, the illusion-of-truth dwindled, before returning again and again. I began rejecting his guardianship of me, and battling for my rights as an adult, mother, and wife. Steven and his parents viewed me as an entitled, ungrateful, raging bitch, when in-reality, Mom was paying for the gas in my car, and clothing for our children. Steven thanked her by calling my mother the same names that he always called me and refused to appreciate or even acknowledge what she provided to us, emotionally and financially. In fact, she supported him on every single one of his new financial ventures, which took place for years on end. We patted Steven's back, and provided his frail ego hope, positivity, and assurance, all of which were later erased from his brain. But as one job followed another, the lies followed as well, and my rage intensified. His parents blamed me for every failure; they perceived my rages as abuse and his as self-defense. What came first the chicken or the egg, I began asking myself, as I passed through the various stages of enabling.

One evening I noticed the mirrored spoon holder in the dishwasher after it had spent a decade of collecting dust in the dining room credenza. I also began waking in the wee hours of the night, as I heard the rumbles of Steven's Harley Davidson circling in from around the corner, waking up the neighbors and our kids. Our dogs, Lily and Louis waited downstairs for Daddy to get home, before sprinting up from their kitchen beds the instant that they heard the roar of the bike from blocks away. The kids later admitted that they frequently found hidden pills between the couch cushions,

Narcissists squander money and when caught they respond by saying. "Get over it! It's done!"

But it's never done, and victims threaten back with retaliation, before pitying, allowing, and feeding into the cycle all over again. Each time I ranted he wallowed in self-pity to his parents on the phone. Ron and Sam offered several times to put their poor son on the next flight to Florida, to stay for an indefinite amount of time. "Get away from her!" I overheard Ron say more than once. "She's toxic!"

Enablers fail to consider the responsibilities of co-dependents, and fail to treat them as grown adults, breadwinners, spouses and parents.

Jason's big event was looming, and I was fully responsible for temple and event preparation. The little agreement Steven and I had made about raising our children Jewish if everyone agreed to celebrate the faith and teach me along the way, got broken long ago. "Steven, I need to pay off the temple dues and DJ today," I expressed.

"Just charge it all Chrissy and I'll pay the bills at the end of the month. The money will hit the accounts by the end of the week Chrissy," I heard again, "calm down."

"The D.J wants to be paid now, Steven," I expressed again on Friday.

"Leave me alone!" he yelled back, "stop harassing me for money!"

"But you were the one who wanted two parties." I replied.

"Go talk to your mother, or figure things out for yourself. Stop relying on me for everything!"

*Y*ears later in therapy, I kicked myself again for feeding into the illusion-of truth effect for so long. My tendency to believe false information repeated so often that it got embedded in my brain as truth. In fact, the human brain is "built to default to truth," notes author Michael Dregni, "and the side effect is being easily deceived by the occasional sociopath."

"Occasional," I told myself, nodding in dismay.

In many therapy sessions I discussed my troubles as a Catholic and raising my children differently. I adapted well in the beginning,

I expressed, as Ron and Sam flew up for Rosh Hashanah and Yom Kippur and attended temple with our family. They mailed Jason and Stephanie eight small gifts on Hanukkah, the Festival of Lights. I loved to watch them unwrap the apple from Harry & David on day one, followed by the dreidel and chocolate coins on days two and three. Sam prepared five foods for the Seder plates on Passover as well, I explained, and we all celebrated the Jewish culture together. And Jason, Stephanie, and Steven celebrated Easter and Christmas beside me and my family as well, out of respect for my religion.

But over time the inconvenience and costs overshadowed their faith, and the family fell short. As I continued carpooling back and forth to Hebrew School three times a week, I started developing resentment as well. Steven put zero commitment into family traditions and upbringing, I explained in therapy, that he fought so hard for before marriage.

I can't blame them for disliking me, I expressed in another session, due the burden of my brain and my raging reactions to their son's behaviors, my inadequate mothering, and lack of earnings. Perhaps I failed to meet my in-law's monetary and non-monetary expectations. Perhaps their over-involvement in parenting worked for everyone back then and went underappreciated. Perhaps I wasn't following their advice about fulfilling their son's basic needs.

But soon enough I tallied up my mother's donations, which exceeded Steven's earnings by a longshot. Soon enough I wondered why they acted as if his repossessed cars were his fault. "If they held the right to dish out crap to me, then they why did they refuse to do it my other half?" I asked my therapist.

Victims of gas-lighters and narcissists add to the spreading of madness by continuously taking blame and looking for solutions to an incurable disease. These self-righteous types manage keep reverting their victims back to the never, ending cycle of guilt and paranoia.

"Cancel the party!" Ron shouted over the phone the week of the celebration. "Who told you to have such an expensive affair?" he shouted.

"They did," I chimed in.

I called my mother, my savior since brain surgery, as well as a marital enabler, I discovered years later. "It's a day of hell," I cried out, "I have to cancel the affair. I'm sorry Mommy."

After all the years of commitment, preparation, money, and challenges, we cried together, not necessarily for ourselves, but for Jason, his own years of commitment, effort, and study. Not having a lavish party was fine with me if paired with honesty and lower expectations. As Mom rambled on the other end of the phone line, I pondered about Jason's nerve-wracking practice sessions with his Hebrew tutor, and the stress of having to prepare to speak before hundreds of people about the Tsunami earthquake in Indonesia. I pondered about the Jewish customs I have learned beside him, and of the Jewish history that brought him to his thirteen-year-old milestone to begin with.

Steven eavesdropped on our conservation and belittled me with more lies just to get his adrenaline pumped up again. "Stop the crying again!" he lashed out to me. "She's nuts," he said to Mom, "for making up stories in her head. I have a big transaction at work, finalizing on the 25th for God's sake."

"Steven, you should have thought about this already, planned and budgeted," Mom shouted. "Why did you leave Chris with all the responsibilities? How can a parent do this to their child at the last minute? Now what?" she asked him angrily.

He snickered cynically "And your mother wanted this too Steven," I said, "yet neither of you thought about the costs?!"

"You should be ashamed of yourself!" Mom said. "Jason is my grandson, and I can't do this to him Steven. I'm disgusted with you," Mom bellowed one last time, before wiring fifty-thousand-dollars to us the following day.

He promised to repay her by the end of the following week when his big deal closed. As two enablers, Mom and I kept our fingers crossed. Two altruistic souls continuously feeding into the mind of a master manipulator on a precarious cycle of swindling. I was not only his codependent and enabler, but his alter ego as well, I unmasked later in therapy, one half of his split personality. He has been mimicking my words, tones, and gestures, I expressed, with admiration and jealousy, as if he wanted to become a part of me. Narcissists convince us we are inferior. They never ever stop acting out, because acting out their own pain serves a purpose. It helps them obtain money, sympathy and further control, and Dr. Sarno notes, a release from responsibility of arduous labor. *

Premature victims of abuse are prone to over-the-top altruism, and any mere possibility of dishonesty gets wiped away, right beside their history. Even people with normal brains who get involved with a narcissist can watch their lives play out until they have nothing left. A damaged or depleted amygdala makes it nearly impossible to perceive intentions. The brain fails at linking perception to knowledge and knowledge to execution, so it continues to recycle its mistakes. She will be fine, was Steven's biggest motto. In five minutes, she will forget this even happened. This proves again that every speck of the convoluted brain holds a unique domain, that only a guinea pig can describe.

It turned out that the rabbi agreed with Steven and Sam; he was not keen on a B'nai Mitzvah either. The former Rabbi that just retired had approved of it, but the new one did not. "These rare sibling occasions should get promoted," I argued back, "plus two celebrations in two years not financially feasible."

"If you ain't got it, then don't spend it!" I heard Dad in the background again, lecturing his normal lecture, while Steven's self-destruction spread through my brain like a cancer. One afternoon at Applebee's I watched Ron and Sam chatting face to face like usual, as I ordered my customary unsweetened iced tea with lemon. They paid for everything, and this began making me extremely uncomfortable as a grown adult, epilepsy free. Let us pick up the tab for dinner once in a while, I begged Steven. "We are adults! Aren't you embarrassed about anything?" I asked.

"I'm never paying," he chuckled, "I'm taking as much as I can get from them!"

Like usual, Sam was snooty to the server. Finally, Ron looked up and ordered the normal diet Coke for himself and black iced coffee for Sam. Her nose oozed from a sinus infection, I vividly recall, and the nasal drips reminded me of Steven's. His nose sprays scattered all around the house for various reasons. I kept quiet for the time being, admiring their loyalty toward one another, and common interests like golf and yachting. But I couldn't help loathing Steven. Unlike Ron and Sam, he often humiliated me in public and shunned me in private. Unlike his mother and father, he contradicted every word that came out of my mouth. As I watched them laughing together without a care in the world, I thought about Steven using drugs. I thought about the night before, when I scolded him quietly in the office for another lie, before his rage had spread into the den again like a wildfire. Once again, addicts play victim, and enablers get scorned. But the blame game was getting old.

As parents they have every right to know, I told myself at the lunch table again. If anyone approached me as a mother to express worry about my child's addiction and well-being, I would never take it with a grain of salt. Instead, I would thank him, hug him, and jump across the Earth to seek help for my child, whether fifteen or fifty. The last thing in the world I'd consider is to place blame on somebody else. I am not a five-star parent by any means, but I keep an open mind and welcome in opinions, rather than discount them just to avoid spending my time and energy.

This is an inversion technique, which represents a crucial, right hemispheric skill held by unconditional thinkers, those that occasionally drive the brain in reverse. It is because high-stake decisions involving hefty consequences, require not just right-brain intuition, but the power to overturn the status quo.

That day at Applebee's I finally opened my mouth. "Steven is an addict," I blurted out.

"Your marriage is none of our business!" Ron replied.

"It's not about our marriage, rather about your son and his well-being," I snapped, "your flesh and blood. He needs help, and I'm the only one willing to help him?" I asked.

By the time Stephanie's Hebrew school began winding the following year, I pined for Stuffed Pink Piglet, Bella, and Mr. Bridge again, but my unconscious comrades took a back seat from my painful reality. Steven lost another job, remained in full-fledged denial, and failed to get himself out of bed in the morning. The bedsheets soaked from the sweat of his withdrawal. When a friend told me he saw Steven riding his red Harley on Grand Avenue, I replied, "It's blue."

"No, it's red," he said. "I'm sorry I said anything," he replied kindly to my shock response.

Steven concealed a third Harley on our landscaper's property, I soon learned, which he had hidden from me. By this point I was working with an overtaxed and overspent brain, having to prepare for another celebration without the full components to heal or prioritize. I needed a healthy prefrontal cortex to plan, budget, organize, and execute the best decisions possible. Even simple decisions such as how much to pack for a trip or what to prepare for dinner requires the prefrontal cortex to digest the input and reflect on all the options and alternatives available to save time and money. My brain had many variables to choose from, between party favors, invitations, themes, food, centerpieces.... Too much white noise and too many time constraints for a brain to live in the immediate moment like mine.

The differences in decision making between our right and left hemispheres fascinate me. Stephanie's brain works like mine since the apple does not fall far from the tree. Like me she felt as if mundane choices like a party theme were not crucial in the grand scheme of the celebration. "Let's just book the party," she said indifferently, lacking worry and strategic planning. "I trust your choices Mom," she expressed, "and I'll give you my list of friends when I get a chance. I'm going to the mall now, bye."

These drivel choices get left for the left hemisphere. It is the right that contains the most intelligent parts of the mind, used to make acute, rational choices through its intuition, gut instinct, and last-minute execution. As the stakes rise the brain relies on these deeper, more complex, higher processing powers in the emotional right mind. It indulges the brain in unconscious chaos before making the swift, accurate decision, and before ordering the left to execute it instantly.

In the meantime, my left hemisphere took a backseat. No choice but to let the theme of the party play out in my right mind first-and-foremost. An autumn theme, my unconsciousness, already knew, one based around the festival of Sukkot. This decision required no conscious thinking, processing, or selecting among options, because my automatic pilot established too rapidly. It selected autumn crops, agriculture, and harvest, all in celebration of Sukkot, my favorite Jewish holiday, also representing the beginning of the end of the Jewish season.

It's risk that triggers insight and intuition, sanctioning the decision spot on. Unlike my left hemisphere over-rummaging and worrying, my right follows natural hunches, notions, and ideas, unable to be explained through conscious reasoning. Introverts are not fond of verbal exchange, time constraints, opinions, or schedules. We rely more on mime, gesture, freedom, and randomness. A schedule makes me cringe and following one feels nearly impossible. A right mind lives by chance and listens to its inner voice, rather than opinions of outsiders.

Don't get me wrong the dominant left holds our majority of explicit memory, knowledge, and information to form associations and make daily decisions. What most don't know however, is that the higher power used in split-decision-making, which is vital for a surgeon, pilot, or professional athlete, lies in the right hemisphere. Deciding where or when to open a skull, land a plane, or throw a fastball makes or breaks a game or saves a life. The decision-making process of the quarterback is so crucial that it's listed in a special category called Intangibles, notes Jonathon Lehrer. This side of the brain holds goodwill, and even in the accounting world goodwill represents a priceless, intangible asset, lacking space and weight.

Rather than Stephanie selecting her love of basketball as a theme, we selected a broader theme, autumn, and Sukkot, both lacking lines and discipline. I called Joe at the local nursery five days before her party to place my order of centerpieces and growth. Joe owned a massive garden center a few towns over, filled diverse living flora in every shape, size, texture, and color. Each year Joe and Michael supplied me with bright red and white azaleas in late spring, mountains of pink and white impatiens in the summer, burnt orange and violet mums in the fall, and arrays of glorious tulips in the spring. I had spent thirty, forty thousand dollars on landscaping over the years for sure. "That's where the money went!" Steven often reprimanded, and he was right. I spoiled my lands.

"Joe, I'm not spending over five hundred dollars for all of my centerpieces," I expressed. "This isn't a wedding."

"OK shoot," he replied.

"I'd like a hefty burnt orange chrysanthemum on each table, surrounded by two smaller burgundies."

"Ok keep going."

"One medium sized pumpkin per table, figure around twelve adult tables in all."

"Got it."

"Some small yellow squashes and orange gourds surrounding them, oh and a small stack of hay as well. And some brown and yellow corns."

"You got it, Chris. I'll drop all off on Saturday morning. Let's say three-hundred-fifty."

"Thanks again Joe, love you."

A brisk Friday afternoon before the weekend celebration, and Lily and Louis heard the leaf- blower retire and dashed outside with their dwarfed, doxy legs. They headed directly toward the swing. We all sat beneath the canopy and faced the western sunset, I rocked them forward and back, with the cool breeze and fresh cedar mulch wafting through the air. I closed my eyes and heard zone-two of the sprinkler system slapping against the Japanese maple. Twelve zones of water dusted various points of my gardens seven hours a day. The three of us treasured our primitive mindsets, holding over magnified senses of sight, sound, smell, and movement. Like the animal, my temporal lobe is gifted to differentiate between the sounds of each zone, drumming up against every stone, trunk, shutter, and pole.

I fell asleep. My prefrontal cortex shut down as my limbic system turned on. I began dreaming of my childhood earthworms again, this time crawling beneath the Japanese Maple rather than the dirty sidewalks of Broadway. I picked one up again just like I had done long ago and felt it crawling between my fingers. In the immediate moment, The Little Man expressed to me that, "Earthworms hold distinct brains separated from other parts of their body, so when they get sliced for scientific purposes they can still move around the environment."

I saw the weeds that my earthworms fed on long ago and I saw the poisonous mushrooms and fungus they avoided. It took over a decade for me to understand why I found them crawling between my fingers again, and between the cracks of the dirty sidewalks of Broadway. The tune, stuffed with sentiment, struck a chord twenty-four years later, a semiconscious chord I failed to understand. I cried, laughed, and grieved badly. It turns out that Uncle Dominick visited me in Niantic for my ninth birthday in 1975, gifting me with my very first 45-record again, "Rhinestone Cowboy." The song strikes a familiar place for unfamiliar medical reasons, as if the cracks in the sidewalk feel like the cracks in my brain.

Fat Louis began snoring beside me before I dozed off again on the swing with my ancient football helmet, the one with the blue horseshoe logo on each side. "I must wear the helmet again," I shouted in my dream, "to protect myself, since something quite peculiar is going on!"

When we dream, the brain begins to encode memory of the present day, before searching for other weaker associated memories from the past. Next, the brain combines them into a dream narrative, note authors Zadra and Stickgold, before exploring association that it would never consciously consider. In addition, my sixth sense in my heightened temporal lobe provides me with deeper awareness than normal and tracks my dreams and hallucinations more subjectively. It perceives impending danger and pleasure before they appear real time. Ironically, the lack of the amygdala and hippocampus, used to perceive danger, get made up for in my dreams. *

My exceptional precognition conceives of future high-risk situations lying just around the corner. Clairvoyance is observing events before they become normally perceivable; telepathy is communicating thoughts from areas beyond the brain's normal senses; and precognition is the ability to foresee the future before real time. My brain holds all three abilities.

It turns out that less than thirty-five percent of Americans are right brainers, who detest hierarchy. We live with high emotional and creative intelligence, but often fail at displaying it. We eat up the lands, soils, and animals, rather than Chanel bags or Givenchy shoes. See brain healing is not accomplished by the brain alone, but by the mind, body, and bare hands as well. It doesn't get accomplished solely through speech therapy, but with communicating through mime and gesture as well. Talking hurts my mouth, mood, and brain, and unbelievably, only seven percent of communication is through verbal tongue. In addition, a universal right mind lacking a true autobiographical self feels devoid of time and borders, which lands, and seas fail to hold.

On Saturday morning my outside landscape looked like something out of Better Homes and Gardens. Michael and his team appeared one more time for a final leaf blow. The deep orange chrysanthemums, purple asters and burgundy sedums bloomed gloriously beside my tall, fuzzy grasses and six-foot cannas.

That evening when Stephanie began her candle lighting, Steven was nowhere to be found. When we reached candle number twelve for Michael, Michael was nowhere to be found. I gazed through my magnificent centerpieces, adorning each table with autumn life. I gazed through my browns, burnt oranges and burgundies, that before the celebration, had felt cool and crisp. The air tasting like warm apple cider with a touch of cinnamon suddenly dissolved. While everyone paused for the men to appear for the candle lighting, my unconscious mind fled again in fear. It fled back to Amy Levy in high school, teaching me about the "four species," mentioned in the Torah about Sukkot, all representing the blessings of nature. They include the fruit of a citron tree, the green, closed frond of a date tree, the leaves of the myrtle tree and branches of the willow tree, all symbolizing grief and decay, hope and revival and do not forget, the beginning of the end.

One lobe cannot alter or get removed from the brain without it affecting all four. It's nearly impossible. The crisp air that morning before the bittersweet celebration cleared some of the negative pathways in my brain, my fear of Steven again. The pumpkins, autumn leaves and rusty foliage mounting along my landscapes exhilarated my occipital lobes, the sound of the sprinkler dusting up against the tall, brown grasses calmed my temporal lobes, and the droplets of morning dew along my burnt-orange chrysanthemums stimulated the sensory cues in my parietal lobe. I was an avid gardener in my right mind, right beside my dearest friend Michael. He shared his endless horticultural expertise with me. He was like a member of the family, which is why we all selected him to be an honoree to light a candle at Jason and Stephanie's celebrations. Once again though, I relied on my poor sensory cues to make this decision. While Stephanie was lighting her Bat Mitzvah candles, Steven and Michael were busy in the men's room, I discovered years later, most likely snorting powders up their bleeding noses. Michael turned out to be Steven's hidden drug trafficker the entire time.

By Sunday afternoon the celebration seemed to have passed in a whim. My four lobes suddenly symbolized the four species of Sukkot: grief, decay, hope and revival. We rocked on the swing again and faced the western sunset. Lily, Louis, and I knew our bullfrog was over drinking, and gulping down his mighty, fine wine behind our backs again. "Steven is not coming up with the money this time either," I heard Lily say, "to pay Mom back for the second party."

"He never keeps his promises," Louis said in my dream, as we all rocked, and soaked up the lands and creatures of the Earth together.

2010 / 2015

Wouldn't you know it, Little Chip got created from another one of my drawings in the 1970s, before reviving after the epilepsy passed on three decades later. Once again, my unconscious mind replaced my unconscious seizures. When Little Chip saw me again after so many years his body crashed into my terracotta pot. I watched him empty his cheeks, the sockets for storing the berries and acorns that I collected for him as a child. I had made the stockpile while he rested beneath the weeping willow tree beside Stuffed Pink Piglet.

Our two sets of glossy eyes locked again. This wonderful critter managed following me from northeastern Connecticut to northeastern New Jersey, I told myself, skipping Long Island along the way, after all, Long Island was our period of latency. An aged playmate from an aged mind, I felt, holding the exact features as long ago. Remember, perception stands still in the unconscious mind.

Over the years Steven and I often joked about the chipmunk's life span, because every season the same little creature with a black dot on one ear sprinted into our garage, on a quest for remnants. One day we watched him hold a tulip bulb with his two delicate paws, before scoffing it up with his overgrown teeth. Our hot dogs Lily and Louis came out of the woodwork suddenly, and chased poor

Little Chip with their short, doxy legs. Dachshunds are hounds with elongated bodies, bred as hunters to tunnel underground and flush out badgers and rabbits. Rather than climbing trees like Little Chip, Lily and Louis preferred digging underground and burrowing. So, of-course speedy Little Chip managed escaping their chase.

Another day the rodent spilled an entire bag of grass seed on the cement floor, and rather than chasing him out of the garage or sweeping up the seed, Steven and I left it for him to savor. "Awe, the chipmunk is back today feasting again Chrissy," Steven said, while he was polishing another motorcycle.

"I left Connecticut quite some time ago," he whispered to me one morning. I bent down on my knees and pecked his nose again. "To keep tabs on you," he said, concerned. "This time I'm protecting you from your husband rather than your father. I am stashing grass seed and bulbs for another winter hibernation as well, and I won't be going anywhere for quite some time. Not until I know you will be permanently out of harm's way."

My consciousness and unconsciousness were discreetly superimposing on one another again, pulling me in two directions in time. Together they stealthily aided in my unmasking process and linked my dreams to waking memory. This linking is an exceedingly challenging task, Zadra and Stickgold said, because most dreams and hallucinations leave conscious awareness by the time the brain awakes, but not mine. For over twenty years, I regularly updated my dream content in this book, and my dreams were slowly strengthening the weaker connections in my explicit memory and waking life as well. Over time my recurring dreams and transferences not only led to problem solving, but to unexplored research and unknown scientific data, which is the reason I chose creative non-fiction as the genre for this book. *

Little Chip was my defense mechanism for so long, prohibiting The Old Christine from being disposed of so quickly. He knew I had to undergo every single stage of grief to heal, from torturous weeping spells to happy euphoria and from anxiety to jubilation. "Your pain is my pain," he often told me.

Days, months or years later I heard him kick an empty plastic bottle in the garage. It rolled and rolled and made noises. He quickly glanced at me to see if I saw what it was. "Another Percocet bottle?" I asked, as he kicked it into his stockpile.

"I will manage this," Little Chip said. "Your brain must rest in order to recover and worry only about itself."

In another dream, my dachshunds stumbled upon Little Chip again. "What's wrong?" Louis asked him concerned, "you look frazzled today."

"It's the motorcycle again," he whispered. "I hate it when he spends money he doesn't have, on various models and colors. It puts Christine in a frenzy."

"And the lies, money, and wasted time and energy riding," Little Chip said. "Besides, Chris's brain sustained enough head injuries for a dangerous motorcycle to remain in her presence every day."

"It turns colors all the time!" Lilly said.

"Where will we all live if Steven doesn't learn from his mistakes?!" I shouted in my dream.

More time passed, and Little Chip continued to stumble over empty bottles and lies. Unlike me, he handled Steven's addiction with composure. "How do you weather the storms so calmly?" I asked. "Is it because you can tunnel deep into the ground during the cold, winter months and take a break from it all?"

"No, I never take a break from it all, because your sadness and happiness are mine as well," Little Chip replied. "Plus, I have all the parts of my brain available to help me deal with chiselers. And even so, you are the strongest person I've ever met, and I know you will pull through this on your own. Still, I must stay warm and safe under the ground for next season, for all of us to play chase again."

"But I fear for your life during the blizzards," I replied, "so, can you come inside this winter and cuddle with me in the guest room under the warm blanket? I'm afraid of him Little Chip."

"Like I said I must hibernate in the winter months. It is how chipmunks live, not throughout the entire season though."

"Why?" I asked.

"Because we retreat to our burrows and wake up every few days to raise our body temperature back to normal."

"So, you retreat down into the basement with your candles and berries?" I asked Steven in another dream. "You retreat with your berries until your bottles are empty and your withdrawal kicks in again like always? Then you get chills and sweat, and begin rage at me again?"

"Spring is just around the corner," Little Chip expressed, "and it is ok to be angry at him Christine, because anger means opening the floodgates and embracing your emotions, rather than neglecting them."

When you're gone how can my brain carry on? I heard ABBA on the outskirts of my limbic system. You make me feel alive, but someone will die, I fear, I knew.

"Reality and acceptance will overpower your life someday. Keep pushing your brain to its maximum potential Christine. It will rise to the top, I promise."

Little Chip's residue was far from psychotic. It was very real. In fact, he represented a psychological phenomenon to science, holding activity from an earlier time. The operation twenty-eight years later happened to relaunch the period of my 1971 cardiac arrest. In 1999 my brain finally reacted its original insult! Such odd miracles emanate from the basal ganglia and amygdala, Sacks notes, before slowly creeping up and out to the newer, conscious parts of the cerebral cortex. My selective lyrics from selective artists follow the same trail: Carly, Fleetwood Mac, ABBA. In fact, Sacks labels this as *raw music*, and neuroscientist Dr. Konorski notes that this rare form of music begins coding after the third or fourth strike to the brain as well. *

They all carry intense emotion, initially lacking meaning, and association. For a decade, my unconscious mind failed to associate my selective music to my grievances. My brain felt like it was on top of the world, looking down on The Carpenters creation again in 1972. These distinct choices touched upon unknown catastrophes or joys, and weeping spells or elation, whether I was driving, cooking, or working out. I was experiencing the death of someone or something I knew very well. I begged Steven to get me the cassette-tape single in 1999, and I began rewinding it hundreds of times over the next ten years like a druggie. The same with "S.O.S." by ABBA, as I felt so far while standing so near, as Gordon kept me alive, but something died, I feared.

A Sacks patient named Mr. L. once asked him, "Aren't children's minds too poorly formed to record such early events?"

It turned out that Mr. L.'s brain scans revealed a disturbed prefrontal cortex from childhood trauma as well, presently affecting his emotions and poor ability to maintain healthy adult relationships. He continued dreaming and envisioning his mother dying all over again at age two, which is a critical learning time for emotional attachment, when the parent or caregiver provide the infant with love, connection, trust, and security. These attachments need to be continuously reinforced through nonverbal gestures like hugs, kisses, humming and positive facial expressions. Infants need to experience and re-experience these interactions repeatedly to regulate their emotions and socially connect to their environment. It is a major reason behind Dr. L., Steven and I losing the ability to attach to others, to trust, love, and hold on to them.

In another recurring dream Mr. L. sensed that he was losing an object that was a big part of him, while unsure if the object even ever existed. He suffered depression and despair, and was desperately in search of something. With his limbic system continuously activated, he kept re-experiencing his loss in the now, as his past and present felt the same. Over time he realized that the missing object was related to his desperate search for his mother. He finally sought therapy and expressed that in another dream he was a man holding the missing object, the big wooden box carrying a heavyweight inside. More time lapsed until he finally found a connection to the box. It was his childhood toy box, he expressed, as well as his mother's coffin. During all these years I was carrying around the weight of my mother's death, he cried out. Suddenly he heard a stranger saying, "Look at what you paid for this box."

The stranger disrobed himself. Mr. L. noticed his leg scarred and scabbed, holding protuberance and feelings of death. "I didn't know the price would be this high," he expressed to Sacks.

Sacks finally realized that the words linked to his growing realization of his mother's death, which had slipped into silence for way too long. Mr. L. cried out, "Can't you see after this terrible loss, I have to be depressed right now!"

He started having weeping spells like a baby, covering his face, and putting his hands in his mouth like a two-year-old, all before breaking out into loud, primitive sobs. "I want to be consoled for my pains and losses, yet don't come too close to console me. I want to be alone in sullen misery. Which you can't understand. Which you can't understand. It is a grief that is too big."

He visited his old house again later, this time searching for adult possessions. In this dream his motherly ex-wife answered the door and welcomed him in. Her gentle mothering and warm welcome slowly helped him emerge from isolation. As she began consoling him in the very house that he grew up in, Mr. L. began finally entered the positive stages of healing. Like me, he began reproducing his implicit memories through transference to befit his present stage of grief. This complex process of unmasking implies the existence of a higher mental activity mapped somewhere in the unconscious right hemisphere. Only after grieving and acknowledging his pain did he gain the strength to visit his mother's grave for the very first time. He was no longer withdrawing from the harsh realities of life, rather, placing them in his conscious memories to rest. He reached the last stage of grief: acceptance. Freud notes our memories are very plastic and do not remain unchanged forever.

In addition, there is a clear history of childhood trauma repeating itself through dreams in brains with distinct personality characteristics, such as being trustworthy, altruistic, creative, sentimental, as well as what the late Ernest Hartmann once noted, "thin psychological boundaries."

"*Y*our crocuses and daffodils will bloom brightly in spring," Little Chip assured me, "and I'll be feasting on the acorns beside you and the dogs again. Love you Chris, and you will be just fine," he whispered, before blowing me a kiss and recessing down the burrow.

But as soon as Little Chip burrowed, The Wicked Witch of the West reappeared. "I'll get you my pretty and your little dog too!" she shouted, with her green, boogeyman face, pointy nose, and chin. "I'll get you," I heard Steven screech, "You will never ever win! You will die broke!"

My mind got reduced to the level of a child again, waiting with dread for the hourglass to dispense, and for the sand and blow up my innocence. The REM dream played a big role in portraying everyone's negative emotions for sure, as I found my body sitting next to Dad's again on the sticky sofa. His empty Schaefer Beer cans reeked of urine. "The brewing company is in Milwaukee," I heard him say again.

I looked up at the TV again to see Scarecrow screaming, "Help, I'm burning, I'm burning"

The Old Christine longed for The Good Witch to reemerge again, but Glinda was nowhere to be found. Instead, the Wicked Witch's wooden broom handle banged against Dad's as the humanoid creatures of havoc chaotically commanded power. I'm sure that Dad was sweeping another pile of dirt under the rug. As Joey and I finished dinner, the poles slapped our legs beneath the tabletop. Joey jerked his arm, before his napkins flew alongside the Flying Monkeys. The kitchen corrupted.

The following evening, I sat on the edge of the jacuzzi to watch Steven shave. "Why don't you love me anymore?" I asked.

"Stop being so needy," he replied, without turning his head. "And years ago, you pointed at my stomach fat, remember?" he asked. "You have no filter!"

And boy was he right. It turns out that the hippocampus, the horseshoe figure, between 200 and 300 million years old, acts as a vital filter, filtering our behaviors, thoughts, and actions before blurting them out candidly in one big run-on sentence. The hippocampus manages our heart rate, memory, and self-protection. People take advantage of it in their everyday planning, such as vacations and future finance. For me, making a reservation for dinner feels worse than rubbing my fingernails on a chalkboard, since I only live in the immediate moment. Remember, the hippocampus acts as a hub as well, between short and long-term memories.

Our childish affection had faded with time, to be replaced by marital duties, broken promises, and self-seeking gains. I walked out of the bathroom, only to wait for him on the bedroom couch, still seeking attention. I waited for him to finish his forty-five-minute stunt in the bathroom again. When he did, he ignored my presence, got dressed and stomped downstairs.

Later that evening I dressed in pretty pajamas again and lay in bed, hoping for a miraculous change. I turned on CNN and waited for him to come back up at nine like usual. Perhaps he will crawl under the covers with me and watch a movie, I tried convincing myself. But nothing changed. He tucked me in bed like a child, with a peck on the cheek and a "Good night, Chrissy."

"Do you want your water now, Chrissy?" he asked kindly.

"Yes," I replied. "Watch television with me ok," I pleaded in vulnerability.

"Here's your water Chrissy."

"Stay with me," I said.

"I have work to do, Chrissy. Here, take this with your water," he said. "It will relax you for a bit, and I'll come back up when I finish my work ok," he said nicely, before watching me swallow a pill, Ambien.

Moments later I felt as high as a kite for the very first time. I craved munchies just like he did every single night. I got knocked out instantly. He fed me one of his prescribed sedatives every night from that point on, just so he could go downstairs and use. I got addicted.

"You're about to lose it all!" his father exclaimed to me over the phone again later that month, "your marriage, home, and even your children!"

I was being gaslit again, doubting my events and perception, while knowing deep down that Steven's parents were always his biggest enablers. Half of me knew they had no right to take my children away from me; but maybe I really am crazy, the other part considered. It was always three against one, and over time, five against one, as they all convinced my children that their mother was unfitted to parent.

"Steven it's time to come up for dinner!" I said from the top of the staircase.

"Steven dinner is on the table," I shouted down ten minutes later.

"It's time for dinner!" I screamed in rage fifteen minutes later, smelling the flowery scent arising from the basement, before the piney, skunk smell over-rode it.

"Chrissy, if he wants to chill in the basement after a long day at work then God almighty let him!" Ron shouted. "He has a new job with full medical benefits, so what do you want from him?"

He's submerged in the basement, surrounded with candles, powders, pills and pipes, I wanted to rage back.

"We're here to spend quality time with our grandkids," he replied like usual, "not to hear you screaming all the time."

I spoiled another dinner by reacting to his moaning, heavy breathing, and diminishing body. The following evening, I went upstairs to freshen up for dinner out. I opened the bathroom door, and I will never forget the sight of his head bending backwards as he snorted powder up his nose. It was treacherous for me to witness.

That was what the rolled-up dollar bills in the bathroom drawer were being used for, I told my therapist years later. And the white powdery stuff that I cleaned up in his drawer was not styptic powder for shaving, but rather cocaine.

My brain poisoned like his. "Was it my surgery or circumstance that steered us away from normalcy? I asked myself aloud.

Most likely both, I told the therapist. After all, Dr. Jeffrey Kreutzer states that, *"Guilt is the tie binding many people to a dependent stranger, inhabiting their spouse's body after brain injury. But guilt is not unique to the caregiver who might also fantasize about getting away. Couples just 'hold on to hope' that they will overcome these challenges…and that's simply not going to happen."*

In therapy I began unmasking where his patterns stood when we met compared to when I awoke eight years later. Was I was trying to reproduce something that never existed to begin with? I asked her. Were Mom and I the only ones to witness his four-hour naps every day? He scoured through people's medicine cabinets, and was too often tired, withdrawn, and irritated, I said. It was just pot at the very beginning, perhaps mixed with a few pills here and there, but either way he was always on something.

Over time more poignant memories resurfaced. He left the house five, six, seven times a day for hours at a time. He always volunteered to go to the supermarket for me. His sweaters in the closet reeked of cigarettes and weed. ADHD pills went missing from our daughter's bedroom. "Did my seizures and brain surgery provoke his desire to use like he always said?" I asked my therapist, "or was he genetically prone to addiction before we even met, or a little of both, maybe?"

"I think you can answer that for yourself at this point Christine," she replied.

So, we were just people with two shattered brains struggling to coexist in one habitat? I asked aloud. So, my faulty fight-or-flight responses were not the only source of my fear and anxiety? Did our environment stimulate our overreactions as well? The answer is yes, I later learned, since fear releases more adrenaline, and continuously reinforces trauma.

On a rainy December afternoon, I overheard Steven scouring through boxes of old Playboy magazines and thirty-three records on the unfinished side of the basement. He came across our wedding responses from 1991, as well as the dusty eight-track tape buried between them. When he walked upstairs, I saw him gently place a piece of paper on the countertop in sweet disdain. The yellow lined paper fluidly scripted a light flowing stream of cursive made me cringe. I could barely recall how attractive my writing had once been, since my penmanship turned into chicken scratch years ago. Remember, the left side of the brain controls the right side of the body. This romantic letter dated back to December 16, 1990, a year before our wedding day, and my last sentence read: "I can't believe how my heart has taken over my mind."

What a fluke, I thought, because by this point, I watched him race past me each night after work, straight upstairs to the bathroom, slamming the door behind him. I followed and overheard him ranting on the phone to his dad again. "Dinner, check," I told myself again, "kids homework check, I told myself again, "laundry, check," I told myself again.

"I need to get away from her…I know she's toxic Dad…. but how do we…she makes me nuts…Dad I know she's abusive…" I heard from saying from the bathroom door.

What his father did not know was that he sweated, trembled, and seethed. Pills and gaslighting became my husband's primary mean of survival. This included spinning and omitting information to benefit his present needs. My paranoia added more critical strands to his cunning web of betrayal.

"I'm sorry," I cried out again in the bathroom, begging for forgiveness. "Please don't leave me or keep telling your father I am bad. Give me one more chance."

Other than walking out on Steven, all I had left to do was bargain, since some power felt better than no power at all. Bargaining happens to be another stage of grief. I started regulating his doses by hiding the Oxycontin bottles in inconspicuous places. I went from the tampon box across the house to the dusty dining room credenza, but in the end, addicts always manage finding their pills. They skillfully keep their victim's brain off track as well, paranoid.

Their impulse, risk, and reward centers instigate further avoidance, stealing, and turning the tables on their victim. Trained to walk on eggshells with an alcoholic father, I struggled for control. He started overdosing on sleeping pills as well, so one night I called the police to have him dragged out of the house and placed into overnight rehab. But he dressed himself before dawn and insisted that I pick him up, promising me he would finally fix himself. I had to believe him this time around, because I was preparing to throw a big Christmas party that Friday evening, and I wasn't keen on calling eighty guests to cancel it. So, I lapsed back into denial again to befit my present needs. The party was an enormous success, but just after the new year I hauled him to another doctor, an addiction specialist with forty-five years of experience. Michael, of all people, recommended him to me. That morning I gave him another false threat. "Get out of bed or I will throw you out of the fucking house for good!"

The specialist got the same runaround from Steven as he had heard from every other addict in his forty-year practice. "It's all under control," Steven expressed with confidence and anger. "I'm just in a lot of pain, and I don't take pills on good days," he snickered at me, "I can stop anytime."

"He takes two dozen pills a day," I said, intervening.

"You don't need to be here!" he replied, glaring at me in disdain.

The Doc's response was powerful, one I will never, ever forget. "Good luck fighting the disease on your own," he expressed calmly and authoritatively. "It will never happen. You need to hit rock bottom, and sorry Mr. G. you have not done that yet. It will be rehabilitation or death, and I've seen the latter too many times." *

We walked out. I continued my mission of resolve, expecting nothing more than a shortcut to escape the unyielding torment. I still insisted on immediate resolution and gratification, because by this point, I certainly deserved it, I told my therapist.

Pharmacists were not trained back then to catch the red flags, the double dosages, and scripts. At this point he sought pain killers from his internist, orthopedic surgeon, dentist, and pain management specialist, and when they finally halted, he bought them off the street for thousands a month. "Calm down Chrissy," he continued, "the money will be in the bank for the electric bill tomorrow."

"My card got declined at the gas station again today!" I shouted back.

"Shut up.... all you talk about is money...my parents say the same thing...everything is just fine Chrissy.... The bills always get paid...You must learn to relax.... You will have your fuc.. money tomorrow for the electric!" I heard him scream again, as I awoke in fear and sweat.

"Calm down Chrissy. We have leeway. It's all ok," he whispered again, just before the electric shut down.

So caught up in his pathological webs that he believed his own schemes. Addiction emanates from a genetic predisposition, as well as from childhood development, and worsens through time. Steven and Joey's brains unintentionally ripped off by their sibling's lifelong disabilities as well. Steven's sister's learning disability and my epilepsy soaked up too much of our parent's pruning and care, leaving our brothers' needs inadvertently unmet. One turned to drugs and the other to alcoholism. Joey was a closet drinker, masking his pain while Steven smoked weed in his bedroom with the door open. They sought attention differently. Dad verbally belittled Joey and critiqued his every move while Ron and Sam provided Steven with too much liberty as a child to learn how to make the right choices. Premature amenities can lead to a lack of earning potential to finance them later on.

He watched his parents sell their multi-million-dollar business before reaching fifty. He watched them break car leases for new ones, change mansions, and R.V.s, as well as spoil our children early on. Steven and I followed the pattern for years as well, after all, we were being bankrolled. Family narcissism, codependency, enabling, and entitlement are all blood cousins of addiction that overshadow reality. Co-dependency and enabling can get fixed, however narcissists reap what they sow, and when these maggots spend their entire lives building up false egos and refusing to change, they will internally die a slow dance of death.

Years later I asked my therapist a couple of questions: What gives his disease the right to lie, cheat and scheme, but not mine or anybody else's? What gives drug addicts the right to allow victims to go bankrupt without consequence? How can a brain, with four missing pieces necessary in survival, conceive reality over time and continuous therapy, but an addictive one cannot? Which brain is more medically damaged? I know that addiction is not a disease of choice, I expressed to my therapist, but what about all the underlying damages it causes? Even if the addicts' frontal lobe, amygdala, and hippocampus get damaged from drugs, not even removed like mine, then why can't their judgment and decision-making improve over time? Is it choice or refusal? *

Ill brains are certainly modifiable to change, but of course only to a certain extent. Dr. Doidge expresses that, "When you pile up every memory of things that went wrong, how you were hurt, how you hurt others, what you lost emotionally, physically, financially, socially, legally etc. it becomes like adding too much weight to a car, or over packing the trunk. At some point, you'll overtax the system, and it will break, unable to carry the burden."

Years passed. On a Sunday afternoon my in-laws took a flight back to Florida, and first thing Monday morning I called New York University Hospital to make an appointment with neurologist, Dr.

Orrin Devinsky. I need a brain scan, I insisted, an MRI or EEG. I am convinced that I'm insane.

*R*emember Bogen's comment? "We all look forward to the day when the implications of split-brain-research emerge in a form that can help guide human society toward an improved understanding of its own internally conflicted creativity."

The Old Christine met up with Raggedy Andy from her childhood again as well, finally getting the pleasure of watching him climb up the massive apple tree that she created on construction paper with her colored pencils long ago. Clementine, his long-haired Calico with white and orange stripes nestled tightly in his arms for the climb. Her mouth was wide open with excitement, and her sensitive whiskers twitched with anticipation. Andy bore the exact blue and white striped overalls I colored, with detailed patchwork on the knees. His red sleeves puffing out on the shoulders matched his oversized bow tie and baker balloon hat. The apple tree appeared more massive this time around, as the vibrant green foliage extended beyond the page.

With a new, robust occipital lobe, my brain grasped the beauty of the tree from afar, the twisty branches, and dark green leaves growing individual blades. I gazed at my bright-pink and white impatiens, my mini-mountains of beds extending along the entire width of the house. One September afternoon I plopped my body down Indian style with my peaking mini valley behind me. My twelve-zone sprinkler system targeted the flower beds at all hours, showering them disproportionately, and creating mounts of colorful, majestic blossoms. The good Michael and I created picturesque gardens with our own bare hands. Out of nowhere, the good Michael appeared, and snapped a picture of me sitting in front of my mini mountains reaching above my head. A few weeks later it appeared in the local newspaper.

One afternoon as I rummaged through boxes in the office closet looking for a bill, I stumbled upon that quiescent shoebox from very-long ago instead. Right beside it sat my magical manila folder, collecting dust alongside my college textbooks and C.P.A. review cassettes. When I looked at the folder, I saw that kind black lady with the hunchback again. This time I hugged her, and she still felt a warm and soothing as long ago, just like my Nana. Memories admixing with real time again. As we opened the box together, we smelled the moldy pencil lead and waxy crayon from decades ago, the scent of moist, rich soil and wet leaves.

Except that now the pencil widths, lengths and color all amplified: longer, wider, broader, richer.

A defect in the brain during its early developmental years produces a hierarchy of talents, and gifts the brain with various elevated fields, one including visual agnosia, a higher order defect allowing me to draw, paint, plant, decorate, copy, and create scenes that an average occipital lobe cannot. The elements behind composing even one, single scene, Sacks notes, get analyzed meticulously. Of course, everything was silently maturing during my epilepsy.

From my office I could hear Stephanie stomping down the stairs. She stomps with dead weight, just like her dad. I rushed to the kitchen with my manilla folder in tow. She was thirteen years old and on her way to the mall, but I stopped her. "Will you look at the pictures with me first?"

"Ok?" she said in a form of a question "What pictures?"

We heard Daisy, our white Burmese sipping the milk from the bowl of Frosted Flakes. "Ok Mom you were thirteen years old," she said.

"See my prairie girls?" I asked, mesmerized. "See my little red and brown barn house resting sedentary on top of the valley? See their heads turning sideways gazing at one another, and the basket of fresh fruit and long-stemmed purple wildflowers and....?"

"Really, Mom?" she asked, "look how old you were."

"How do you know how old I was?"

"Mom you signed your name C. Vennari and dated it 1979 on the bottom corner of the page."

"You're right," I replied.

"You were thirteen years old!"

Yes, I was a young teenager like you, I told myself, still coloring childlike depictions with colored pencils. Coincidentally

Stephanie was thirteen at the time as well, but rather than drawing birds with smiley faces she was making real teenage plans with her friends.

"I'm done!" she exclaimed, as the horn outside honked, "bye Mom."

My experiences bring me back to Dr. Schiffer's questions again: "If the unconsciousness can make decisions or oppose the conscious mind," he asks, "then why can't it get studied in isolation? Further, how could analysts describe the unconscious, tell us it was primitive or childlike, had wishes, memories, fantasies, and yet say it did not exist, but existed only as processes?"

One cannot experience something that by definition he/she is not aware of, Dr. Sarno notes. Well, my drawings and characters answered a few medical questions, as my lifelong births, joys, grief, sadness, glee, and deaths were all brought to conscious awareness.

Next, Freud wanted to know what instructs the unconsciousness to keep some memories or ideas repressed and censored, and yet others revealed, and by now we all know why Carly, Stevie, Three Dog Night, ABBA, and Andrew Gold took the prizes.

Take the brain of a veteran that endured multiple blows to the head. He/she may regress back in time as well, and unconsciously relive the war through their implicit memories, unable to classify their past events by time, place, or context. Although most times the brain can barely recall the incident, the emotions linger. The flashbacks elicit uncontrollable sorrow and grief. Time stands still.

Jimmie G., another Sacks' patient held short-term memory deficits caused by alcoholism. As a veteran he lived out his life feeling helpless, demented, and disoriented. He developed amnesia and retreated to 1945, his first years in the Navy. He spoke of the past in the present tense, the same way I did with Nixon and Watergate.

We held another profound attachment, that of horticulture. Like me, Jimmie G. felt trapped inside a house that he felt was no longer his own. The lands and oceans signify home because they lack rooms, walls, and restrictions. We humans do not get separated from other living creatures of the Earth, so we must treat them the way we expect to be treated. Heidi Wachter states that "It's not about right to the land; it's about responsibility for the land."

The difference is I knew real time all along, even when my perceptions failed to match up. Unfortunately, Jimmie G. never healed.

A split brain does not deliberately lie to others as does a sociopath or schizophrenic, but it often lies to itself instead. It tarnishes and polishes from loss of episodic memory and dire need to fill in the blanks. It tarnishes and polishes due to two sides contradicting one another so often as well. One side presents itself as very social and warm while the other as withdrawn, lethargic, and socially inept. Overall, I am an introvert, content in isolation from poor face recognition, perception, and memory, but often I appear to be extroverted as well, due to lack of filter and hippocampus. This cerebral duality led me back to the same question again, "How can I associate with loved ones and friends when I feel cut off from my Self?"

My right hemisphere always longed for support and validation from its pal on the other side, but it got left besieged for a very long time and left to fend for itself. Or was it the other way around, I began asking myself through time. Before the surgery, Levy concluded my brain holds mixed dominance, equal partnership between the right and left hemispheres. I was uncertain if this was true, but in a way it illogically was. I turned into a complicated simpleton, an asymmetrical savant, continuously shifting her powers around.

Doidge notes that no two savants are ever alike. Imagine removing two chunks of Play Dough from the dinosaur, then trying to remold it to the exact size and structure as before. It's impossible. Doidge says that when pieces of the brain get severely injured or removed, the whole becomes different than the sum of its parts! The vacancies provide more space for the remainders to spread out, and to fill in the voids any way they can. The brain re-transposes into a brand-new whole. Unlike a sandwich, half the brain does not make up for half the mind, Doidge says, and the brain needs to economize on its remaining, healthy functions. *

Savant Syndrome affects the entire cerebral cortex: temporal, frontal, occipital, and parietal lobes, so when a wire snaps in one, it sends jumbled signals to the others as well. Then when the healthy cells begin interacting again, they influence each other differently than before. I felt the physical and mental movement for an exceptionally long time. I felt the tangible and intangible re-structuring, persistent thumping, competition, and compromise. Nothing felt whole or uniform like before, but disproportionate, autonomous, and self-governing.

One hemisphere puts on a sneaker while the other walks away to begin her shopping list. I cannot hear myself speak so I scream. I'm oversensitive to other people's voices so I cover my ears. The imbalance in my auditory cortex promoted imbalance in my occipital cortex. Visual creativity versus tunnel vision. Driving perfectly between the lines versus trouble judging depth and distance. I place my cup on the end of the counter only to watch it spill. I drop things, curbside drive, trip over my own feet. But get this: I type the letter f on the keyboard rather than g and type the letter k rather than j. It is a perfect imbalance on each side, because some brain areas hold the pseudo-stereo effect, where sights get processed from different channels, causing them to get amplified or reduced. Other brain areas hold the stereo-visual effect, the binocular disparity between images of objects in the right and left eyes. Over dramatic, magnified, augmented, showcased, tapered, blurry, narrowed, deficient, yet somehow leveled off.

Savant Syndrome does not just pertain to autism spectrum disorders, but frontal lobe and neuro-developmental disorders as well. It is why *The Brain That Changes Itself* began competing in my brain with *Charlotte's Web*. Once again, it has a lot to do with boundaries, face recognition, perception, and memory. The

Welcome To state signs are still especially important to me because they remind me of where I stand in the world at the present, and that I indeed exist in the here and now. I need this edge since my brain depends more on implicit, procedural, and working memory than normal brains. I need this edge because my brain relies on dreams, insights, hallucinations, sixth senses, and intuition, all holding no edges. Yes, these uncanny abilities emanating from a gifted temporal lobe extend beyond the normal scope of rational, but they crave margins just as much.

Brain surgery was the third and final blow to my brain, but rather than sensibly feeding into my existing amnesia, it overturned it instead, and activated an old lost life when The Old Christine called her weeping willows Gentle Giants. Over time her Gentle Giants began providing her an oasis-of-shade again to repress her reality. As their distinctive shapes and textures grew and changed, each branch developed their very own resourcefulness. "They're one of the fastest growing trees of the Earth," The Little Man expressed, "growing nearly two feet high in a single season and peaking as high as fifty feet in fifteen years with an equal spread!"

We all remember Raymond, played by Dustin Hoffman in *Rain Man* from 1988, the autistic savant living with noticeable disorder, a silent sixth sense. He adhered to routines impeccably, such as watching reruns of The People's Court the same time every day. His brain held the ability to make instant calculations on the exponential level, far beyond the normal range. He held an astounding capacity to memorize entire phone books and baseball stats, but most entertaining was his ability to count a six-deck shoe at the casino, quickly scoring 80,000 dollars, and even prompting the floor people to call up the eye in the sky! This is where brilliance offsets underdevelopment and rises to the occasion.

Doidge described a brilliant woman holding exceptional skills that coexisted with retardation. She holds trouble understanding simple concepts from back in kindergarten. If her brothers attended the same school as her, she wanted to know why she was not allowed to leave her class and visit theirs whenever she wanted. An injured frontal lobe holds trouble understanding rules while an injured amygdala tries to change them.

As a savant, my left hemisphere began ruminating and over analyzing every thought, action, and behavior. It needed to replace the destructive powers of rumination with reflection and constructive thinking, but it did not know how. It needed outlets to regulate its maladaptive behaviors emotions and impulses, and to channel them more evenly. Yet, I also needed my left hemisphere to remove my right from my past torment and bring me forward. I healed through therapy.

One evening I had the honor to speak with Dr. Schiffer on the telephone. After I explained my inability to let go of the past, he gave me an exercise. He told me to cover my left eye, in order for me to see only through my right. Remember, our left hemisphere controls our right vision and vice versa. When I covered my left and looked through my right, I felt a sense of peace, livelihood, color, depth, and optimism. Yet, when I covered my right eye and looked through my left, I felt doom and gloom, depression, and darkness. So, this implied that rather than my left hemisphere, my right, aged hemisphere had never fully healed from its past traumas. This is another fine example of Doidge's Plastic Paradox.

So, after I hung up the phone with Dr. Schiffer, I continued his form of dual brain therapy, and over time, patience, and repetition, these two conflicting hemispheres began coexisting in unison. Each hemisphere holds their own liabilities and assets. I may have trouble finding the right word to complete a sentence, however, look at my book, the research, writing, and ability to teach others a bit about the human brain. This is neuroplasticity at its finest.

Finally, Dr. Doidge sums up neuroplasticity by stating that it gives rise to both mental flexibility and rigidity. And before my hemispheres learned teamwork, each side had to appreciate the depth of its own triumphs. So perhaps Levy saying that my brain holds mixed dominance was bizarrely true all along.

Well, Devinsky's team sent me home after my checkup, stating that I was not going insane like Steven and his parents suggested. In fact, I was undergoing multiple PTSD, post-traumatic stress disorders, and the overlaps that were pushing me over the edge.

Psychiatrist Dr. Leslie Rawlings notes that, "In times of crises, threat and upset, our brains cannot process information ordinarily, because the traumas cause an overload in our sensory processing. However, our traumas get indeed stored, whether we desire them to be or not."

Depressed, bitter, and guilt ridden, Dad failed to grasp and accept Joey's death. Joey died alone in Atlanta, Georgia from complications of alcoholism. I cannot begin to fathom how it feels for a parent to lose a child from alcoholism or drug overdose, while failing to understand that the road to recovery involves courage, fortitude, and the ability to recognize the disease. Mom told me many times that she wished she had provided the same moral support to her son Joey as she did to Steven. And unlike drug abuse, alcoholism doesn't destroy families financially. As my Capgras waned over time, the guilt and grief of losing my brother intensified, and at various points it overridden the pain of losing my Self. Again, it was easier for me to remain angry or in denial since they both feel a hell of a lot better than pain.

Dad could not manage Joey's loss, and at some point, his alcoholism took over as well. By 2008, the delusional soul decided moving far away, and he asked Mom to join him. He wanted to leave his soiled life in New York behind and move out west to Las Vegas, Nevada. Tried to convince himself that a better life was waiting for them in the middle of the dessert. Absolutely bizarre, I thought, since my stingy Dad was far from a gambler. In fact, he was a penny pincher. I despised my father, but my heart shattered once again. I had every right to remain angry, but unfortunately other emotions often overshadow the anger. I was subconsciously grieving the loss of so many people at once, as my system overtaxed once again.

About a year later, Dad admitted that the grass was not greener on the other side of the country, and he begged Mom for another chance. My distorted frontal lobe pitied Dad the same way it pitied Steven, I later discovered, as I attempted to convince Mom to accept him back. "He's made a lot of mistakes Mom, we all have," I expressed, "and he never seized your strengths."

I knew that his brain lacked the ability to carry such a heavy burden on his own, especially guilt about Joey's death five years earlier in 2003. Maybe seeking couple's therapy together and sharing each other's feelings and concerns will save your marriage, I suggested. Maybe it will help you both come to terms with Joey's death, I expressed, knowing deep down that I was fooling myself. So, Mom took Dad back, and his behaviors significantly improved.

Unfortunately, AA and therapy must be continuous to maintain a long, healthy life and relationship. Alcoholism is a chronic disease that is debilitating for family members as well. Neither of them actively working on saving their relationships, and like Steven was by the time I left him, Dad was far gone. When Mom set boundaries and rules, Dad took off to Sin City once again.

As a child we took another drive from New England to Long Island. On I-95 in Madison Connecticut, I dozed off beside Stuffed Pink Piglet, and my white helmet with the blue horseshoe logo on each side. Like usual I prompted Mom and Dad to wake me up just before reaching The Big, Big Bridge. "Dad don't let us miss The Big, Big Bridge again!" I exclaimed, "Or the Pumpkin Place near Nono's! Don't let us sleep through it again!"

The suspension bridge over the East River took charge of my immature mind again, right beside the toy store at the TSS shopping center in Queens. The big, big bridge runs nearly three thousand feet and holds six lanes, The Little Man reminded me, and thousands of cars pass over it every single day. Just two main cables support the Throgs Neck Bridge, which are held up by suspension towers! I indulge in bridges, their conjoining, as well as their separation between towns, boroughs, and states. I yearned for such boundaries so people would not take my altruism for granted. To me a bridge doesn't represent a definitive separation, rather a healthy edge allowing both individuality and relationships to prosper.

Dad spoiled the fun again and failed to wake me up the sensational way that I looked forward too. At the toll booth along The New York State Thruway, we heard him shouting at the money basket. He woke us both up. "From fifty cents to seventy-five and now a buck twenty-five, just to cross over this stupid bridge!' he yelled.

Stuffed Pink Piglet and I knew exactly what was coming next.

"Choke!" he yelled, tossing the change in the basket.

TSS and The Pumpkin Place sitting along the Nassau Expressway oozed out of unconsciousness as well. As an epileptic, The Pumpkin Place signified another important landmark for me, the one dividing Queens and Nassau County. Well, it turns out that TSS stood for Times Square Stores, I later recalled, a chain of discount stores on Rockaway Turnpike in the 1970s. Part of TSS included "Lionel play world," the magnificent toy store with the big, orange, smiling pumpkin!

Years later I discerned this trip took place in early 1973, a few years after my fall, as my helmet with the blue horseshoe logo on each side rested beside us in the back seat. I heard Carly Simon bolting out her brand-new hit single on AM radio, "You're So Vain" as well. You gave away the things I loved, I cried out to Dr. Gordon, and one of them was.... Another seizure erupted in full force. I was six-years old again, and I felt my fingers clenching, heart palpitating, and nausea traveling up my little body into my brain. Stuffed Pink Piglet placed the helmet on my head, before grasping on to my hand tightly. I had another dream of clouds in my...and I stared at Joey in the car, and he looked invisible. "I don't like it when she loses oxygen and breath," Stuffed Pink Piglet said to Joey, nudging him. But there was nothing to nudge, just spirit.

So now you know that "You're So Vain" and "Dreams" remain in my implicit memories, stuck in real time, and incorporated into my sense of Self without conscious thought or deliberation. Imagine a song sounding brand new upon every replay. This implies that the beginning of my mental demise in the early 1970s remains unhinged, and still connects to my present Self. Sacks confirms that the self and mind both remain unaffected during the earliest stages of epilepsy. It's the autobiographical self, the personality that relies on explicit, episodic memory, which over time, gets virtually lost. *

The year after Stephanie's Bat Mitzvah Mom underwent a mastectomy. By this point in 2009, Dad was back from Las Vegas for the second time. I can't recall much about how or why she accepted him again, however I can recall that Dad was completely sober, Unlike Steven, Dad financially provided his family with food, homes, college, clothes, and cars. Even when he took off for Vegas, he left Mom with their entire lifetime savings. Before Steven's addiction drained her resources, Mom had enough money to live another lifetime. Dad and I both helped Mom during her breast cancer treatment. I spent three nights with them, before Steven and my in-laws demanded that I come back home. But I had no room left in my brain for Steven's shenanigans. "Get home Chris," Sam said on the phone three or four days later. "We need to get back to Florida!"

I not only wanted to be there for Mom the same way that she had always been there for me, but I desperately wanted his parents to fix Steven during those few days as well. I even tried to use Mom's cancer as their wake-up call, and I detested the idea of going back to face the bloody pillowcases and drenched sheets. Let them see what he is all about, I told myself, refusing to strip him of consequence and guilt. Let the parent's witness the son's bloody nose and let them hear the continuous messages that the pharmacies were leaving on the answering machine, questioning his scripts and refills.

It took me too long to realize that Mom is the strongest woman I know, my hero. Sure, she was overly altruistic and gullible, but the day came when she finally decided to never repeat the same mistakes again. During my years of Capgras, I failed to express my pride in her courage, self-respect, and liberation. She finally decided NO MORE and DETACHED herself completely from Dad the narcissist after fifty-plus years of verbal slander. Earlier in my journey, I felt compelled to battle the family dynamics, and overturn the generations of disease. Since Nana lacked the means and education to exercise her strengths and escape the ditches, I felt compelled to do it for her. Remember, escaping narcissism and gaslighting takes a lifetime of understanding something relatively simple, but exceedingly difficult to implement. The life of a narcissist will not be different tomorrow, and the self-destruction mutilating inside them carries forward to the victims if we allow it to. So, I needed to end the family sins for Nana, but I failed to realize that when all said and done, Mom already did this for me. *

*A*s Nana was hanging the wet clothes on the line with the wooden clothes pins, she watched Belle, Stuffed Pink Piglet, and I from the corner of her eyes. We had the last piece of dough in tow. Nobody budged. So, I tossed the mini meatball high as the sky, and everyone watched the gull gulp the dough in midair. Nana winked at us.

"She knew about the bread all along," Belle said.

"Yeah, I think so," I replied.

"She knew about the Robbin Hoods stealing the crumb to feed the hungry." Stuffed Pig Piglet expressed with a sigh of relief.

"It's all good," I said. "Altruism can still be good."

*A*dam and I communicated periodically, and the fall of 2008 he invited me to an epilepsy fundraiser he was sponsoring on The Upper West Side. At that point I was nine years seizure-free, and still buried in my Capgras Syndrome as well, and elated to see him. While gathering eight friends rather quickly, I turned others away as well, due from information overload, and peer pressure. I got myself mixed up in two cliques, for lack of a better word. So many school moms and friends that I failed to filter out the bad eggs from the good ones, and I insulted some dear friends along the way. By the time my judgment, reasoning, and decision all improved, my mistakes had already caught up with me. It took a long time for my frontal lobe to ascertain the false pretenses behind friendships.

I held an inferiority complex around people as well, and as I began healing, this complex turned into anger and the anger had me facing some ugly truths about myself. I had to experience this anger to stop making a doormat out of myself. Most people in the clique were not devoted friends, I learned over time, and my anger facilitated my healing. Adults in such situations, Dr. Firestone expresses, continue to blame our singleness on external forces.

However, in long-term partnerships, we fail at recognizing that we are not as open to new relationships as we think we might be. It took five years after my divorce for my brain to release its inferiority complex, preventing me from experiencing happiness and pleasantry. Now, I expect from others what I release, unconditional trust, and Sacks calls this matchless.

The night before the big event, Steven copped out as a designated driver, but the big shot paid for a limo instead. I later discovered that he did this to provide himself run of the house to use.

The thought of seeing Adam generated the exact chills as it had nine years before, falsely activating my brain's emotional reward centers. I am not a big fan of alcohol, but my sentiments for this man were a fine reason for me to down a glass of Pinot Noir before leaving the house. By the time we reached The Palisades Parkway, just ten minutes from home, I had downed my second glass. I preferred Pino over Cab back then, since it's less vigorous and sweeter around the edges. When the limo crossed over the George Washington Bridge, I was already drunk.

Dana the socialite recognized faces and worked the crowd during cocktail hour. Compared to the insipid-looking guests, we all looked radiant, dressed for a black-tie affair. Right away I saw Levy and Gordon glance in my direction with the corner of their eyes. Instantly, Sarah McLachlan triggered again from the outskirts of my mind. As I stared into space I overheard, there lived in darkness seeping in the night, you gave me a sense of nothing, but oh you gave me life.

I was a happy and sad drunk the same time. I started thinking about my first postoperative visit with Gordon three months post-surgery. It took place on the Jersey side of the bridge in Teaneck. That evening I vividly recalled him tinkering with a gadget behind his desk, failing to look up at me. It reminded me of my first encounter with him and my parents in 1999. Rather than greeting The New Christine with warmth or compassion like Adam, he kept looking down, frustrated with his brand-new 1999 Blackberry. When he finally looked up, I recalled this:

"How did you get here?" he asked, just like Levy.

"I drove," I said.

"You're not supposed to be driving," he said, just like Levy.

"The seizures are over," I said again.

"How are you feeling?" he asked.

"Great!" I responded, acting out a part.

"It's a different type of aura than before," I finally said. "It's musical. It also feels as if a seizure is about to erupt while I know full well that it is not."

He explained to me that post surgery auras feel real, but they are fake and are known to spring up occasionally as well, but are not followed by a later seizure.

"I get lost in my familiar surroundings now," I blurted out next. "My very own neighborhood feels unfamiliar to me, and the fire hydrant in front of my house appears out of sorts."

I fiddled with my fingers and waited for him to say something, and when he did, it wasn't much of anything.

Within fifteen minutes I walked directly toward him and shook his hand. I couldn't recall sending him my eighteen-page memoir in place of the post-surgical questionnaire that he asked me to fill out. But he started talking about it right away. I resented him for closing my surgery like a business deal, ending with a handshake. But by this point, my anger gone. In fact, it got instantly replaced by warmth, kindness, and concern.

I looked like a different person, free from medication and epilepsy. My body was lighter, my skin clearer, my mind smarter. He asked me about my depression and personality changes, before stating that he had come across other patients with similar behavioral changes, some even leading to post surgery divorce like mine. I just wish he had warned me about this in the first place, I wanted to say aloud.

I cannot explicitly recall much of the event, but my pages did it for me. Apparently, my group managed amusing ourselves throughout the stiff event. In fact, we laughed so loud that an old bag over at the next table whistled at us all night to shut us up. But Adam amused as well, which was all that mattered to me. "Adam, are those girls sitting at your table yours?" I asked.

"No, they're my nieces."

"Adam are those girls at your table your kids?" I asked again later.

"No, they're my nieces," he replied again.

"Wait, I thought you have two sons!" I expressed.

"Dr. Levy she's a little drunk!" Barbara said

"I can see, I like it," he replied.

"Did you give your speech yet Adam?" I asked, "I'm waiting,"

"Chris, he already spoke!" Barbara said.

"When?" I asked, "Can I speak too Adam? Did you bring your children?"

"They're not my kids," he replied, still smiling. "And no, you cannot speak, but next time ok."

My Capgras Syndrome was very real, and Dr. Levy managed this in the utmost professional way. We all acted like mischievous middle schoolers, breaking all the rules. At another point Barb and Dana walked my drunken ass to the lady's room, where I bumped into a lady in costume. As they walked directly past her toward the stalls, I stood there motionless.

"Evita!" I shouted out.

She is a performer, I knew, preparing to take the stage. She ignored me. "Chris, go pee already," Barbara said.

I kept my promise...I began singing...you keep your.... Barb and Dana walked away, leaving me alone in the bathroom. As I stumbled back to the table by myself, I heard everyone cracking up, so loud that the mean lady pointed her finger at us again. "We need to all leave now," I expressed to the girls. "I need Adam to get on this right away. Where is he?" I asked Barb.

"What are you talking about?" Liz replied.

"I saw a bride in the bathroom and we're holding up her wedding, and why did you two leave me in the bathroom?" I asked.

"Because Chris, there's no wedding and no Evita and you are drunk!" Dana replied.

"You didn't stop singing and congratulating that lady on her wedding. It wasn't her wedding, and you made an ass out of yourself. The lady got pissed!" Barb said.

The following morning Dana filled me in. It turned out that Adam had to say goodbye to me four times, because I did not want to leave him. I would not get up off my chair, so everyone walked out and left me sitting alone at the table. The room was spinning, I recalled, and my stomach felt vile. The second time Lisa returned inside to get me, she shouted, "Chris your husband is paying for every minute the limo sits outside. Now let's go!"

When we reached The Palisades Parkway, I was ready to throw up, so Tracy covered my face with napkins while Barb told the driver to pull over. I vomited. Twenty minutes later two friends dragged me inside and upstairs to my bedroom. They undressed me and put me into bed like a toddler. They began cracking up at something, and I covered my ears. "Stop laughing, my head is killing me!" I shouted.

"I can't believe what's under your dress!" Dana exclaimed. "A ripped bra and high waisted, Hanes underwear."

"They sell them in three packs in the supermarket!" I said, "now go home."

That morning I also discovered that Dana had introduced me to another brainy woman, a writer named Loryn. She snapped some pictures of us "The Jersey Girls," and asked Dana the reason we were attending. Loryn emailed the pictures to me the following morning, attached with a beautiful note. After we exchanged some kind words, she asked me some questions about my epilepsy, brain surgery and my relationship with Adam. I found myself tongue-tied, unable to answer her it in just a few sentences, so I wrote, "It's too complicated to explain, but if you're interested and someday have time, you can read this. Attached is the first summary of my memoir, eighteen pages. Then I hit send.

I was off to the gym, dry cleaners, and Starbucks, and forgot about the morning communication with Loryn. However later that afternoon, I felt like a homosexual coming out of the closet. Loryn wrote that my story filled her with tears, enlightenment, pain, joy, intrigue, admiration, and deep sorrow. This was when I sat back on my swivel chair and swiveled for a few moments. I got up and began salvaging the dusty papers from inside the closet. I wound up scanning through every page piecemeal, including articles, letters, magazines, research, until I came across that Newsweek issue from 2004 with a cover portraying the human brain from a side angle. I reread the folded page again, the Letters from Readers. I reread what I wrote, "I do not regret anything…five years for my brain to reach its maximum potential.…

This was bogus! I thought. I was trying to convince myself that life after brain surgery was manageable. "Goodbye for now to a very special person," I read next in my letter to Dr. Levy.

My journey was far from over, I told myself. God will further challenge my brain with as much at it can handle. I was ready for future challenges or meaningful purpose. One evening shortly after, I hallucinated Glinda, The Good Witch, again. She was floating above and watching over me through The Cumulous Clouds. I reached up high to grasp on to her beautiful spirit. I saw my brother floating peacefully beside her as well, but in dreams we cannot touch. But their unconscious presence provided me encouragement and hope, as I began surrendering myself to the process again, to reopening my story and picking up where I had left off.

Mom afforded me the strength to fight my weaving threads of bad luck. I started going out with my friends just to stay away from Steven. Hijacked by narcissism and gaslighting again, leaving me with mixed emotions including hate, over-altruism, disgust, hope, and fear of the unknown. The potency even spread to our children like a cancer, and at various points they believed their father's words about me. "You are nuts Mom," I heard. "Stop fighting, leave Dad alone!" Steven's favorite threat was saying, "Do you know how much I have on you?" before chuckling condescendingly.

I spent years figuring out where I went wrong, before learning that was just a false threat by a meaningless bully. I said the rose is red and Steven said it is green, and he twisted the kids into believing it is green. The apple doesn't fall far from the tree, yet I felt determined to break the family cycle for the sake of my children.

Loryn put my book on hold on temporarily, while Steven continued to spiral downward. "How could parents remain blindsided by their own son's behaviors right before them?" I wanted to know. "How did brain surgery award me the wisdom that other's so glaringly lack?"

*A*nother tax season and another launch of my radiant spring blooms. My purple crocuses and yellow daffodils already getting admired by passersby in February and March, before my white and pink hyacinths flowered, providing a sweet scent along the walkway. And my tulips. Michael and I planted over a thousand bulbs every December right after the first frost. In 2008 we selected Dutch bulbs shipped directly from Holland and created a spread of thirty-inch-high snow-white tulips with a stream of dark eggplant along of my beds. Each spring cars and passerbyes stopped to look at the ten-day magnificent scene.

But by April, smack in the middle of their striking display, another trauma dented my reward system. Tuesday morning, April 15, with tax season officially over, the emotionless robot began stomping heavily down the hardwood stairs. By this point he failed to get out of bed before eleven am, and each morning I had to drag him into the shower. His sheets drenched with sweat from withdrawal symptoms. That morning when he arrived downstairs, I watched him make himself a cup of coffee with the Keurig, before sinking his frail body down into his filthy sofa cushion. He howled a long, loud weeping spell of death. His brain and body were collapsing before me, dwindling into a skeleton. I wanted to hold him, slap him, kiss him, encourage him, but he wanted no part of me. He grasped on tight to Lily and sobbed. Lily moaned alongside him. He threw himself down landing flat on his stomach on the floor and wailed like a baby to Louis. Titled his doxy head sideways, before sadly licking his Daddy's tears off his face.

"Chrissy, I'm an addict," he finally admitted, "and I need help, just like the doctor told us last year."

I cried proud tears. I hugged him, before reaching for the phone to call the overnight rehab center to seek information. His face was pale and expression cold as stone. "Don't you dare!" he raged suddenly, before instantly jumping up and racing out the door. I followed him panic stricken and watched him hop on his motorcycle. "But you need help!" I shouted, as he sped off in search of another fix. "I'm so proud of you," I shouted following him, "don't give up now, please come back!"

I watched his bike zoom away, right past my Dutch flower display for one more fix, before the real beginning of the end. By the end of the week, I suffered another nervous breakdown, smacking myself and pulling my hair. With my elbows over my ears again I screamed up at God. "Haven't you put me through enough," I asked Him angrily, "I'm only one person with one frail brain!"

Mommy, together with my Aunt Sina and Uncle Norman raced up from Long Island immediately. It took Norman, a retired New York police officer, less than fifty minutes to arrive. I dropped to the floor, sobbing and my Mommy wiped away my sweat, tears, and runny nose. We touched, cried, and rocked our bodies up and down, squeezing one another for well over ten minutes. She was my mother again, I felt for the very first time in nearly ten years, my flesh and blood. The poignancy was bittersweet.

Uncle Norman raced out to pay Steven a surprise office visit at work, but upon arrival, Norman found his bike gone. "He's using somewhere again," I expressed to him on the phone, "because I got another e-email from the bank and the balance is low. He's probably on the other side of the G.W. in the Bronx, I said, so come home."

Later that day Norman appeared in his parking lot again. This time he disconnected the motorcycle wires and waited. Two hours later Steven appeared. They came to an agreement. Uncle Norman reconnected the wires only if Steven agreed to follow him home. But my uncle arrived without Steven in sight. He U turned on The Palisades Parkway, Norman explained, heading back toward the bridge again. Altruistic Aunt Sina and Mom prepared him a plate, before heading back home around eight. I took an Ambien and conked out on the kitchen chair. By this point I failed to sleep without them.

The following morning, I felt the stakes at their greatest, so my right hemisphere went into high gear. The unconscious mental toughness kicked in again, so rather than considering about what might happen, I focused on what needed to happen. I called his parents and insisted that they to book the next flight to New Jersey to help me save their son. And they finally heard me and did just that. For the very first time the three of us thought rationally together as a team. Ron and Sam calmly and efficiently found a drug rehabilitation program for Steven. Impressed by their efficiency and extremely grateful. Working together as a team, they promised me a resolution by the weekend. "Hold on tight," Ron expressed calmly.

Don't get me wrong I struggled to block my shattered nerves and worked proficiently alongside them. I was anxious, angry, relieved, scared, disappointed, and incredibly nervous. On Saturday afternoon their plane landed at Newark Airport, and by Saturday evening Steven's drug rehabilitation sponsor from Oakland, California landed as well. By eight pm, everyone, including Jason and Stephanie, gathered at a nearby hotel, while Mom was driving to our house from Long Island. Steven was nowhere to be found.

During the meeting, I listened to my two young teens, fifteen and sixteen, express their father's trauma to the sponsor, professionally, flawlessly. There was no underlying anger or resentment like Mom, rather fervent desires to get care for their father. Shockingly surprised by their maturity and proud of their values and love for their father. "How did you know so much about withdrawal symptoms?" I asked Stephanie years later, "and the long-term effects of overdosing? Why didn't you tell me you found Dad's pills between the couch cushions?"

"Mom, he wasn't ready to help himself," she replied.

"Grow up Mom," Jason said another time. "It's not about you all the time. It's about Dad, and he needs to go away and get clean."

His bike roared in past one AM, I later learned, while everyone was asleep, but Mom. She got from the couch to face him. He gazed at her stoned, spreading both arms out as if he finally surrendered. The day before his body looked like a corpse and his eyes sagged with hopelessness. Mom, the altruistic one, offered Steven food.

"Thank you anyway," he quietly declined, before going down to the basement to sleep. I believe he was aware that the end was near.

By the following morning, everyone fully prepared to follow the series of steps that the sponsor explained the night before. We had to begin a structured group conversation, non-argumentative and peaceful. But this shit should not have happened to our family, part of me thought. The asshole should have grown up like me, but I beg your pardon, Lyn Anderson hummed from afar, life is far from a rose garden.

On Sunday morning the doorbell rang promptly at 9:30. Ron shot downstairs to pay his son a surprise visit. The first challenge was to get Steven upstairs, and the second was to have him agree to surrender to the counselor. Everyone relieved when Steven walked upstairs and displayed no shock or confrontation "What do you all want?" he quietly asked us.

Everyone had to express one by one how much we loved him and how we feel hurt by his poor behaviors. But Steven was nice to everyone but me. In fact, he acted hostile and angry toward me, and the family blame game fueled once again. But everyone was in crises mode and undergoing mixed signals, so his parents indirectly shifted the blame to me, struggling for control. Sure, we were all instructed not to play the blame game, but this was normal family dynamics during this type of crisis.

By the mid-afternoon, the car pulled out of driveway and soon after the plane took off to Oakland California with Steven on board. I felt like million pounds of nothing. He is finally under surveillance, I told myself in the stage of shock, where he can no longer inflict harm on himself.

My tulips appeared dead to me. I had no earnings, but I had to focus on "myself," Ron and Sam kept insinuating. The bills piled up, but I had to focus on myself. I had to grasp on the concept that like epilepsy, addiction is a disease and not one of choice. Before flying home, Ron and Sam advised me to go out and seek a job, earn money, explore new opportunities, and begin rebuilding a new life with my children as a single parent. But I could not breathe. Sure, his parents and mine kept us financially afloat, but this did not ward off my anger and bereavement, as well as the shock that I had to endure once again. During that time, I slept from the moment I dropped the kids off at school. I only forced myself to wake up moments before afternoon pickup. The dirty laundry piled up, the bedrooms unkempt, and litter box reeked. "He's in a safe environment now," I told myself. "His brain and body are detoxifying, and that's all that matters."

But people saturated with havoc do not resort to self-medicating, I told myself. I must forgive, forget, and stop looking back, I told myself next, only forward. My perpetual tears represented release valves for the stress and toxins to drip out. Another post- traumatic stress disorder, I later learned, inflicting my present nightmares. Zadra and Stickgold note that, "Scientists have yet to determine the extent toward which progressive changes in dream content contribute to post-trauma recovery."

My dream content contributed the most to my post-trauma recoveries, and their narrative structures and characters should help science understand how the brain selects its memories to relive, and what it selects to reconstruct and unfold. These two brilliant authors were still unsure of what guides the behaviors, feelings, and personalities ascribed to the characters in our dreams, but I am not.

I rocked on the swing again, this time dozing off beside Mom. This time I had a happy dream, and Zadra and Stickgold note that only twenty-five percent of dreams are happy dreams, with most holding minimum dream recall as well. My new brain not only holds exceptional dream recall, but exceptional ability to couple my dreams with future creativity, exploration, and resolution. The hippie on the beach permanently reverted me back to the gypsy that I was, loomed one last time to tighten the loose ends. I heard "Delta Dawn" admixing with "Gypsy," only this time through my conscious auditory cortex rather than my unconscious limbic system. "Delta Dawn" finally asked the hippie what's the flower that she had on? A twelve-year-old hallucination tagged for later processing finally unmasked before me on the swing. In this dream, I found myself surrounded by Nono's flowers, blooming in her front yard. "There they are!" I shouted in my sleep.

"You're dreaming again Chris," I heard Mom say from afar.

"The purple and white flowers on her flip flops," I shouted, from 1972!"

"They're Dahlias Mom!" I shouted, before she nudged me again.

"Flowers that signify encouragement and dignity!" I shouted, fully awake.

I started flooding my neurons with literature about drug addiction. Dr. Doidge explains that addiction involves lifelong changes in the brain's neuroplasticity, and moderation can be impossible. Cocaine makes the pleasure-giving neurotransmitter dopamine more active by transmitting rewards and releases, and triggering an exciting, immediate pleasure and energy without having to work for it. When scientists placed electrodes in the septal regions of the limbic system known as the brain's pleasure-centers, trial patients experienced powerful, joyous euphoria, similar to the effects cocaine and sexual pleasure. It affected their personality, decision making and emotion. As they were blocking Steven's pain sensations, they were targeting his emotional and financial escape at the same time.

By now we realize that addiction speeds up over time, beside peer pressure, marital woes, financial distress, and verbal battering. As the drugs wear off more rapidly, the internal pleasure follows, and the external rages heighten. By the time my internal epileptic rages desensitized another form began from other sources. The misconception of why the addict goes back for another fix is the sense of immediate pleasure, and the avoidance of withdrawal. But addicts take drugs even when there is no prospect of pleasure, Doidge notes, and when they know they have an insufficient dose to keep them high. The craving increases and the withdrawal kicks in, before the craving increases once again. Wanting and liking are two different things, I learned, and sensation leads to increased wanting, though not necessarily liking.

Home from rehabilitation and relapsing often, which is normal and expected, the counselor explained. Steven began pilfering family medications. He got an abundant number of legal scripts from doctors as well, to replace the illegal ones he had gotten before. Five, six, or seven bottles at a time. some necessary, others to fill his pallet. When he began Alcoholic Anonymous rather than Narcotics Anonymous, I failed to understand why. AA gears more around learning skills to help others while on your own journey toward sobriety. NA gears more around coming to terms with the pain the addict caused on himself, as well as others in their lives. He married the twelve-step program, and attended twice a day, seven days a week, in search of a Higher Power. He made people believe he was committed to helping himself, but his parents and peers failed to witness other people's prescribed drugs disappearing from the house, or the late nights out after the program ended. To him and his family, it was a case of heads or tails. I either fully supported him or I was a piece of shit.

I finally reached out to Loryn again, because by this point, I wanted to complete my book. You are back in denial again, she expressed, and not anywhere near ready. So, we struck a deal. As a temporary editor and friend, she asked for a telephone interview with Steven. Jeez, I said to myself. I need to precondition him beforehand, I knew, warn him to act like a mature adult, embellish our lives, adorn the relationship, and kill it with kindness. A better quality of life is just around the corner, I tried to convince myself again for the sake of my book, emerging when my book is complete. Then, he will be proud of me, I told myself, and his parents will be as well. But over a decade later, pride was furthest on their list.

I pleaded internally for false adjectives such as "terrific and radiant," the very ones Charlotte used to describe Wilbur on her web at The County Fair. But he just returned from rehab, still struggling with his own demons, I thought. Besides, his statement upon arrival was far from terrific and radiant, a gut-wrenching scene to say the least. "I'm responsible for taking care of only myself now, and you're responsible for taking care of yourself," he told me.

"Really?" I replied in anger.

To begin with, he returned too quickly. With only five weeks gone, I was still in shock, anger, and dismay. "Suddenly you're responsible for only yourself, after your parent's dished out over thirty thousand dollars for your program?"

"It's always about money with you!" he replied.

"You expected them to send you spending money for snacks and cigarettes as well, while failing to feed our family and pay the mortgage? The kids were crying and shouting from internal mayhem. Are you kidding me Steven?"

He was numb to our presence and fully detached. He failed to acknowledge the family emotional and financial crises, and this is exactly what addiction can do to the brain when the twelve steps do not get met in full. It gets fueled with contempt and stays numb to consequence. Everyone is peeling off their layers of grief, I tried to tell myself, and God is assessing my brain again to see how much neuroplasticity it affords me.

In the meantime, I had to revive a broken relationship and rely on wishful thinking, because The New Steven, clean of coke and pills, was just as problematic as The Old One. I still woke up each morning to spilled milk or soda on the countertops, cookies on the carpet, Taco Bell remnants between the sofa cushions. And I am responsible to take care of just myself? I asked myself angry. What a crock of hogwash.

Steven failed to consider the seven Cs taught to him in drug rehabilitation, two of which state: communicating feelings, and making healthy choices. His parent's business was none of my business, I knew, however, everyone was in each other's business regarding the dollar bill. They created a monster. And I am solely responsible for taking care of myself? I shouted in my dreams, without ever expecting it to take so long. It turns out that it takes the brain nearly as long to unmask the bad habits, as it did to form them in the first place. *

*O*n a Sunday afternoon as he slouched on the couch watching football, the phone rang. I stood behind him folding laundry on the kitchen table. I hope he focuses on me, I prayed, not himself. "How did you feel watching your wife materialize into someone new? Loryn asked him on speaker phone.

Steven shut off the speaker, and within moments I heard him saying things like I got captivated by the beauty of her disease....I had my own demons when we met......I've had problems with addiction my whole life....and blamed Chris, because I got away with it......Oh yeah it started with weed in my bedroom at thirteen and I left the door open for my parents to smell it and give me attention since my sister got it all....All I got from my parents was money and I take as much as I can get........Over time I escalated from Oxycontin and Percocet to cocaine.....The uppers and downers, the rich man's drugs.......

Forty minutes of self-indulgence poured into the phone like liquid puke.

My ego mounted when I saw the involuntary finger and lip movements at the ATM, I heard him say, and I never suspected that my seizures augmented his false power, nor that they built a haven for me to prolong my adolescence.

"She screams, I scream, we all scream," he said, laughing.

The passive aggressive behaviors worsened. My epileptic rage, Dad's rage and Steven's rage. The outbursts localized in my prefrontal cortex felt like neurological surges of electric energy that were out of my control. A brain repeatedly on fire, and the burning rage surpassing my cognitive knowledge and executive control, prevented my rational left from modulating my irrational right.

As an epileptic survivor I had to learn how supervise myself, and to rely on trustworthy cousins or friends when I couldn't do it myself. I often reached out to Barbara and Michele when I'm uncertain of my decisions or make repeated mistakes. Barbara has been my best friend for nearly three decades. Aristotle stated that, "Anyone can become angry—that is easy, but to become angry with the right person, to the right degree, at the right time, for the right purpose, and in the right way—that is not easy."

I even managed manipulating a drug counselor in West Palm Beach to give me a private room…Yeah, I got shipped to Florida after Oakland California failed me…. I think they were a cult…. oh her……I sought an urge when we met…. risk and intrigue…. captivated by her seizures, not necessarily by her……. I wanted to control her destiny……. I got away with buying three motorcycles in three colors and managed covering them with towels or hiding them on our landscaper's property………

The admissions and bragging were wretched. Overspending like this gets rooted from our emotions as well, and placed right beside addiction, immediate resolution, and gain. Long-term fiscal goals and consequences get ignored, because the addict's impulsive emotional brain fails at fully comprehending interest rates and debt payments, even on their own behalf. Their emotions run on immediate stimuli rather than future gain, so impulsivity prevails over common sense.

His tongue circled around his lips as if he was savoring a spoonful of chocolate mousse, topped with homemade whipped cream. Another cyclical battle between pleasure and pain. "What challenges did you face living with an epileptic?" Loryn asked him, I later learned. "How did it feel watching your wife materialize into someone new?"

.... Problems with addiction my whole life .... but after her surgery she eventually caught on to.... way before my parents did.... but I continued because nobody ever listened to her.

"Let's go back to your wife," Loryn responded.

One Achilles then another......four or five herniated disks in the lower Ls.... addicted to painkillers and nothing was going to stop me....... hundreds a week, thousands a month....

Over time I learned that as my epilepsy worsened, I peeked to a higher level on his narcissistic chart, providing him the ability to shadow his very own. Pearl Harbor Day, I recalled one day, the beginning of the end.

This selective recollection made me wonder when the "beginning of the end" started for us in the first place, because over time I learned narcissists undergo three stages in relationships: idealizing, devaluing, and discarding. Over time and unmasking, I discovered that the first stage did not last long at all.

I finally showed face. I pointed my finger in his face the same way Zia Melia pointed to her pupils in Naples. Then my attention shifted suddenly. I looked at the football game on television and saw the white helmets with the blue horseshoe logos on each side. They are sort-of-like the hippocampus, I thought, the seahorse figure on each side of the brain. Unlike basketball and baseball, football fails raising my endorphins like a true American, but this time was different. It was not the game itself, but the helmets and jerseys. I touched a random player on the tv screen, thinking, "That's my helmet, my childhood helmet!"

I gazed at number eighteen, soon learning that I belonged to Peyton Manning. Great looks, I told myself, and a great number, but not the same one I grew up knowing and loving, not The New York Yankees third baseman number eighteen, Scott Brosius, 1998 World Series MVP and one of my favorite Yankee players of all time. "Move away from the tv!" Steven shouted. "Sorry Loryn," he chuckled in the same breath.

After the slander I left the room and went to Google number eighteen on the team wearing the helmet with the blue horseshoe logo on each side. It turned out to be Peyton Manning and the Indianapolis Colts. I just learned about this famous five-time-league MVP winner, born in New Orleans, Louisiana in 1976 played in college for the University of Tennessee, before selected by the Indianapolis Colts as first overall pick in the 1998 NFL draft. I soaked up facts and stats like a starving fish. Even better was me learning that the white helmet with the blue horseshoe logo on each side, originally designed for The Baltimore Colts, signifies luck and happiness, and the white background signifies integrity.

As Steven presented himself with a lack of integrity on the telephone, I finally unmasked more about my childhood helmet, and understood where it had always belonged: 1971. Loryn was right the entire time, I eventually discerned. The Old Christine had not yet fully steered away from childhood, nor her present life. She was not ready to surrender herself fully to the healing process.

January 24, 2011, just a few moments past midnight, so it was really January 25 and seconds after the transition period from one day to the next. In ancient Roman times midnight fell between sunset and sunrise, The Little Man noted, and varies according to seasons. AM represents ante meridiem, or before noon and PM represents post meridiem, or after noon, yet neither are quite correct since noon is neither before noon nor after noon, and midnight can be equally twelve hours before and after noon. This is how my brain can work.

January 25 and I saw myself staring at my computer screen again with Petunia purring atop my pages. In needed to learn more about Dr. Oliver Sacks, the Brad Pitt of the brain world, and that night I learned he was born in 1933 in London England into a family of physicians and scientists. He earned a medical degree at Oxford, and residences at Mt. Zion Hospital in San Francisco and U.C.L.A. A practicing neurologist in New York since 1965, and in July 2007 he got appointed The Professor of Neurology and Psychiatry at Columbia University Medical Center.

I found his name in a Newsweek article titled, THE MYSTERY OF EPILEPSY-WHY WE MUST FIND A CURE. So ecstatic that I emailed Dr. Levy to insist he get the issue. Adam was heading to Seattle, but he picked up the magazine at the airport and promised to read it on the flight. I read every word of every page and waited for his plane to land for commentary. It turned out that Adam impressed as well, and he informed me that Sacks was speaking at Columbia in a few weeks to promote his new book *The Mind's Eye.*

On Feb. 10, 2011, I found myself standing five feet from the podium at the Kaufman Concert Hall, just three feet away from world famous Dr. Oliver Sacks. A packed theatre at the Hammer Health and Sciences Building at Columbia, directly across from Adam's office. Like usual I arrived just in time, not a minute too soon or too late. Without a vacant seat left or room to stand, I sucked up the nerve to weasel my way down the stairs directly toward the podium, where I stood for nearly two hours, hearing every sound, movement, and gesture. Emailed Adam with trembling fingers and directed him to cross the street and join me. My ill brain just expected a doctor to leave his practice on demand, and to cross the street to join me at the podium. The tickets were all sold out Chris, Adam emailed me soon after.

I stood behind him motionless, and all eyes and cameras directed at him meant they directed at me as well. He impressed his audience with eloquence, fluency, articulation, and vast neuro-psychological knowledge. The English accent was a charm. This exemplary physician spoke about hallucinations of the deaf and blind, and heightened visual imagery the brain impaired like me hold, through pictures, paintings, images, hallucinations, and ideas. His random flow of thoughts graceful, fluent, and philosophical, and his bravery challenged unmapped territories, and encouraging me to follow a path.

Analyzed his perfectly groomed grey mustache and beard. While dissecting his large round glasses, black shirt, and sneakers, I saw about fifty young adults as well, Columbia students sitting on the floor in front of him, looking physically disheveled and mentally worn out. Some were getting antsy while others fell asleep right in front of him. I wanted to shake them awake, but Sacks failed to look down or notice.

"They were probably up studying for the past twenty hours," Adam joked the next day, "Been there done that."

At the end Sacks took random questions, and that was when my ego got the best of me. If anyone deserved the right to stand up and ask Sacks a question, I thought, it was me. When the director turned her head and pointed the lights on me, I felt like I found the Golden Ticket! "I read about Natasha K. in *The Man Who Mistook His Wife for a Hat,*" I said, "and when my left frontal lobe and hippocampus got removed, my personality didn't temporarily alter like hers, it permanently altered!" I asked, "Why?"

The audience was awe struck, Sacks appeared awestruck and caught off-guard as well. "I didn't know that striking these areas would leave me with a permanent residue, and alter my very identity," I said.

"The subject is too deep, with too little time to delve into it now," Dr. Sacks replied aloud. "Come see me at closing to further discuss."

Abrupt and skeptical at first, but then he warmed up. I promptly explained my past and present circumstances and praised many of his books. He handed me his card and told me to email my story to him. I exited The Kaufman Concert Hall swarmed around questions and praise. My fifteen- minutes of fame, I thought, as I strolled outside toward my car proudly.

Ten days later I found a hand-written envelope in my mailbox. I placed it on my heart and then read it while swinging on the swing. The letter written in pencil like chicken scratch, holding misspellings, and cross-outs and corrections. The writing of a paradoxical genius, I thought. He admired my story, thanked me for sharing my identity crises with him, my sense of estrangement, and other mysterious aftermaths. Apparently, he had other patients who had trouble accepting themselves after brain surgery, but none were able to express it like this. Neuroplasticity, I told myself again.

This consummate scientist inspired me to integrate my life one book, blend my old autonomy with my new one, and my dreams with reality. Sacks was the one inspiring me to tolerate the uncertainties and unfinished business no matter how long it took, to ignore schedules and allow my creativity to prevail.

More happened later in that year, 2011. The forty-five-year-old Christine made a semi-conscious decision to visit a tattoo parlor in Rockland County, without fully comprehending the event itself. Imagine getting drunk before finding yourself at an out-of-state tattoo parlor on an unsafe end of a town. The Old Christine instructed her needs to the artist without full hemispheric cognizance. She asked him to create her a fat, green bullfrog resting on a lily pad in a pond, gazing upward at a butterfly, with cattails growing behind him. I want placed along my right shoulder. He looked at me awe struck but interested. More memories of exceptionally long ago, inactive in my limbic system, triggered, and slyly leaked out, yearning for recognition. The emotions felt as powerful as a child's love for his new puppy.

According to my writing it took another six years for me to match the bullfrog with my memories. It turns out that my plump

Jeremiah epitomized multiple emotional aspects of my life. Number one, the toad lived in Nana's pond on the lily pad beside the cat tails and reunited with us on our new journey to repel all the insects in my life. Number two, he embodied my bullfrog as well, my "Joy to the World," the song that happened to debut in 1971. He brought joy to my fishes in the deep brown pond and joy to you, me and every other living organism of the Earth. Number three, The Lifeguard with the frog tattoo, the young man who saved my life in Long Island. I subconsciously replicated his tattoo along the same shoulder decades later. Number four, I named him Jeremiah without knowing why.

Like Stevie and Carly, my stout, warty, short- legged amphibian still carries on in real time as well, in my brain and heart. Tattoos not only develop on human skin, but from an inner self, and they often link to pain, pleasure, freedom, and change. Jerimiah epitomized different things along my various stages of growth. Another interpretation of Axton's bullfrog comes from the prophet Jeremiah in the Bible. His distinctive call is God's voice that stands out in nature. Nature provides the broadest pleasures of humankind

And I never had a doubt that "Joy to the World," embodied God's desire to unite people in happiness, notes writer Hoyt Axton, and on my backside, he gazes up at my butterfly serenely.

*R*emember Freud stating that, although reality tells us our loved one is gone, its orders cannot be obeyed at once. My brain failed at looking for a job as a temporarily single parent because grieving and unmasking are far from one linear process. The overlapping, looping around, and failure to stop at a particular point in time all get muddled. But as years pass, the cycles age, crack, or die off, leaving the brain for newer, sturdier, more modern ones to develop. At one point Stuffed Pink Piglet and I stopped relishing the surges of Mr. Bridge, his sways back and forth between land and sea vibrations. One day we looked up, only to find a man above the bridge, sitting in a metal cage box and dangling back and forth with the current. He appeared to be focused on the task at hand. "A real human with a real brain," Stuffed Pink Piglet said, "maneuvering the gears instead."

"Yeah, controlling the land and sea traffic," I replied.

"Was Mr. Bridge just a drawbridge?" Stuffed Pink Piglet asked.

"Yes and no," I replied.

Just a faded rose from the years gone by, Tanya Tucker expressed to us.

"Mr. Bridge will be in our hearts forever," I said, "but he has peacefully met up with Joey now in Tanya's mansion in the sky.

2015 / 2021

The Old and New Christine fully assimilating into One.

Earlier in this book I stated that Dr. Scheinin got taken aback after learning that outer pieces of the brain, holding newer memories can only get restored only after the more primitive regions do. One evening Petunia covered my keyboard again and purred loudly. I looked up at the clock and it read 1:31 am. With her sandy tongue she licked the salt off my favorite snack, Lay's Potato Chips, before we decided Googling information on primitive brain structures and ancient cerebral networks. Instantly, amazing archives on such topics popped on the screen, with depictions of various living stimuli. Petunia and I saw images of nucleus acumens, the brain makeup of a chimpanzee, a dog sitting on the sand staring at the ocean, a baby's brain-size, and then…He suddenly appeared again from nowhere. "We found he Golden Ticket!" I said to Petunia.

Buried within these various structures appeared a selective childhood depiction, fancying me to eternity and back. His head tilted to one side, resting on his hand. There he sits, I thought, the legend that happens to represent our primitive brain structure as well. It was the notorious Willie Wonka himself, the famous and fabulous Gene Wilder sporting his renowned brown hat, purple velour suit and silver bow tie!

A carefully selected character buried in my brain since 1971 inadvertently reappeared when I Googled primitive brain structures.

But over time as my primitive mind matured, Wonka began disappointing me as well. The Old Christine perceived him as a trustworthy leader, benevolent and altruistic, when in fact he resembled another member of the movie's cast of brats. While Joey, Jason, and Stephanie discerned the underlying darkness shadiness behind his character, for a long time, I did not. It's because their brains hold the ability to distinguish a good egg from a bad one, as well as read intentions through eyes. But I felt perplexed by Wonka, even while being betrayed. Is he really that good deep down, or condescending and cynical like Dad and Steven? I asked myself.

My abstract thinking and ability to comprehend freely must have improved over time, because the more I watched the more I picked up on the charades and pretenses. In fact, Wonka began feeling dark, shady, and a bit creepy. It is funny when *Willie Wonka and the Chocolate Factory* pops up on television on Christmas or Easter, I make Jason and Stephanie watch it with me every single time, and every single time they spit out laughing at the aged technology and characters making spectacles of themselves. The English brat falling down the garbage chute, the German brat falling into the chocolate river, and not to mention my spitting image, the American brat, Violet Beauregarde, who ignored Wonka all together. "I would rather you didn't take it. See I haven't got it quite right yet…there's still one or two things…" he said to her, unemotionally while rolling his eyes.

"Oh, to blazes with that," Violet continued to reiterate in my primitive mind, before deciding to taste the tomato soup. The more the true nature of Wonka's cunning character seeped into my consciousness, the more that I questioned his desire to find an honest successor to take over his magical factory. Then, just like Jason and Stephanie and the rest of the world, I had finally concluded that Wonka had intended to maintain control over the factory the entire time. I stopped marveling at Wonka the same way I stopped marveling at Steven. Their grandiose sense of importance was all gibberish, I learned, and the two frenzied adults couldn't handle losing power and control. Narcissists are ambiguous, self-righteous people without souls.

Wonka stood out for me for other reasons. Like, Wilbur and Charlotte, both were based around timing of my fall. But most important of all is that Wonka's rare brain exemplifies a genius as well, which is why his face appeared on my screen, right beside the nucleus acumens to begin with. Wilder's grin, smirk, fine craft of perversion, and black satire captured minds and imaginations all over the world. His shady brain holds exceptional mental powers and right hemispheric dominance like mine, a metaphorical inference of endless possibility. *

I thank my brain for its strength, resilience, and ability to salvage its emotions for my mother and children. I recall long ago when I studied Jason and Stephanie's childhood parodies and spoofs and struggled to connect to them. By this point my fake-it-till-you make-it strategies finally leveled off. I raised my children using my two minds: rigid and free spirted. Neither strict nor neglectful. I was a permissive parent in handling everyday decisions and circumstances, but when the stakes heightened, my conscious left hemisphere surrendered itself to the unconscious powers of my right, where my insight and liberty took rein.

Over time I developed a pattern in my parenting skills, a go with the flow approach to motherhood. Right hemispheric parenting like mine does not insinuate slack or negligence by any means, rather provides freedom for children to grow, prosper, and expand their horizons without strict instruction holding them down. I was not a helicopter mom who micromanaged every spectacle of my children's lives, because for starters, my brain does not hold such ability. Yet, as adults, Jason and Stephanie told me that I helicoptered them quite often, without executing stringency.

Steven and I didn't allow them to throw large high school parties in the basement but didn't prohibit them either. I brushed off a few lies and buys to allow them to appreciate their teenage years and soak in the memories that I failed keeping. This softened approach to parenting eliminated overthinking, which allowed Jason and Stephanie to learn from their mistakes and make better choices for themselves later in life. Once again, this parenting pattern has everything to do with right brain intuitive thinking, allowing the mind to decide, rather than just the brain. I believe excessive helicopter parenting not only produces pressure for children to over-achieve or impress others, but can lead to anxiety, depression, and lack of self-esteem as well. A helicopter parent can counteract a teenagers' ability to find their own healthy niche down in adulthood and navigate around our vast planet freely and independently.

Jason and Stephanie certainly use their prominent left hemisphere endlessly just like everybody else, while simultaneously maintaining the right hemispheric faculties to make astute, swift decisions that hold long- term effects. Once again, this ability to forecast and project is vital when people decide which job offer to accept, stocks to invest in, or roommates that will work best with their personality and income. Too many options can lead to decision-making problems that hold high stakes, which overstimulate the prefrontal cortex. The conscious left brain needs to take a break to digest all the information, before the unconscious right decides without thought and contemplation, so the left can then implement it instantly. Perhaps, I lost some ability to walk the straight line as a parent, but I knew exactly when to helicopter in successfully.

This approach has everything to do with utilizing the powerful, unconscious tools of the right hemisphere again, where the brain is wired to make high-stake decisions precisely. This hemisphere doesn't reflect on too many options like the left does. Contemplating too many alternatives such as the theme of Stephanie's Bat Mitzvah felt like a waste of space and energy in the brain. I selected the primitive glory of nature by not consciously thinking the entire decision-making process through, rather finding more reflective channels through unconscious reasoning. This approach helped Stephanie to become an expert in her field, with two of the four largest accounting firms in the world negotiating to hire her when she was twenty-five years old. She holds gut and intuition not found in the left brain, filled with hunches, inklings, notions, and ideas when decisions get made, characteristics that cannot get explained through conscious reasoning. Conscious reasoning is vital and mandatory, but so are random chance, trial, and error.

As a mother, each time I sensed emotional or financial turbulence, grief, worry, or dismay in my children, I managed helicoptering my way back in to help them make the right decision.

2017, fifty years old, and hitting nearly twenty-five years of marriage. While I still had mixed emotions such as frustration, anger and confusion, as well as forgiveness and empathy, my right mind finally gained enough courage to make the right decision and walk out. The last straw was another vacation in Florida playing golf with his parents and dining at the clubhouse afterward, while leaving the children and I with no money yet again. "I'll send you one hundred by Friday," he exclaimed, before dashing out to the airport for five days of sun and relaxation. By the end of that week Stephanie discovered she could not register for the CPA exam due from unpaid school fees. "Dad!" she shouted over the phone, "I need my graduation certificate from the last summer to register for the exam and five hundred dollars for registration as well! I cannot believe that you still owe the school! Are you kidding me?" she raged.

We heard things like: LEAVE ME ALONE! I AM ON VACATION! YOU'RE NUTS LIKE YOUR MOTHER! GET THE MONEY FROM SOMEWHERE ELSE!

Still calm and civil, before my verbal mayhem intensified again, and they thought I was nuts. Stephanie and I were left in fear and upset again, in another episode of fight-or-flight mode.

MY PARENTS THINK YOUR NUTS! THEY'RE LAUGHING AT YOU RIGHT NOW CHRIS I'M NOT COMING HOME AT ALL SO SHUT THE FU.. UP!

By the end of the week, Mom, the tailor still working, used our trust to pay off the remaining fees, as well as the cost of her CPA registration. Throughout everything my mother kept her logic and financial priorities. We loathed those in Florida, refuted them.

My landscapes had died years before from loss of love, money, and most important of all, Michael. My personal designer and dear friend passed away in his forties from an overdose of pills and cocaine. I mourned Michael right alongside Joey's dead roses and green rose hips. By this point, I had lost so many living beings and fauna, that the last thing my brain needed was more gaslighting and financial infidelity. At this stage my brain felt like a hollow ton of bricks. My husband of over twenty years provided me an allowance of one-hundred-dollars-a-week to support our family and myself, I recall, five crisp twenty-dollar bills counted out proudly right in front of me. I was his charity. His parents remained blind to his control, theft, rages, and threats. More crap like this: IT'S MY HOUSE NOT YOURS! Continued for years AND I'M NOT GOING ANYWHERE UNTIL THE BANK TELLS ME TO. YOU'RE GETTING NOTHING FROM ME, NOTHING AND MY PARENTS THINK YOU'RE INSANE!

They're the only ones who do, I knew, as I packed up my belongings and left him for good to restore my sanity.

I walked out on him in 2017 with nothing but fifty grand in legal fees, and Mom's trust account. On my very first evening away from the wretched man, my girl was alone with her father. Jason had moved out to Hoboken just weeks before, and Stephanie had already made plans to move to Hell's Kitchen in Manhattan. I prayed she would be OK living in the house with her father during this short-time frame. Leaving my child alone with a recovering addict was the hardest decision I had to make as a mother. I offered Stephanie the guest room in my apartment in Englewood, however she declined. "I'm studying for the CPA exam," she replied, "and I don't want to move all of my material twice. Pus, I need to take care of the three guinea pigs."

On Stephanie's first night alone with Dad he got high as a kite from sleeping pills and he texted a young woman in his program right in front of her. She cried at the sight of his phone, before leaving the room and calling me. We wept together, and I begged to pick her up from Englewood on her first night home without me. My guilt disabled me even more than Steven's mental abuse, but I knew that in order to care for my children, I had to care for myself first. My darling little girl, my young lady that I grew to cherish and adore like a rose petal, was undergoing her very own lifelong PTSD, and amygdala stress, I later learned.

It turns out that Stephanie's anxiety from kindergarten continued to hinder her brain, growth, and development. She had her own childhood agonies to unmask, I later learned, and it saddened me to realize how the brain surgery had affected on my loved ones. After twenty years of holding her tongue about selective mutism trauma, Stephanie finally unraveled the reasons behind her silence in the classroom. At twenty-five years old, she finally explained to me she felt like a victim of social isolation, stemming from her mom's inability to maintain the bond we had shared during her first four years of life.

Suddenly, I recalled her lack of eye contact as a toddler, and blank facial expressions. My darling little girl may have been suffering early amygdala damage as well, I thought, from her own inner childhood distress. It took two decades for her spit out the reason behind her decision to speak, smack the middle of first grade. "It's because you were there, Mom," she said, "it was that simple."

I grasped her tightly and sobbed. "I love you more than anything else on the planet," I said, "and I wish I could have done better."

"It's OK Mom," she said. "Do you remember when you read my class your favorite Christmas story, The Polar Express to my class?" she asked, laughing, as I wiped tears and laughed back.

"I never blamed you Mom," she said, "the surgery wasn't your fault."

I left thirty-five hundred square feet of suburban space filled with bad karma for an urban apartment of one third the size. But it has twelve magnificent sliding doors, all sunny and free from northern exposure. The sunlight seeping in throughout the entire day helped my brain heal and my dracaena trees to thrive. I thirsted for isolation as well, the same way a human stuck in the middle of the Mojave Desert thirsts for water. The urban traffic, honking horns, police cars, and roaring fire engines replaced the chirping birds and spatting sprinklers of my suburban home, but I knew I needed change, and that I would grow to love it, the same way that a young adult leaves home for the very first time. The half urban, half suburban dwellers in Englewood tend not to stop or chat with a passerby, which works well for an introvert like me. In fact, this melting pot of various races, cultures, religions, and ethnicities, feels more like home to me than Connecticut, Long Island, or northern New Jersey, because my brain flourishes around peaceful coexistence rather than intense friendships, or peer pressure. My aged right hemisphere never let go of the late 1960s movements, including fairness, equality, social justice, and variety. Stevie tells me that my brain will always feel freedom with a little fear.

I had a project to complete, I knew deep inside. There was more unmasking to do. I needed solitary and independence to finish this book. Kelly Azevedo notes that, *"All your plan has done is given you a path from where you are now to where you want to be. You still get to decide how you get there, how long it will take, what it looks like, and a thousand other small details."*

*W*hen Jason and Stephanie first visited, they screamed the same way they became accustomed to growing up. But suddenly, I covered my ears and insisted for the screaming to stop! * My brain set new boundaries almost overnight, ones that I never had the right as a mother to place on them before, restrictions that were opposed or mocked by Steven and his parents. I threw Stephanie out of my apartment one evening for bad-mouthing me. "I need to heal," I shouted, "so if you retort in defiance one more time, you are out of here!"

She walked out sassy, but sobbing as well, I later learned. It took me running away from narcissistic abuse for my children to learn the most valuable lesson in life: respect. I was silently ripping off more layers of skin and developing a sense of self-worth.

Mom suffered through every wound alongside me, never depriving me of encouragement, strength, rest, or support. I realized that there was a single soul who had provided me with the care that I coveted all along, showering me with patience and hope during my stages of unmasking and Capgras Syndrome. She bathed my brain like a newborn, iced it and massaged it even when it failed return her love. As our memories evaporate, our relationships widen. Introversion feels good, but isolation can feel paralyzing. The brain-injured get often left with a shrinking support system. Friends and peers expect them to remember, speak and act normally, when they simply cannot. I've watched my previous friends shake their heads at me in frustration and talk behind my back, believing I that I concocted my shortages, or played dumb for attention.

In 2019 I endured another operation, this one to remove a twenty-year-old metal screw from my left hemisphere. However, the simple neurological procedure aggravated my pain, memory, and coordination. It provoked additional wounds and caused more behavioral and cognitive issues. Healing from a broken brain is not as simple as healing from a broken leg, and the mental and physical pain remain lifelong struggles. Outside frustration makes the victims further insulate themselves in cocoons, another reason I quit my decade-long book club.

The struggles are very real, so let me say that it's imperative not to shout at brain-injured people when we mis-comprehend a sentence or forget a name. Rather than displaying frustration, repeat your statements in low pitch and adult language. Give us very simple choices of where and when to meet, without providing us with too many options to process at once. Revise, restate and repeat.

The dwindling Capgras Syndrome was a psychological miracle in- itself since brains holding this oddity fail to detect their flaws in perception, and more important to ever fully recover! * But my neuroplasticity grappled with this problem for over ten years and struggled to overturn it through therapy, photo albums and cognitive, behavioral strategies like Free Association.

This brings me to the marvelous theory of Hebb's Law, founded famous Canadian neuropsychologist Donald Hebb. His theory suggests that neurons that fire together wire together. The more we practice positive experiences, behaviors, and actions the stronger the positive synaptic connections in our brain become. The more we exercise patience and good intent the better we build healthier, long-term relationships, and the less we act out on compulsion.

Compulsion represents the second theory of Hebb's Law, stating that neurons that fire apart wire apart. Doidge notes that not acting on compulsion will eventually weaken the link between compulsion and the idea that it will ease our anxiety. The brain maintains its subconscious habits, skills and thought patterns from early childhood and repeats them over a lifetime. Habits such as lying, cheating, drinking, compulsion, and using can break, only through long-term therapy and various forms of counseling. Hebb's theory of "use it or lose it" tells us to continue therapy, reading, writing, socializing, exercising, sleeping, and practicing good habits, so the brain can grow new cells and keep them alive.

Miraculously, after fifteen years, I perceived my cousin Angela the exact way as I had before the operation. She became like my sister again, and I invited myself to her house regularly, lacking novelty. As my brain slowly developed new mechanisms of attachment, association, and communication, it was learning to decide who to embrace and who to reject as well. When I left the suburb, I left faux friends behind and kept the few worth preserving.

It's commonly perceived that action follows feeling, however, action and feeling go hand in hand as well. Learning to regulate actions indirectly regulates feelings as well. My children encouraged me stop the habit of holding grudges after arguments with family. It was an unhealthy habit that I developed from my large, stubborn family, they said, of not speaking for years over spilled milk. The aphorism fake-it-till you-make-it-until-you- rock-it finally processed. I learned to honor and respect myself, which provided me the ability to honor others. Honestly, I never expected to experience the pride and bond of motherhood ever again, the unconditional love, and ability for my children to count on me as their leader no matter what.

According to Jason and Stephanie their father was always a good parent and their love for him remains no different from their love for me. I found this problematic to accept and understand, because as young adults their brains do hold the ability to distinguish between moral and vindictive, rational, and irrational. They should be able to understand the crises that their father inflicted on their mother, grandparents and even on themselves. I knew it was impossible for me to manage an addict, narcissist, and gas lighter, so I pressured my children do it for me. Yet recently, my two friends, Barbara S. and Michele S. wholeheartedly disagreed with me, and in fact always have. They filled in some gaps in my explicit memory as well, applying some logic to my illogical thinking. It takes two to tango and break up a marriage, Michele reminded me, as Steven and me both tangoed and failed.

Subconsciously, I know my children love their father no matter what. Even as adults, children should never get placed in between warring parents, Barbara argued, and disparaging comments about exes only makes matters worse. Children have no control over poor financial decisions. I failed to understand that their primary sources of safety got unraveled from my poor decisions as well, and that their future relationships could get negatively affected if I didn't stop involving them. In addition, I tended devaluing Steven's positive attributes during my unmasking process as well, failing to bring them to consciousness. It's simply because I did not want to! Stop focusing on the negatives, Barbara repeated, they rent too much space in your brain. She reminded me that I woke up from brain surgery needy and unstable.

Only then, I recalled calling Steven multiple times at work just after my operation, like an infant in need of care. It was the same year we met Michael as well, so I am uncertain whether Steven began using by that point or not. Michael started coming over after work, and meeting Steven in our garage just about every evening. I suspected something shady but discounted it. Besides, I had just undergone brain surgery, so what the hell did I know? I'm still uncertain of whether my husband provided me with any stability or reinforcement. I knew he was a hands-on Dad, involved in carpooling, golfing, and coaching, always on the go...and always looking for and reason to leave the house.

Ron and Sam remained integral pieces Jason and Stephanie's entire lives as well, Barbara reminded me, providing them with knowledge, insight, money, culture, vacations, and emotional support (although usually working against their mother). You need to stop focusing on how you were getting stripped of everything and appreciate the two happy, healthy, successful children that you have today in Hoboken and Chelsea, Barbara advised. I decided to take another step back from rumination and negativity and accept that their bonds with their father are very real, and that I should stop trying to alter them. Stop trying to alter them and begin fully detaching from him, I continued to tell myself, however fully detaching from a narcissist and following the NO CONTACT RULE is impracticable when so much money is involved, I thought.

Narcissists generally fail to make timely alimony payments, mortgage payments, property tax payments, college payments... which keeps the ball rolling for victims for an insurmountable amount of time. Brains with NPD hold zero apathy, break laws repeatedly, fail to follow judgments and learn lessons from past mistakes. Narcissists never, ever stop trying to scheme the system. They seek so much control that they wish death upon their victims.

During the early 1990s when Steven ended our courtship, I held the ability to follow the no-contact rule, because my unhealthy habits were not yet fully pruned, the uncertainties, fears, restraints, and anxieties. But as long-term financial and emotional infidelity grows, the road to nowhere follows, and spoils the brain's ability to maintain the boundaries necessary to protect it. Any narcissistic marriage is a paradoxical disservice to both brains.

Studies prove that altruism is not only a biological response toward life, but it can get hard-wired in the brain at birth as well, and ironically in the primitive right hemisphere. It represents a sense of humanity and is even considered above the higher ranks of the left brain, resting right beside intuition and perception * But there lies an exceptionally fine line between humanity and enabling and crossing line this brings you to "no real, definitive means to an end." The only means to an end is one hundred percent DETACHMENT and NO CONTACT, just like Mom finally had to do with Dad. But always remember, that for a brain to succeed, it must repeatedly fail, as well as fight for its neuroplastic changes.

Dr. Schiffer wrote of a philosopher named William that described men as constantly struggling with inner destructive impulses. "Their spirit wears with their flesh, they wish for incompatibles, wayward impulses interrupt their most deliberate plans, and their lives are on long drama of repentance and of effort to repair misdemeanors and mistakes."

"Impulses wearing out the flesh." I thought. "Wishing for incompatibles rather than partners." Wayward noted. "Impulses disrupting plans…. A long drama of repentance and effort to repair mistakes."

The endless search for the perfect partner to control and patronize usually leads to bankruptcy, egomania, loneliness, and a mind ablaze with financial creativity. It never, ever stops.

Lehar explains that "Unless you experience the unpleasant symptoms of being wrong, your brain will never learn how to revise its models. Before your neurons succeed, they must repeatedly fail, and no shortcuts exist during this painstaking process."

If my brain can act as a charioteer assuming the responsibility of controlling my horse, then yours can too, I tell victims. One must stop people-pleasing and fully detach to become one's own authentic self. Only then will the Lost Father Syndrome and fear of emotional abandonment fade into the shadows, beside the default-to-truth mechanisms that led us astray to begin with. Transparency, Gladwell notes, is a common-sense assumption that really turns out to be an illusion. Only when we allow our gut instinct to offset our illusions are we finally comfortable feeling that it is OK to be unliked by certain types, and even to be view as their villain.

Saturday morning February 15, 2020, six am New Jersey time, three am Las Vegas time. The phone rang. I looked at the caller ID, and by this point I had already reached the last stage of grief: acceptance. Like narcissism, the Peter Pan Syndrome never goes away, I told myself, and Dad and Steven will always have the body of an adult and the mind of a child.

"Chris, I'm very sick," Dad said quietly, "I'm at the end of my life now."

"What happened? Are you ok?" I asked, concerned.

"I'm ill," he replied, "and my body is shutting down. I just wanted to let you know."

"I'm going to call an ambulance right now," I said, "so stay put Dad, please." I insisted.

"I already called one," he replied. "Chris when you get Vegas go to Wells Fargo across the street from my development and ask for Peter. The money is all yours now. It's a lot of bucks," he said, ailing.

"Dad, I don't want your money!" I cried.

I called Dad's number day after day for three days straight, but no answer. Finally on a Tuesday, four pm Eastern time, I picked up my cell at work. I never answer an unknown caller ID, but this time I had a hunch.

"Sorry Chris, my cell shut off. I'm still in the hospital, but I am much better now," Dad expressed, with vitality and energy I never heard before. "I left the hospital and I'm in another building now. Going home real soon."

After working in senior care for eight years, I knew what his sudden surge of energy meant. "I love you Chris," he said for the very first time. "I'll call you as soon as I get home ok," he said, before hanging up.

"Love you too Daddy," I replied, too late.

As the rain washes us clean.... resurfaced from my temporal lobe suddenly...we know. Stevie's background voice humming through my auditory cortex again.... We will know.

I kept calling, but I failed to reach him. Finally, on Friday, February 26th, I received a call from a hospice nurse. "I'm sorry, Christine, but your father has less than seventy-two hours left," she said. "Yes, I suggest you fly here to say your goodbyes by Monday the latest."

I booked a flight for the following morning, Saturday, February 27, 2020, and just as I left for the airport, the phone rang.

*D*r. Seuss's gating mechanisms deferring my grief finally subsided as well, and my unmasking was forever winding down. The New and Old Christine were becoming one. "THREE TREE Three fish in a tree...Fish in a tree.......How can that be??" I asked myself one last time just before the water surged into my bedroom.

As I wrote this paragraph after my dream, I suddenly recalled Dr. Alexander Luria's striking piece about dreams, expressing it is possible to lose track of time and begin living in a world of isolated impressions. I dreamt of crystal-clear water rushing through my sliding doors, streaming on to my hardwood floors, and flowing beneath my bed along the entire length of my rectangular bedroom. I saw two feet of pretty feet of small, pretty, swirly waves flowing into my closets and bathroom. I awoke for a brief second to check for water damage but fell right back asleep again into my dreamy state, into my beautiful landscape and visual imagery. I was having more high-running frontal lobe activity and exceptional dream recall. I finally watched Seuss's bright goldfish escape the dreadful tree, swimming tranquilly though the fresh water beneath me. The mild waves drew them directly into my jacuzzi, overflowing with fresh water. I watched my fishes hop and dance in glee, with their gills finally expanding after so many years of dreadful heat.

One Fish Two Fish Red Fish… were swimming back and forth from REM sleep to wakefulness, emerging and re-emerging from consciousness, before finally escaping my limbic system for good, and entering my cerebral cortex, real time. I saw healthy scales along their fins in various, colors and shapes, and I'm sure that their alertness and clarity returned as well. They all dwelled safely and interacted socially, freely, energetically, and fearlessly in fresh, clear water.

Maybe I missed out a bit on life as an introvert, I thought, since like fish, humans inevitably need social interaction as well. All living organisms exist with a heart and mind, bred in need of security, assurance, and love. But to reach this point, I finally accomplished what Dr. Doidge notes as the need to turn the ghosts into ancestors. and let them go.

Stuffed Pink Piglet and I witnessed their last stages of vegetation. Long ago we moved our caterpillars one by one into small mason jars. We placed the jars on the deck railing, loosely covered by Saran Wrap. She poked holes in them for the air and sun to seep through, and fed them grass, insects, and willow leaves. The rainwater afforded our host plants nourishment, and our celery and fennel remained preserved for decades.

The baby jars and host plants finally ended their duties of harvest. In this dream, Stuffed Pink Piglet and I witnessed our green and orange creatures grow out of their own skin. Their plump bodies underwent a series of molts, as the shed their skin before us. "They need more space," Stuffed Pink Piglet said, "and twigs, in order to hang upside down and spin themselves into silky cocoons."

Stuffed Pink Piglet fixed the blemishes, and we watched their bodies transform into beautiful orange, green and yellow hues, just before the magnificent butterflies flew away to live happily ever after.

Constantinople and Timbuktu are desolate no more. It turns out that Timbuktu lies in Mali, a country in northwestern Africa, I learned, and Constantinople changed its name to Istanbul in 2008. It turns out that these two countries appear in Dr. Seuss's famous picture book HOP ON POP from 1963, which my Uncle Louie gave me for my sixth birthday in 1972. The book unconsciously pleased my pathways in 1999, but something was still missing. Finally in around 2015 Suess's resurrected: one is my other brother....my brother's reads a little bit...little worlds like if and it... and big words too like Constantinople and Timbuktu....

*L*ike the animal, our right is less civilized than the left. Animals are keen, bright, and perceptive, yet hold more trouble accumulating knowledge, contemplating outcomes, and thinking logically outside the box. They communicate mentally, physically, and empathetically through mime, sounds, gestures, and expressions rather than words, specific to the human species. In addition, animals' frontal lobes are smaller and less developed than humans. We can read expressions from afar, but have more trouble understanding connotative, intellectual activity. We perceive through denotation, often lacking meaning or feeling as well.

Sensory cues like vision, hearing, smell, touch, and taste are the fundamental gifts in our perception. Dr. Jill Bolte Taylor describes our sensory systems as a complex cascade of neurons, where each group within the cascade alters and over time enhances the whole, refines it and redefines it. If any cells along the pathway fail functioning normally, she notes, then the final perception skews away from reality.

This adds to the cyclical reprise of others using you monetarily, sexually, and psychologically. Self-esteem that is built around caring for others can allow them to exploit the giver. Over time, our inferiority complex festers with inner shame and anger, and this had me facing some ugly truths about myself. Remember, pathological altruism admixed with pathological narcissism feels like quicksand, the more we consent the deeper we sink and the more elusive our self-forgiveness becomes. Dr. Sarno says, "The person who feels perpetually compelled to make a doormat of himself and do pleasant things for others can take stock and decide to curb the tendency."

*A*t the end of my journey Nono re-appeared from dormancy one final time. I watched her pruning her roses in the dead of winter, rambling in Italian to me about how pruning eliminates dead, diseased canes. Joey's mini dried-up roses surfaced simultaneously, specially, the small, plastic pot that I brought home from his funeral in January 2002. I saw the pair of ceramic frogs that I bought when he passed away. One still lying on my nightstand, and the other resting beside his grave. We buried Joey in a black suit and for some strange reason, The New Christine decided on wearing a black dress to his funeral, rather than a hippie one. I wore black boots and a black hat as well, and Steven remarked I looked like I was attending shul.

In 2019 my Gentle Giants thrusted into consciousness one last time, my aged prizes thriving around the Connecticut streams, rivers, and wetlands. The braided, dense roots protect our lands from flooding. They thrive in masses and flourish around any form of standing water…My information system reminded me…. There are nearly four hundred species and varieties of willows as well, holding roots aggressive enough to lift sidewalks or interfere with sewer lines! Their wood makes the flute and broom handle, however beneath the handy bark lies unique symbolism as well. In fact, the magnificent tree represents balance, learning, growth, and harmony, reminding me of the magic of the brain's neuroplasticity. The willow holds flexibility just like the human brain, and ability to bend and readjust to life's changing environments without snapping.

Rather than the battling the weathering storms they hold no control over, they have learned over time to accept them, and acceptance is the last stage in healing. The brain holds the ability to flourish as well, combat its commotion, restructure itself, and mature into something better than before. Life can indeed change for the better over the passage time, just like Sacks vowed to me a time long ago.

I saw the orchids and chrysanthemums from Joey's wake as well, flowers that represent mourning. But this time his roses buried beneath the winter snow. No sense of time or order in my dreams, rather imperative emotional growth, integration, expression, and progression. Nono told me that rose stems are essentially canes and must get cut regularly just above leaf growth to eliminate fungus, mildew, and yellowing. I awoke from my dream for a moment, only to find myself amid another weeping spell. Joey's poorly groomed rose bushes extended above the dirty, winter snow. Each mini, green rose hip mounted along the prickling stems. My gardens neglected for years, due from my lack of ambition and care. "The conditions to maintain the perfect groom," Nono expressed again, "cannot be less than perfect."

I grieved Nono, the grandmother who sat next to me to watch Dynasty; the grandmother that made me eggs over medium with homemade Italian sausage when I got home from school. Nono pruned her vegetable gardens at 5:30 each morning. She placed fresh string beans, plum tomatoes, cucumbers, eggplants, and butter crunch lettuce into baskets. Nono understood English, but like Nana, she refused to speak it. I wailed out loud again and woke myself up. "Are you ok?" Jason asked.

"Please get me a cold cloth," I replied, sweating.

I undressed myself and threw on flannel pajamas, before dialing Mom. She was quiet, pensive, reflective. "What's wrong Mom?" I asked. "I just had a nightmare," I said.

"Nothing," she replied sadly.

I awoke briefly again before sunrise. The outdoor spotlights reflected along the dirty snow. Next, I saw fresh powder falling from above, whitening the dirty snow. I saw individual crystals rather than chunks, unique in molecular structure. I tulips blooming above the fresh snow, not in bunches the way I plant them, but in one, long, straight line instead, individually separated by ten feet. Red and yellow tulips with long, wavy stems. My dream choices were not solely stemming my auditory cortex, but from other regions of my temporal lobe as well, those specifically responsible for song selection! Over time Dr. Penfield finally assured me that such ceaseless activity, stemming from the basal ganglia and other parts of the limbic system, indeed result from frontal lobe deterioration. These implicit memories represent personal reflections of an earlier life, eventually making their way to the temporal lobe, the consciousness, which was exactly what finally happened to me.

Just remember during the winter…. I heard Bette sing. I saw Joey floating above Carly's clouds in my coffee once again, resting peacefully on the light froth with a cinnamon swirl. My brain bombarded with multiple senses, gifts, coincidences, and imageries. I read of another victim, Michael Chorost, who underwent similar experiences following a cochlear implant to partially restored his hearing. His new implants began dismissing his prior auditory hallucinations, "Like the sun blocks out the stars," he explained. "It's as if my overworked auditory cortex has been angrily saying to me, if you won't give me sound, I'm just going to make it up!"

It was sunrise, January 14, 2019, exactly sixteen years after Joey's death. "That's why Mom sounded sad last night," I thought.

I fell back asleep, and as my instincts went up and inhibitions went down, more mixed dreams followed. Underneath the bitter snow… Bette repeated…lies the seed.

Love is not only for the lucky or the strong, I told myself, because I always loved my brother, even during my brain's epileptic latency. That with the sun's love, I heard, as the rose bushes quadrupled in size right before me, flourishing right above the bitter snow. Within seconds time moved from winter to summer, and I found myself at the shoreline again, treading water beside the raft. "You made it to the end this time" I said to Joey in glee.

I treaded water beside him and watched him circle and ponder about whether to climb up the ladder. He paddled idly for quite some time. "Chris!" I finally heard from afar.

"What?" I asked

"Knock, knock," he repeated from long ago, just after he finally decided climbing up the raft and into The Cumulous Clouds. He stretched his right arm out toward me.

"Who's there?" I replied, "Who's there.... don't disappear on me again!" I shouted.

"Olive."

"Olive who?" I asked.

"Olive you," he said, before floating up to the joyous angels and silver stars.

Joey is no longer with me, I finally understood, whimpering for the very first time.

*N*earing the end of our lives as we knew it. Mr. Bridge was already resting above The Cumulous Clouds beside Joey, Belle, Little Chip and Silver Sylvia. Our flock of seagulls, holding the higher powers of intuition and insight appeared one last time.

"We're all in this place for a reason," I heard them from overhead, "and closing an old chapter means opening a new one."

They descended upon Stuffed Pink Piglet and I one last time, reducing their speed and circling in unison. "Thank you," they told us, "Christine, Stuffed Pink Piglet, and Belle for feeding us the remnants of Nana's bread."

I jumped up to kiss them.

"Continue sharing your resources for the time you have left on the planet Christine and letting your altruism shine through without expecting back."

Stuffed Pink Piglet and I looked at their long slender wings and forked gills, casting their shadows along the water. "Share your challenges, learn to release what you cannot control. Make a difference in other people's lives."

Stuffed Pink Piglet reached upward to salute them.

"Just like the seagull, they said, use your right architecture to your advantage. Your brain is finished unmasking now, and it holds the ability to move forward with clearer prospects. Thank you again for being our friends, but now it's time for us to take care of ourselves just like you must do."

"I love all of you!" Stuffed Pink Piglet shouted upward, before suddenly re-appearing on the plastic cover of my record player again, stuffed with plastic pellets.

"We will retire as well," they said, "to a private haven away from the beaches. Our gulls are weakening we must avoid our predators."

"It's the circle of life," I heard Glinda, The Good Witch say. "Your scars have healed. Your brain had the power all along my dear."

"The vast globe lies right before you," my aged flock fi expressed, before soaring away into infinity.

<u>The 17 Powerful Songs
Along My Journey of
Unmasking the Mayhem</u>

"Alone Again Naturally"	Gilbert O' Sullivan
"Delta Dawn"	Tanya Tucker
"Dreams"	Fleetwood Mac
"Everywhere"	Fleetwood Mac
"Gypsy"	Fleetwood Mac
"It's the Real Thing"	COCA-COLA COMPANY
"I Will Remember You"	Sarah McLachlan
"Joy to the World"	Three Dog Night
"London Bridge is Falling Down"	Tommy Thumbs
"Rhinestone Cowboy"	Glen Campbell
"Rose Garden"	Lynn Anderson
"The Candy Man"	Sammy Davis Jr.
"The Rose"	Bette Midler
"Seasons in the Sun"	Terry Jacks
"S.O.S."	ABBA
"Top of the World"	Carpenters
"You're So Vain"	Carly Simon

Bibliography

1.   Caroulis, Jon, "Brain Injury," A Silent Epidemic, (PENN MEDICINE, Spring 2002), 9-15.

2.   Zengerle, Jason, "A Brain With a Heart," (New York Magazine, November 12, 2012), 50-53.

3.   Begley, Sharon, "I Can't Think!", (Newsweek, March 7, 2011), 28-33

4.   Meacham, Jon, "Epilepsy in America": What Must Be Done, (Newsweek, April 20, 2009), 2

5.   Meacham, Jon, "A STORM THE BRAIN", (Newsweek, April 20, 2009), 38-41

6.   Adler, Jerry and Gray Eliza, "IN THE GRIP OF THE UNKOWN," (Newsweek, April 20, 2009), 42-47

7.   Axelrod, Susan, "AGONY, HOPE & RESOLVE," (Newsweek, April 20, 2009), 49

8.   Zellmer, Amy, "CONQUERING CONCUSSION," (EXPERIENCE LIFE, July, August 2020), 72, 73

9.   "In the Region"

http://www.nytimes.com/2005/12/16/nyregionspecial2/18liline.html
?pagewanted

(The New York Times Company, 12/16/2005), 2-14

10.   Twedt, Shelley, "SUPPORTING TRAUMA VICTIMS,"

(http://www.examiner.com/article/supporting-trauma-victims, May
27, 2012), 1

11.   Wikipedia, "CRISES MANAGEMENT,"

(http://en.wikipedia.org/wiki/Crises_management), 1

12.   HW, Lisa, "Does Something Good Always Come out of
Something Bad?" (http://lisahwareen.hubpages.com/hub/Does-
Something-Good-Always-Come-Out-Of-Something-Bad, May, 11,
2005), 1, 2, 6

13.   "Life is Symbolic. Start Interpreting," (http://www.whats-
your-sign.com/symbolic-meaning-of-giraffe.html, 2013), 1, 2, 3

14.   Wikipedia, "Savant syndrome,"
(http://en.wikipedia.org/wiki/Savant_syndrome.   05/25, 2021), 1-6

15.   Burgess, N., Jeffery K.J. Jeffery, O'Keefe J." The
Hippocampal and Parietal Foundation of Spatial Cognition,"
(OXFORD UNIVERSITY PRESS,
http://ukcatalogue.oup.com/product/9780198524526.do,
12/31/1998), 1

16.   "Traumatic Brain Injury Resource Guide- Occipital Lobes",
(http://www.neuroskills.com/brain-injury/occipital-lobes.php), 1

17.   Borade, Gaynor, "Buzzle 1960s Hippies Fashion",
(http://www.buzzle.com/articles/1960s-hippies-fashion.html,
01/10/2012), 1,2

18.   NIH Consensus Statement, "Surgery for Epilepsy,"
Functional and Stereotactic Neurosurgery Surgery for Epilepsy,
(http://neurosurgery.mgh.harvard,edu/epil-hih.htm, Mar 19-21,
1990), 1-8

19.   The University of Washington, "The Hippocampus,"
(http:usd,sagubaw.k12,mi.us/-mobility/hippocam.htm), 1, 2

20.   Wikipedia, Passer and Warnock, "Capgras delusion,"
(http://en,wikipedia.org/wiki/Capgras_delusion, 1/31/10), 1-5

21.   Schwartz, Theodore H. MD, "Excite Epilepsy Focus—
Epilepsy Surgery,"
(http://excite.healthology.com/focus_article.asp?f=epilepsy_surgery,
06/14/21), 1-4

22.   Dasheiff, Richard M., MD, Ryan, Christopher W. Ph.D.,
Lave, Judith, Ph.D., "Epilepsy Brain Surgery: A Pittsburgh
Perspective,"
(http://www.ttuhsc.edu/pages/neuro/ttep/surgery/e_surg05.htm,), 1-3

23.   Restak, Richard, M.D., "Complex Partial Seizures Present Diagnostic Challenge," (Psychiatric Times, September 1995, Vol. XII. Issue 9, http://www.mhsource.com/pt/p950927.html), 1-6

24.   Wikipedia, "Charlotte's Web,"

(http://en.wikipedia.org,wiki/Charlotte's_Web, 04/25/2011),1,2

25.   Shammi, P., Stuss, D.T., "Humor appreciation: a role of the right frontal lobe," (Oxford University Press, http://brain.oxfordjournals.org/cgi/content/full/122/4/657, 2010), 2, 3, 5, 8, ,9, 10,

26.   Holmes, Gregory L. M.D., "Frontal Lobe Epilepsy," (http://www.epilepsy.com/epilepsy/epilepsy_frontallobe, 10/21/06), 1

27.   Medscape, "Left Mesial Temporal Sclerosis (MTS): Discussion," (http://www.medscape.com/viewarticle/481142_3) 1994-2009), 1

28.   Wikipedia, Thomas Mann, (http://en.wikipedia.org/wiki/Thomas_Mann, June 5, 2021), 1, 2

29.   Wikipedia, Alexander Luria, (http://en.wikipedia.org/wiki/Alexander_Luria, 12/29/09, 2010) 1-4

30.   "The Theory of Memory, the Hippocampus and H.M.," (http://sps.nus.edu.sg/-huyihuyi/pub/sp2171/node9.html, 05/04/2004), 1,2

31.   Devinsky, Orrin, M.D., NYU Medical Center, "FACES,"
(http:/faces.med.nyu.edu/about-us/our-history/letter-from-our-
founder, 2010),1

32.   "Limbic System,"

(http://thalamus.wustl.edu/course/limbic.html,) 1-5

33.   "Epilepsy Information," (Columbia Weill Cornell
Neuroscience Centers,

http://wwwnypneuro.org/healthinfo/epilep.html, 2001,) 1-5

34.   Matlack, Gerry, "An Imposter in the Family,"
(http://www.damninteresting.com/an-imposter-in-the-family, 02/07,)
1-3

35.   Friedkin, Christine, (Newsweek Letters and Live Talks, Mail
Call: http://www.msnbc.msn.com/id6700294/site/newsweek, Dec,
20 2004), 19

36.   "The Temporal Lobe,"
(http://www.geocities.com/CapeCanaveral/Launchpad/3937/tempor
al.htm

37.   "Memory, Learning, and Emotion: The Hippocampus,"
(http://www/psycheducation.org/emotion/hippocampus.htm,
10/07/03), 1-6

38.   WiseGEEK, "What is Declarative Memory?" (http://www.wisegeek.com-what-is-declarative-memory.htm, 2003-2010), 1,2

39.   Wikipedia, "Declarative Memory," (http://en.wikipedia.org/wiki/Declarative_memory, June 11, 2010), 1-10

40.   Wikipedia, "Episodic Memory," (http:/en.wikipedia.org/wiki/Episodic_memory, April 13, 2010), 1-6

41.   Buchtel, Henry A., "The Wada Test," (http://www-personal.umich.edu/~gusb/wadadesc.html)   February 23, 1999), 1

42.   Wikipedia, "Cluttering,"

(http://en.wikipedia.org/wiki/Cluttering, Jan. 28. 2021), 1, 2

43.   Brain Wave Entertainment Technology, "Left Right Hemisphere Brain Processing," (http://web-us.com/brain/lrbrain.html, 1995-2009), 2, 3

44.   Wikipedia, "Joke," (http://en.wikipedia.org/wiki/Joke), 1

45.   "When Injuries to the Brain Tear the Hearts," (The New York Times Health,

http://www.nytimes.com/2012/01/10/health/when-injuries-to-the-brain-tear-at-hearts.html?..., Jan. 10, 2012), 1-6

46.   Carter, Sheryl, "Oliver Sacks,"

(http://www.oliversacks.com/about.htm, 2007), 1

47.   MovieAddict2010 from UK, Airplane!,

(http://www.imdb.com/title/tt0080339/usercomments, 2009), 1-5

48.   Wikipedia, "Queens,"

(http://en.wikipedia.org/wiki/Queens), 4,

49.   Wikipedia, "INTUITION,"

(http://awakening-intution.com/Intuition-definition.html, 2000), 1-3

50.   Devinsky, Orrin, M.D., Lipson, Scott E., M.D., Sacks,
Oliver, M.D., "Selective emotional attachment from family after
right temporal lobotomy," (www.sciencedirect.com, March 23,
2003), 340-342

51.   Johnson, Glen M.D., "TRAUMATIC BRAIN INJURY
SURVIVAL GUIDE, MEMORY,"

(www:tbiguide.com/memory.html, 2010), 1-11

52.   ScienceDaily, "Researchers Identify Decision-Making Area
Of The Brain; Results will Aid Treatment for Brain Disorders Such
as ADHD,"

(http://www.sciencedaily.com/releases/2002/11/021105080438.htm,
1995-2013), 1-4

53.   NEWSWEEK MEDIA LEAD SHEET,

(http://www.google.com/gwt/x?Q, December 6, 2004), 1, 2

54.   Tingly, Kin, "The state of concussion studies illustrates the biases of medical research – and how they can lead to serious gaps in understanding," (The New York Times Health, June 30, 2019), 16

55.   Gupta, Sanjay, M.D., "Keep Sharp, Build a Better Brain at any Age,"(A.A.R.P.) 36-38

56.   Ambrosio, Frank, Department of Philosophy, Introduction to Philosophy, (Georgetown University,) 1

57.   Allen, Shannon, "Free Spirit For Life: 7 Struggles Of Being A Free-Spirited Woman,"

(https://www.elitedaily.com/life/culture/struggles-of-free-spirit-woman/993046, April 12, 2015), 1-6

58.   Wikipedia, "John, Hughlings Jackson," American Psychiatric Association,

(http://en.wikipedia.org/wiki/John_Hughlings_Jackson, 1999), 1-8

59.   Rawlings, Leslie, LCSW.ACSW-R CASAC. MTS, "Trauma and the Brain," (December 12, 2010), 2

60.   Wikipedia, "Neuroplasticity,

(http://en.wikipedia.org/wiki/Neuroplasticity, April 3, 2013), 1-16

61.   Moisse, Katie, "What happens in the Amygdala...Damage to the Brain's Decision-Making Areas May Encourage Dicey Gambles," (SCIENTIFIC AMERICAN http://www.scientificamerican.com/article.cfm?id=amygdala-loss-aversion, April, 2013), 1,2

62.   Mobbs, Richard, "Our Four Brains," (http://www.le.ac.uk/users/rjm1/etutor/resources/brain/brain4brains.html, December, 20030, 1-3

63.   Grandin, Temple, Johnson, Catherine, "Animals in Translation," Chapter 3, "Animals emotion is simple and pure; Similarities between animal and autistic emotion," (http://www.grandin.com/inc/animals.in.translation, ch3.html), 1, 2

64.   Three Dog Night performer, Hoyt Axton writer, "Jerimiah was a Bullfrog," (https://www.lyricsfreak.com/c/creedence+clearwater+revival/Jeremiah+was+a+bullfrog208066617.html), 1-3

65.   Family Caregiver Alliance, "Coping with Behavior Problems after Head Injury," (http://www.caregiver.org/caregiver/jsp/content_node.jsp?node.jsp?nodied=396), 1-4

66.   Prowe, Gary, "Letter to My Wife's Family," (http://www.brainline.org/content/2011/05/letter-to-my-wife's-family.html, 05/11), 1-3

67.   Neumann, Dawn, Ph.D., "Emotional Mis-communication Changes Relationships after Brain Injury," (Facebook, http://www.lapublishing.com/blog/2010brain-injury-emotions-relationships/, May 25, 2010), 2, 3. 4

68.   Cavazos, Miguel, "WHAT IS THE MEANING OF INTERPERSONAL RELATIONSHIP?" (http://www.livestrong.com/article/229362-what-is-the-meaning-of-interpersonal-relationship/, June 14, 2011), 5,6

69.   Dymkowski, Alyson, "Life After Brain Injuries: Are We Still the Same People?"

(http://serendip.brynmawr.edu/exchange/node/1689, 01/03/08), 1-3

70.   Psycheducation.org., "Memory, Learning, and Emotion: the Hippocampus," (http://www.psycheducation/org/emotion/hippocampus.htm, 10/07/03), 1-6

71.   "Mystery of Human Consciousness Illuminated: Primitive Consciousness Emerges First as you Awaken from Anesthesia," (Science Daily, http://www.sciencedaily.com/releases/2012,04,120404102140.htm, April 4, 2012), 1-4

72.   MITnews, (http://web.mit.edu/newsoffice/2005/basilganglia.html, February 24, 2005, 1, 2

73. Smith, Alexandria, MA, LPCC, "How to Stop Ruminating," (Experience L!FE, October 2020), 72- 75

74. Gladwell, Malcom, "How to Talk To Strangers," (Experience L!FE, April 2020), 13

75. Smith, Alexandria, MA, LPCC, "Toward Self-Forgiveness," Experience L!FE, April 2020), 14

76. Promises Treatment Centers, "Addiction Recovery & the Negative Effects of Not Letting Go,"

(http://www.promises.com/articles/addiction-recovery/addiction-recovery-the- negative-eff...), 1-5

77. Madsen, Joseph M.D., "When Epilepsy Surgery Offers the Chance of a Cure," (The New York Times, http://www.nytimes.com/ref/health/healthguide/esn-epilepsy-espert.html1?pagewanted=all, 05/16/08), 1-5

78. Merzenich, PhD., "About Brain Plasticity," (http://merzenich.positscience.com/about-brain-plasticity/, April 16, 2008), 1,2

79. Cohen, Marla, Sukkot: "Tips for decorating your sukkah...and more," (JEWISHLEDGER, Sukkot, Https://www.jewishledger.com/articles/2010/09/16/news/news/10.txt, September 15, 2010), p 1, 2

80.   Cherry, Kendra, "The Anatomy of the Brain," (About.com Psychology, http://psychology.about.com/od/biopsychology/ss/brainstructure_2.htm), 1,2

81.   Wikipedia, "Flower power," (http://en.wikipedia.org/wiki/Flower_power), 1-3

82.   Roth, Rebecca, "A Look at Humor, Laughter, Tickling and, of course, the Brain," (http://serendip.brynmawr.edu/exchange/node/2053, 02/13/2008), 1-7

83.   Wikipedia, "Free association" (psychology), (http://en.wikipedia.org/wiki/Free_association_psychology, September 3, 2010), 1-3

84.   Heid, Markham, "WRITTEN IN THE GENES?" (TIME, THE SCIENCE OF ADDICTION,) 1/24/20), 18-20

85.   Wikipedia, "Selective Mutism," (https://wikipedia.org/wiki/Selective_mutism, May 26, 2021), 1-4

86.   Berto, Patrizia, "Quality of Life in Patients with Epilepsy and Impact of Treatments," (http://ideas.repec.org/a/wkh/phecom/v20y2002i15p1039-1059.html, 2002), 1

87.   The National Aphasia Association, "Aphasia Frequently Asked Questions," (http://www.aphasia.org/Aphasia%20Facts/aphasia_faq.html), 1-5

88.   Ponchomeg, LifeRecreation-People, "Traits of a Modern Bohemian Hippie or Free Spirit," (http://www.listmyfive.com/4591f550/The-Top-Five-Traits-of-a-Modern-Bohemian-Hippie, November 2012), 1,2

89.   Grunert, Jeanne, "Interesting Facts About Weeping Willow Trees," (http://garden.lovetoknow.com/wiki/Weeping_Willow_Tree_Facts), 1

90.   Miller, Ashley, "SIX STEPS OF GRIEVING," (Http://www.livestrong.com/article/115001-six-steps-grieving/, May 1, 2010), 5,6

91.   Google Sites, "Oh, The Thinks Dr. Suess Can" Think... (http://sites.google.com/site/ahatfulofseuss/oh--the-thinks-dr--seuss-can-think), 1-3

92.   Wikipedia, "Codependency," (http://en.wikipedia.org/wiki/Codependency), 1-7

93.   McPherson M.D., Mempowered, "The role of emotion in memory," (http://www.memory-key.com/memory/emotion, 1-8

94.   Wikipedia, New York metropolitan area, (http://en.wikipedia.org/wiki/New_York_metropolitan_area), 1

95.   Wikipedia, "Dr. Seuss,"
(http://en.wikipedia.org/wiki/Dr._Seuss), 1-12

96.   Corbet, Bob, "WHAT IS EXISTENTIALISM,"
(http://www.2.webster.edu/-
corbetre/philosophy/existentialism/whatis.html, March 1985), 1-3

97.   Balley, Regina, About.com. Biology, "Corpus Callosum,"
(http://biology.about.com/od/anatomy/p/corpus-callosum.htm), 1

98.   Newman, Judith, "Living with a Thieving Spouse," (AARP
THE MAGAZINE, February, March 2020), 56-59

99.   Skinner, Quinton, "HOW TO CHANGE YOUR BRAIN,"
(EXPERIENCE LIFE, ExperienceLife.com, June 2020), 59-63

100.   Harrar, Sari, "HOW TO BUILD A BETTER BRAIN,"
(Reader's Digest September 2020), 66, 67

101.   Latson, Jennifer, "DISCONNECTION," (EXPERIENCE
LIFE, ExperienceLife.com April 2018), 46-50, 81

102.   Steber, Maggie, "The Girl Who Can't Remember," (People
Magazine, December 30, 2019), 67-71

103.   Williams, Paige, "A Deadly Mistake," (THE NEW
YORKER, Feb. 10, 2020), 28-39

104.   Baily, Regina, "What is the Function of Plant Stomata,"
(ThoughtCo., Aug 15, 2019), 1,2

105.   Sacks, Oliver, M.D., Seeing Voices, (Great Britain, Picador 2009), 58, 59, 61, 63, 65, 75, 76, 82, 86, 87, 91

106.   Taylor, Jill Bolte, Ph.D., My STROKE of INSIGHT, (Plume, Penguin Books Ltd, June 2009), 17, 20, 21, 27, 33, 118, 119, 120, 145, 159

107.   Sacks, Oliver, M.D., The Man Who Mistook His Wife for a Hat and Other Clinical Tales, (TOUCHSTONE, Simon and Schuster, Inc., 1998), 4-7, 13-17, 19, 21, 23, 26-39, 80-83, 103, 133-136, 143-146, 154, 155, 217-231

108.   Genova, Lisa, Still Alice, (Gallery Books, Simon and Schuster, Inc., 2007, 2009), 4, 10-12, 15-17, 62, 63, 128, 129, 200, 251

109.   Bragdon Allen D. & Gamon, David Ph.D., Building Left-Brain Power, (BRAIN WAVES BOOKS- Allen D. Bragdon Publishers, Inc., 1999), 1-5, 11, 14, 15, 59,

110.   Nolan-Hoeksema, Susan, Ph.D., Women Who Think Too Much, (Henry Holt and Company, LLC., 2003), 37, 38, 43, 59-63, 71, 72, 80, 81, 92, 93, 111, S 118, 119, 145, 153, 163, 164, 172, 178, 182, 202, 203, 239, 242, 247-252

111.   Sarno, John E. M.D., THE DIVIDED MIND, (HARPER, 2007), 5, 19, 37, 38, 48, 50, 56-65, 71, 72, 100, 102, 104, 107-109, 143, 144, 148, 149, 158, 168-172, 177-179, 182, 267, 268, 279, 280, 353,

112.   Vertosick, Frank, Jr. M.D., WHEN THE AIR HITS YOUR BRAIN, Tales of Neurosurgery, (Random House Publishing Company, 1996), 1, 3, 9, 21, 23, 55, 213, 214, 222

113.   Gladwell, Malcom, Talking to Strangers, (Little Brown and Company, Hachette Book Group, September 2019), 215, 216, 239,342, 343

114.   Schiffer, Fredrick M.D., OF TWO MINDS, THE FREE PRESS, A Division of Simon & Schuster Inc, 1998), 5-9, 11-24, 30-33, 41-45, 68, 78-102, 123-127, 150, 153,

115.   Doidge, Norman M.D., THE BRAIN THAT CHANGES ITSELF, Penguin Group, 2007), xx, 4, 5,9, 12, 13, 18, 25, 27-43, 52-54, 60, 68, 74, 75, 82, 86, 106-108, 112-118, 121, 126, 170-174, 208-213, 216, 217, 222-244, 248, 249, 252-256, 259-261, 266-272, 278-281, 295-298, 314-318,

116.   Sacks, Oliver M.D., MUSICOPHILIA, (FIRST VINTAGE BOOKS EDITION, RANDOM HOUSE, 2007), xi, xii, xiii, 8, 9, 13-17, 21, 23, 30, 33-38, 41, 42, 57, 61, 83, 86-88, 90, 100, 121-123, 137, 154, 156, 165-171, 201, 209, 213-218, 220-225, 228, 233, 238-242, 277, 306, 309-311, 340-343, 349, 351

117.   Powel, Richard, MIND GAMES, (FALL RIVER PRESS, Sterling Publishing, 2011), 26, 30, 23, 40, 41, 47, 54, 56, 57, 70, 75, 78, 79, 98, 99, 104-106,

118.   Sacks, Oliver M.D., THE MIND'S EYE, (ALFRED A. KNOPF and ALFRED A. KNOPF CANADA, Random House, 2010), 34-38, 41-49, 61, 69, 73, 78, 82-96, 99. 100, 104-110, 131-135, 138-143, 176-181, 195, 204, 219, 221, 228, 232-237,

119.   Zayn, Cynthia, Dibble, Kevin, M.S., NARCISSISTIC LOVERS, (New Horizon Press, 2007), ix, x, 4-13, 16-19, 24-34, 37-43, 46, 49, 54-59, 85-92, 124, 134, 135, 153, 154, 163, 164

120.   Lehrer, Jonah, HOW WE DECIDE, (Mariner Books, 2009), xv-xvii, 5, 8-18, 23-27, 38, 40-42, 48, 49, 54, 55, 73, 87, 102, 103, 111, 115-119, 142, 143, 149, 158-160, 164-166, 168-175, 182, 183, 186-191,198-203, 210, 211, 217, 236-238, 244-250,

121.   Sacks, Oliver M.D., AWAKENINGS, (Vintage Books, Random House, September 1999), xxxii-xxxix, 6-11, 19, 32, 33, 43, 104-109, 112, 113, 141, 142, 148, 150, 159, 160, 181, 228, 229, 239, 240,246, 252, 253, 268, 287, 288,

122.   Zadra, Antonio & Stickgold, Robert, WHEN BRAINS DREAM, (W.W. NORTON & COMPANY, 2021), 10, 13, 18, 19, 21, 22, 25, 27, 32, 42-44, 47, 63, 73, 80, 90, 98, 99, 1-2-105, 109, 111, 117, 118, 144,162-165, 172-172, 176, 179, 200-212215,

123. Tiktok@hauntingfactss

124. Dr. Suess, Hop on Pop, (Random House Beginner Books, (1963)

125. Dr. Suess, One Fish two fish, red fish, blue fish, (Random House Books for Young readers, March 12, 1960)